THE SIGNIFICANCE OF THE SLAVERY MOTIF
IN THE GOSPELS

A Dissertation

Presented to

the Faculty of the Department of Systematic Theology

Dallas Theological Seminary

In Partial Fulfillment

of the Requirements for the Degree

Doctor of Theology

by

Daniel R. Lockwood

August 1982

WIPF & STOCK · Eugene, Oregon

Accepted by the Faculty of the Dallas Theological Seminary in partial fulfillment of the requirements for the degree Doctor of Theology.

Examining Committee

Edwin Blum

John A. Witmer

[signature]

Wipf and Stock Publishers
199 W 8th Ave, Suite 3
Eugene, OR 97401

The Significance of Slavery Motif in the Gospels
By Lockwood, Daniel R.
Copyright©1985 by Lockwood, Daniel R.
ISBN 13: 9781532640759
Publication date 9/19/2017
Previously published by Dallas Theological Seminary, 1985

TABLE OF CONTENTS

Chapter
  I. INTRODUCTION 1

     The Object of the Study
     The Purpose of the Study
     The Justification of the Study
     The Procedure of the Study

 II. OLD TESTAMENT BACKGROUNDS TO THE SLAVERY MOTIF 35

     Introduction
     Delineating the Slavery Motif
     Non-Religious Aspects of Slavery
     Religious Aspects of the Slavery Motif
     Conclusion and Summary

III. CULTURAL BACKGROUNDS TO THE SLAVERY MOTIF 81

     Introduction
     Slavery in Judaism
     Slavery in Greece and Rome
     Conclusion

 IV. THE SLAVERY MOTIF IN THE SYNOPTICS 129

     Introduction
     The Classification of Slavery Motif Passages
     Examination of the Passages
     Conclusion

  V. THE SLAVERY MOTIF IN THE FOURTH GOSPEL 195

     Introduction
     Investigation of the Motif
     Summary and Conclusion

VI. CONCLUSION 247

    The Role of the Slavery Motif in the Gospels
    A Profile of the Slave of God
    The Paradox of Slavery to God

BIBLIOGRAPHY 260

CHAPTER I

INTRODUCTION

The Object of the Study

Slavery Imagery in the New Testament

In the New Testament, figures drawn from common experience often communicate deep theological truth, depicting the vital relationship of the believer to Jesus Christ.[1] However, there is one figure used throughout Scripture to describe the relationship of peoples to their Lord which for the most part is either minimized or ignored: the figure of master and slave.[2] There may be several reasons for this: (a) the figure has suffered at the hands of translators, who, by rendering the word δοῦλος as "servant," have blunted the force of the figure and confused the term with other synonyms.[3] (b) Through an incorrect identification of ancient slavery with the enslavement of the American Black, there has arisen an aversion to such figures as an expression of the spiritual relationship between God and man. But whatever the reason, the figure of master and slave has not received the emphasis it deserves.

This is all the more surprising when one discovers how frequently the imagery of slavery can be found in the New Testament. References

to slavery in the New Testament often have an institutional or secular
reference, as in, for example, the gospel accounts of Jesus healing a
prominent man's slave, the Pauline *haustafeln* regulations of master and
slaves (Eph. 5), or the Apocalypse's description of the Babylonian slave
trade (Rev. 18:13).

But the expressions for slavery and servitude are more commonly
used in figurative senses. For example, Mary calls herself "His [God's]
slave" in the Magnificat (Luke 1:48)--following an Old Testament precedent to express one's humility toward, and ownership by, God; Jesus
seasons His parables with slaves (e.g., Luke 12:35-40), and He utters
proverbs that contain the slavery theme (Matt. 10:24-25). Paul uses
the figure to depict one's "ownership" by such spiritual masters as sin,
the law, lust, and death and to enjoin his readers to become slaves of
Christ. Paul, Peter, James, and Jude all refer to themselves as "slaves"
of God or Christ in senses which seem to designate not only their complete devotion to their heavenly Master but also their decidedly unique
position of dignity in His service.

Summary of related terms

This pervasiveness is demonstrated not merely by representative
examples but also by the variety of terms used to describe the concepts
of slavery, service, bondage, etc. In the New Testament there are at
least a dozen word groups which convey these concepts and which underscore the variety and complexity of the allusions to slavery in the New
Testament.

I. Terms that stress the aspect of subjugation[4]

   A. Δοῦλος, δουλεία, δουλεύω. ("slave," "bonded-service," "to serve as a slave")
   B. Αἰχμάλωτος. ("prisoner of war")
   C. Δέσμιος. ("prisoner")

II. Terms that emphasize the act of serving

   A. Διάκονος, διακονία, διακονέω. ("servant," "service," "to serve, to minister")
   B. Θεράπων. ("servant")
   C. Ὑπηρέτης. ("servant," "assistant," or "officer")
   D. Λειτουργός. ("priestly official," "public servant," or "servant")
   E. Λατρεία. ("religious service," or "worship")

III. Terms which stress the individual's service in relationship to other people

   A. Παῖς, παιδίον, παιδίσκε. ("child," "servant," "maid-servant")
   B. Οἰκέτης. ("member of the household," "house slave," "servant," "steward")
      Other related words include οἰκονόμος, οἰκονομέω, οἰκονομία.
   C. Σῶμα. (usually means "body" but used in Rev. 18:13 as "slave")
   D. Ἀνδράποδον. ("slave")
   E. Κοράσιον. ("girl," "maid," "female slave")

Slavery terms not found in the gospels

Four of these terms are used infrequently in the New Testament and never in the gospels. Θεράπων, which is best translated "servant,"[5] suggests a position of confidence, freer service, and dignity absent from the ordinary designation for slave. Beyer notes that the verbal idea implies a willingness for service with accompanying respect and concern,[6] and Trench comments that the word denotes:

> performance of present services, with no respect to the fact whether as a freeman or slave he renders them; as bound by duty, or impelled by love; and thus, as will necessarily follow, there goes habitually with the word the sense of one whose services are tenderer, freer than those of the δοῦλος.[7]

Its only New Testament use is figurative. In Hebrews 3:5, Moses is called a faithful servant in God's "house." Though there is considerable dignity attached to Moses because of intimacy with God, he is still a servant in contrast to Christ who is the Son "over the house."[8]

Σῶμα almost always means "body" but in Revelation 18:13 is best translated "slave" in the context of Babylon's various commercial enterprises. Interestingly, both σῶμα and ψυχὰς ἀνθρώπων are used to designate those who are sold. The slave is seen in an extremely dehumanized way: both as merchandise to be purchased according to his appraised value (σῶμα) and as a living creature of little more worth than living animals (ψυχή).[9]

Ἀνδράποδον in this form never appears in the New Testament. Spicq identifies this as a technical, legal term that describes the slave as a two-footed beast with the pejorative nuance of "bestial" or "menial,"[10] and perhaps that explains why it does not occur. The word ἀνδραποδιστής--"slave-knapper"--however does occur once in 1 Timothy 1:10 in a list of vices for which the Law passed condemnation.

Κοράσιον in secular Greek literature could mean either "maiden" or "maid-servant." In the latter sense it often depicted a servant girl of marriagable age who accompanied her mistress.[11] It is never used for a servant in its four New Testament occurrences perhaps because, as Spicq suggests, in the Greek culture it often had the connotation of prostitution.[12]

The Slavery Imagery in the Gospels

The occurrences of the imagery of slavery in the gospels are numerous. In the synoptics, for example, there are at least ten paragraphs in which references are made to literal servitude, another ten which describe people doing the work of service, four paragraphs which speak of spiritual service, and six references to individuals who designate themselves as the slave or servant of God. Even more significant are the proverbial uses of the slavery imagery by Christ (in about eleven different contexts). Jesus makes indirect reference to slaves in five of His parables; and in six of the parables, slaves form the central core of the story.

In the Fourth Gospel, there are ten paragraphs in which slaves are mentioned as serving in various capacities. Jesus Himself, of course, becomes the prominent example of the slave who serves in the account of the washing of the disciples' feet. And though slavery as a figure is not used as prominently in the Johannine discourses, there are at least five major discourse paragraphs in which the relationship of the disciples to this heavenly Lord is illustrated by the figure of slavery.

Terms for slavery defined

The terms for slavery or service found in the gospels are

important in isolating the occurrences of this slavery imagery. They
will be briefly defined and distinguished below.

Terms which stress subjugation

Δοῦλος, δουλεία, and δουλεύω. This word group is the most comprehensively used (both for institutional and for non-institutional uses of slavery) and it has the harshest implication of subjugation. Though the basic meaning is "slave," "to act as a slave," and "slave service,"[13] Rengstorf clarifies the meaning of this word group as follows:

> The meaning is so unequivocal and self-contained that it is superfluous to give examples of the individual terms or to trace the history of the group. . . . The emphasis here is always on "serving as a slave." Hence we have a service which is not a matter of choice for the one who renders it, which he has to perform whether he likes it or not, because he is subject as a slave to an alien will, to the will of his owner.[14]

This word thus describes a person whose position is the absolute opposite to that of the master (κύριος or δεσπότης), the freedman, Christian brothers, sons, and friends.[15] The term is virtually a designation of a man's status or even his character; as Trench puts it, "the δοῦλος is a slave apart from whether he serves or not."[16] It is used both in literal and figurative senses, and metaphorically it "stresses the Christian's complete subjugation to the Lord."[17] There are even nuances of "dignity" associated with the use of this term--as seen, for example, in the titular uses of δοῦλος or δούλη to designate such outstanding saints as Mary (Luke 1:38), David (Luke 1:69), and Simeon (Luke 2:29).[18]

Αἰχμάλωτος. Meaning "prisoner of war," this word connotes dependence, forced subjugation, and servitude.[19] It is less significant for this study, being used only twice in the gospels: once in a literal sense (Luke 21:24) of captivity in the end times, and once figuratively (Luke 4:18 quoting Isaiah 61:1-2) to describe one aspect of Christ's earthly, soteriological work.

Δέσμιος. The "prisoner,"[20] or "one in bonds," is the last of the three words that depicts an extreme form of subjugation. It is used in the gospels only of the prisoner that Pilate would release annually (Matt. 27:15-16; Mark 15:6). A root derivative, δεσμός ("bond"), is employed in the normal sense of a fetter (Luke 8:29) and in the metaphorical sense of being bound by disease (Mark 7:35), by Satan (Luke 13:16), or by the legalistic strictures of the Pharisees (Matt. 23:4).

Διάκονος, διακονία, διακονέω. This common group of words for "servant," "minister," "helper," "service," "to serve"[21] may be questioned as to its inclusion here.[22] And yet it is important not only for its underlying notions of service but also because of its interplay in contexts with δοῦλος. Trench says of διάκονος: it "represents the servant in his activity for the work . . . not in his relation, either servile, as that of the δοῦλος, or more voluntary, as in the case of the θεράπων, to a person."[23] Often in the parables, for example, such service is not clearly designated as voluntary or involuntary. Klaus

Hess concurs and suggests that the contrast is not between being a slave or a free man but between serving and ruling--between humility and pride. Additionally, says Hess, the stress is on one's personal help of others in serving.[24] Put another way, these words depict that "special quality of indicating very personally the service rendered to another."[25] While the word διάκονος is close to ὑπηρέτης, it maintains a greater emphasis on service rendered out of love.[26] The literal uses of this term are diverse, often being used of "table service" in the gospels.[27] But its figurative and spiritual uses are worth attention: it is used of Christ's soteriological work (Mark 10:45); the believer's object of service (including Christ, God, the gospel, the Church, and the New Covenant); and the believer's service to Christian brothers.[28]

Ὑπηρέτης. This word, meaning "servant, helper, assistant, officer," is a close synomyn to διάκονος.[29] The word, however, is also used in close parallelism with δοῦλος (especially in John 18:18);[30] and it thus seems to describe, as does the verbal form, a closer relationship to the master than does διάκονος and διακονέω.[31] This word is often translated as "officer" in the gospels and it is used of government representatives (Matt. 5:25), synagogue officials (Luke 4:20), officials of the priests (John 18:18), and Pharisees (John 7:32). This translation is confirmed by Trench's observation that the word was applied to military persons engaging in difficult manual tasks (e.g., as rowers).[32] That the idea of difficult labor is maintained in the gospels is questionable; ὑπηρέτης simply seems to indicate a subordinate who operates with some authority in an official capacity.[33]

Λειτουργός, λειτουργέω, λατρεύω, λατρεία. These last two groups are infrequently found in the gospels and thus are of less direct value to this study. In the New Testament, both are used in reference to cultic service. Λειτουργός, "servant,"[34] is used both of priests and of Christ as the supreme High Priest. There is an implication of "official public service" about this word as it is used of angels (Heb. 1:7) and of government authorities who are responsible to God (Rom. 13:6).[35] Only λειτουργία is found in the gospels (Luke 1:23).

The λατρεύω/λατρεία group almost always suggests service in the sense of "worship."[36] Christ uses the idea in parallelism with "worship" in His rebuke of Satan (Matt. 4:10; Luke 4:8). Such worship must be of the heart "in holiness and righteousness" (Luke 1:74) but can be expressed in such concrete forms as prayer and fasting (Luke 2:37).

Terms which stress the individual in relationship

Παῖς, παιδίον, παιδίσκε. Παῖς may mean "boy, youth, child, servant"; παιδίσκε may be translated as "girl," or "maidservant";[37] παιδίον is never translated "servant" or "slave" in the New Testament. Spicq rightly observes that it is not always clear whether "child" or "servant" is meant,[38] although the παῖς of the centurion who is healed (Luke 7:2-7) is clearly a servant. This ambiguity demonstrates that παῖς and its derivatives are not intended to be legally precise designations but to reflect a more ambiguous master-slave relationship in which the servant is closely associated with the family either (a) by being born in the family, or (b) by being closely associated with the householder and caring for his personal needs.[39]

Οἰκέτης, οἰκονόμος, οἰκονομία, οἰκονομέω. The major word of this series, οἰκέτης, is capable of various meanings: "member of the household," "house slave," "domestic," or "slave."[40] Both Trench[41] and Rengstorf[42] believe οἰκέτης is almost synonymous to δοῦλος, although οἰκέτης expresses "the position of the slave in relation to the world outside and in human society" rather than primarily in relation to the master. Spicq sees the relationship of the οἰκέτης with the master to be somewhat more unique than the δοῦλος-κύριος/δεσπότη relationship. While οἰκέτες is not necessarily a title of honor, it does suggest a closeness to the master (with accompanying affection, rapport, confidence, and intimacy) that may derive from prolonged contact.[43]

Οἰκέτης also has some affinity with παῖς in that both words imply an association with the master's house. This servant is not the one who works in the field but is a domestic who often cares for the master's personal needs. Nevertheless, the οἰκέτης is still a slave who is to obey his master with fear (1 Peter 2:16-18).

The other derivatives--οἰκονόμος, οἰκονομία, οἰκονομέω--are all found together in the parable of the unjust steward (Luke 16:1-13). The only other use of οἰκονόμος is found in Luke 12:42--again of a domestic who has closeness to his master--where the word is parallel with δοῦλος.

The Motif of Slavery

Definition of motif

The <u>Oxford English Dictionary</u> defines motif as follows: "a constituent feature of a composition; an object or group of objects forming a distinct element of a design." As applied to literature, motif is "a type of incident, a particular situation, an ethical problem, or the like, which may be treated in a work of imagination."[44] Originally derived from motive, it has subsequently conveyed the idea of a recurring theme or subject of a work of art or literature.[45]

Motif in biblical studies

In biblical studies, the term motif is often used in a more technical and specialized way. Two well-known applications to biblical studies of the concept of motif are the religious and the literary motif.

The Scandanvian neo-orthodox scholar Anders Nygren is one of the prominent proponents of the religious motif. He defines the "fundamental motif" of his studies as "that factor in virtue of which a particular outlook or system possesses its own peculiar character as distinct from all others."[46] Summarizing Nygren's view of motif-research, P. L. Berger observes: "The concept of the religious motif, which can be used with advantage in any phenomenological approach to religion, outside as well as inside the Christian tradition, refers to a specific pattern or gestalt of religious experience, that can be traced in a historical development."[47]

When applied to literary studies in Old Testament scholarship, the definition of motif is more precise. Shemaryahu Talmon gives one very specialized definition as follows:

> A literary motif is a representative complex theme which recurs within the framework of the Old Testament in variable forms and connections. It is rooted in an actual situation of anthropological or historical nature. In its secondary literary setting, the motif gives expression to ideas and experiences inherent in the original situation, and is employed to reactualize in the audience the reactions of the participants in the original situation. The motif represents the essential meaning of the situation itself. It is not a mere reiteration of the sensation involved, but rather a heightened and intensified representation of them.[48]

Several elements of interest should be highlighted from Talmon's definition: (1) a motif is representative, and as such partakes of the field of imagery and figure; (2) it recurs in a variety of forms and contexts; (3) it is rooted in an actual situation; (4) it is intended to be reminiscent of the original context.

George Coates, however, (in discussing the conquest motif in Numbers) offers an expanded definition of a motif as follows:

> A motif is a "word or pattern of thought that recurs in a similar situation . . . to evoke a similar mood, within a work, or in various works of a genre." The pattern of words may be rather broad, a common idea, *a cultural notion* or a problem (italics added).[49]

That a motif can embrace as an antecedent a "cultural notion" (to which, presumably, slavery would apply) makes the literary use of motif in this study relevant.[50]

Use of motif in this study

There is little unanimity on how the word is used in biblical studies; and the problem is accentuated as more scholars are consulted, for each one uses the word with varying degrees of precision.[51]

Therefore, a basic definition of slavery motif is submitted as follows: a frequent recurrence of the concept of slavery which is identifiable by a locus of words in a similar semantic field, which can occur in a variety of contexts, and which, though representative of a literal reality, is evocative of a meaning beyond the literal and into the ethical or spiritual. Thus, motif is being used more in the literary sense than in the religious sense (despite due regard for Nygren's contributions); and, in applying the idea of motif to the slavery imagery in the gospels, it employs a reference more to a general cultural pattern than to a specific, single historical event.

In the dissertation, motif will often be used synonymously with "imagery," "figure," and "theme." That the word can be used this way is not without precedent in biblical studies. But one is justified in asking, why is the word motif retained instead of simply slavery imagery? First, except for lacking one specific historical event as its antecedent, the slavery motif does fit several of the elements of motif as presented in the precise definition of Talmon: it is representative of a historical and cultural reality (i.e., the institution of slavery); it occurs in a variety of contexts and literary structures in the gospels; and it is rooted generally in both a historical and cultural antecedent (historically, in the enslavement and emancipation of the nation of Israel and in the use of slave to designate honored representatives of Yahweh from Moses to the Suffering Servant; culturally, in the social conditions of Rome, Greece and Judaism).[52]

Second, motif seems a more appropriate designation than slavery imagery because of the frequency with which this imagery appears. Motif is used because it suggests a pattern that has received heightened attention by the biblical authors.

Third, motif is a preferable word in light of the uses of the slavery imagery elsewhere in the Bible. The use of motif to describe slavery imagery in the Old Testament is quite accepted;[53] and certain uses of slavery imagery in Acts and the epistles (e.g., παῖς θεοῦ of Christ in Acts 3:13, 26; 4:27; 30; and Paul's self-designation of Χριστοῦ δοῦλος, Gal. 1:10 et al.) could well fit the meanings of motif as defined earlier in this section. Since this work is intended to build upon the meaning of the slavery imagery found elsewhere in the Bible by focusing on the gospels, the use of the word motif clearly furthers one of the aims of this discussion: to affirm relationships between the gospels and other biblical manifestations of the slavery motif.

The Purpose of the Study

The Purpose Generally Defined

Stated as simply as possible, the purpose of this study is to answer the question: From the perspective of the gospels, what does it mean to be a slave of God? In other words, how is the imagery of slavery used to depict the believer's relationship to his spiritual Master? What are the implications of that relationship? What does this suggest about the Lord's understanding of our behavior before Him?

It is not the primary concern of this dissertation to discuss the legitimacy of the institution of slavery. Neither is it primarily the purpose to discuss slavery as an institution, although imagery often can be interpreted in its metaphorical applications only when the reality from which it springs is understood. For that reason, institutional slavery will be considered as appropriate.

The Purpose in Light of Biblical Theology

This work should be seen as an attempt to make a contribution to the field of Biblical Theology. By investigating the slavery motif, it is the aim of the writer not only to examine the implications of being a slave of God in terms of the accepted parameters and purposes of the science of Biblical Theology but also to provide new insights which can be incorporated into the larger disciplines of Systematics and Christian Ethics.

Meaning of Biblical Theology[54]

James Barr isolates three approaches in Biblical Theology: as a descriptive discipline; as a dogmatic discipline (which takes the Bible as its only source of authority); and as a "descriptive-authoritative" endeavor (in which there is an emphasis on a synthetic procedure, on the unity of the Bible, and on the normative authority of the Bible).[55]

George E. Ladd selects the descriptive approach and summarizes the meaning and task of Biblical Theology which will be followed here:

Biblical theology is that discipline which sets forth the message of the books of the Bible in their historical setting. Biblical theology is primarily a descriptive discipline. It is not initially concerned with the final meaning of the teachings of the Bible or their relevance for today. This is the task of systematic theology. Biblical theology has the task of expounding the technology found in the Bible in its own historical setting, and in its own terms, categories and thought forms.[56]

Application to this study

Several elements of this definition illuminate the task of this dissertation in discovering what it means to be a slave of God. First, Biblical Theology is concerned with the revelation of God as it is historically conditioned. Therefore, it is legitimate to compare and contrast the findings on any theme or motif in one period of biblical revelation with earlier revelation. Thus, the method of approach in this investigation will be to find the antecedents to the slavery motif in earlier revelation (i.e., the Old Testament) and to discover the meaning intended by the imagery of slavery through an evaluation of the historico-cultural setting of slavery.

Second, Biblical Theology is selective. Hence, the focus of this study will be on the gospels with a particular interest in the teaching of Jesus Himself.[57]

Third, Biblical Theology is descriptive, also affirmed by Barr[58] and Krister Stendahl,[59] but questioned by men like Gerhard Vos[60] and Geoffrey Bromily[61] who insist the task must be prescriptive as well. This study will be essentially descriptive, the main concern being to isolate the motif and to describe the relationship between believer and Lord that appears. However, the very nature of the question under investigation is immensely prescriptive, interpretative, and applicational. Thus, applications to contemporary behavior will not be avoided.

Fourth, Biblical Theology seeks to express meaning in its own terms and categories. Slavery to God is not a traditional theological category in Systematics. Nevertheless, it is not only a prominent biblical theme but is one whose theological implications for various areas in Systematics (e.g., ecclesiology, anthropology, and eschatology) are far-reaching. It is hoped that the results of this study can eventually be integrated into areas of Systematics with a greater clarity than if external categories were imposed upon the truths which the gospels are presenting.[62]

The Justification of the Study

A Biblical Justification

The basic biblical justification for this study is the frequent and diverse occurrences of this motif, affirming the truth of the simple hermeneutical rule that frequent repetition implies greater emphasis and importance. It may be objected that such frequency can be explained simply because slavery was one of the most common institutions of the day, and thus is valuable as a universally understood illustration. However, to say that a figure occurs often because it represents a widely known reality is quite different from suggesting what this figure means. The need to understand the theological meaning of the slavery figure is a biblical justification for the study.

A Theological Justification

A theological justification for a study of the motif of slavery emerges against the backdrop of Liberation Theology. The predominance of various liberation theologies in discussion today could easily account for a contemporary unwillingness on the part of many theologians to emphasize the Scriptural image of being a slave to God and to one another (unless, perhaps, it is to enjoin the "oppressor" to serve the "oppressed"). The idea of slavery as a pattern to be followed contradicts the contemporary notion of slavery as an oppression to be eradicated. The seriousness of Liberation Theology and its significance in light of the slavery motif demands a brief investigation.

Scope of the movement

Although a relatively recent arrival on the theological horizon, Liberation Theology has taken root in Europe,[63] in America,[64] and in a variety of the Third World countries, particularly in Africa[65] and Latin America.[66] It is a socio-politico-economic movement that focuses on at least four kinds of oppression: white oppression over blacks (racism), male oppression over females (sexism), elite classes over the masses (classism), and developed nations over underdeveloped nations (imperialism or colonialism).[67]

Essential principles of the movement

The main tenants are as follows: (1) All of history is unified. In scripture the "salvific acts of God" underlie all of human existence. God then becomes the universal God of the oppressed not only in the past but in the present and future, and all the oppressed can be rightly called the people of God for whom He intercedes.[68] (2) The starting point for Liberation Theology is not the Bible but the experience of oppressed people.[69] As Hugo Assmann says, "its 'text' is our situation, and our situation is our primary reference point."[70] (3) There is a need for accurate socio-political analysis of the situation. In many cases--especially Latin America--this analysis is the Marxist-Leninist approach to class struggle.[71] (4) The method of doing theology is sharply differentiated from both traditional theology (which is too academic, isolated, bifurcated from political and socio-economic concerns, and universal) and liberal social action (which fruitlessly tries to evaluate needs from outside the social arena). Rather, theology is defined as *praxis*: the actual involvement with the people who are oppressed. Truth is defined as acting to meet socio-economic-political needs.[72] (5) Theology is necessarily partisan. "Black," "Feminist," and "Latin-American" theologies are encouraged[73] because "there is no such thing as a general, objective or universal perspective for theology."[74] (6) The church itself is seen essentially as a socio-political (in contrast to a religious) community mandated to do the work of God in relieving oppression. The gospel is essentially a "gospel of liberation from opression,"[75] and liberation is not simply "consistent with the gospel but *is* the gospel of Jesus Christ."[76]

Biblical and theological support
for the movement

Despite its denial of a biblical starting point for theology, a primary biblical appeal is to the story of the emancipation of the Israelites from Egypt. J. J. F. Durand says, "it is important for an oppressed people to know that the God of the Bible is known *first and foremost* as the Exodus God. . . . He delivered them solely and simply because they were oppressed" (italics added).[77] Meyners[78] and Cone[79] echo the same idea that the Exodus is to be seen as the event by which all subsequent (and previous) history should be explained. A further line of biblical evidence is found in Jeremiah's indictment of the rich who oppress the poor (Jer. 5:26-28) and Micah's solution "to do justice, to love kindness, to walk humbly before your God" (Micah 6:8). This represents the prophetic message that even Israel was judged by God on the basis of her treatment of the downtrodden. From a variety of Isaiah's passages, Gutierrez contends that God's creative acts are equated with his "salvific" acts, thus universalizing God's work under the rubric of social liberation.[80] There is also frequent appeal to the teachings of Jesus where He claims to have come to liberate the captives (Luke 4:18-19) and where He proclaims the basis for national judgment to be the treatment of the oppressed (Matt. 25:32).[81]

A strong theological appeal in Liberation Theology is made to the justice of God. Regarding the Exodus, Ferdinand Deist observes, "this liberating deed of Yahweh revealed Him as One who takes up the cause of the afflicted and the oppressed,"[82] and Dale Patrick asserts that Israel's elect status was based upon their prior oppressed state: "The just cause of the oppressed is morally compelling ground for election."[83] Thus, the Exodus shows God's essential justice as a basis for His election of Israel in the past and His present concern for all oppressed people.

A brief critique of the movement

Several criticisms of the trends in Liberation Theology can be made. (1) Hermeneutically, starting with the situation rather than the Word of God is inherently weak. It dilutes the significance of divine relation by erroneously perceiving truth not as objective but as subjective (truth is "action")[84] and by excluding other possibilities of biblical meaning.[85]

(2) The handling of the biblical data is somewhat suspect. Using the Exodus motif as a starting point ignores the fact that the Exodus

> *is not the beginning of salvation history*. . . . Abstracted from the larger story of which it is a part, it becomes merely an account of the liberation of one people from the domination and oppression of another. . . . This is to place the exodus *in the context of Babel and its immediate sequel* (e.g., the conquests of Nimrod, Gen. 11:8-11), rather than in the context of the call, blessing and covenants of Abraham (italics his).[86]

Further, certain details of the Exodus story itself are frequently overlooked: liberation came not through the Israelites' rebellion but through Yahweh's signs; liberation occurred only after they called upon God; the Israelite community was as much a religious community as it was a socio-political one; and the primary purpose of the Exodus was not liberation of Israel but the glorification of Yahweh.[87]

(3) Theologically, the movement is unbalanced in its anthropocentrism. Gutierrez "reduces the new relationship with God to being

nothing more than love for one's neighbor," and mistakes God the Redeemer for God the Creator.[88] This emphasis opens the way for a soteriology that is exclusively social (with little emphasis on personal sin), an ecclesiology that is largely political and universalistic, a bibliology that is subordinate to contemporary social ideology (e.g., Marxism), and an eschatology that telescopes the future into the present.[89]

Relevance of the movement
to this study

The movement presents a twofold challenge with respect to this study: (a) it calls into question the very materials (i.e., Scripture) and the methods of theology which will be followed in this dissertation; and (b) its emphasis on liberation, freedom, and emancipation (along with such derogatory remarks that traditional theology teaches Christians "how to be weak without regret")[90] stands in harsh contrast to the repeated biblical picture of the disciple as a slave. While it is not the aim of this dissertation to deal with the first challenge, the second challenge more than justifies this study. For if the theme of liberation is the initial, primary, and exclusive explanation of God's character, covenant, and relationship with men, what does the imagery of slavery mean? What does Scripture say about being slaves to God and being fellow slaves for Him? To sum up: this study is intended to be not a critique, but a biblical counterbalance to the trend of particularized liberation theologies by investigating a motif that is diametrically opposed to their conclusions.

A Practical Justification

Happily, the emphasis in theological circles is not entirely negative. In recent literature there is an increased emphasis on discovering how the message of Christ and the New Testament on servanthood should be explained and applied. John A. MacKay says, "the servant image is the most significant symbol in the Bible and in the Christian religion;" it "has been degraded in our time" and must be restored.[91] This impulse is reflected in a plethora of publications and a variety of approaches.[92] Thus, it is hoped that this study will provide a fruitful contribution to the more practical question of what it means for a minister or a layman to be Jesus' slave.

Research Justification

A final rationale for this study is that, surprisingly, it appears to be an area in which less attention has been directed. The slavery motif in the Old Testament was investigated by Curt Lindhagen in 1926; and Walter Zimmerli's Servant of God more recently has interacted with and expanded upon Lindhagen's studies. Numerous dictionary and journal articles focus on some aspects of the theme. Christopher North's The Suffering Servant in Deutero-Isaiah: An Historical and Critical Study, remains the classic for the study of the Suffering Servant.

In the New Testament, there are a variety of works on the institutional of slavery in general; and many focus on slavery in the epistolary literature, especially the epistles of Paul. S. Scott

Bartchy's Μᾶλλον Χρῆσαι; First Century Slavery and 1 Corinthians 7:21 is a representative example. Kenneth C. Russell's Slavery as Reality and Metaphor in the Pauline Letters is a helpful contribution but also of less value to the gospels.

When the motif of slavery is investigated in the gospels, however, most of the literature is concerned with Christ as the Suffering Servant. Lewis Mudge, who surveys the rather sparse literature in his article, "The Servant Lord and His Servant People,"[93] restricts the "servant motif" to the Suffering Servant. Morna D. Hooker's Jesus and the Servant also deals with this motif.

While investigating the theme of the believer as a slave of God in the gospels, it was discovered that no comprehensive work has been written. Encyclopedia and dictionary monographs are profitable sources; and works on the parables (such as Eta Linnemann's Parables of Jesus: Introduction and Exposition, J. Jeremias' The Parables of Jesus, and C. H. Dodd's The Parables of the Kingdom) are fruitful for discussions of the contexts where much of Jesus' teaching on this issue occurs. Most promising is Alfons Weiser's Die Knechtsgleichnisse der Synoptischen Evangelien, although it limits its discussion to the parables. Therefore, there is a legitimate place for a systematic analysis of the occurrence of the slavery imagery in the gospels that is considered in light of the Old Testament use of the metaphor and in context with the contemporary social understanding of slavery.

The Procedure of the Study

To accomplish the purposes outlined above, the occurrences of the slavery motif must be isolated, explained, and collated with a view toward developing a cohesive and comprehensive profile of the spiritual master-slave relationship.

The motif will be isolated lexically, utilizing the terms defined earlier to find the occurrences of the motif. Once the occurrences are isolated, they will be explained within the larger context of the saying. The focus will be on those paragraph units where the metaphorical use of slavery is predominate (e.g., in Jesus' parables and proverbs). Finally, these explanations will be collated in a framework that will systematize what it means--from the standpoint of the gospels and especially Christ Himself--to be a slave of God.

Cautions in the Procedure

Since a lexical approach is being used to isolate the slavery motif, a word of defense that this study does not succumb to possible linguistic fallacies is in order. James Barr isolates at least four linguistic fallacies: (a) etymologizing, or using the history of the word to elaborate its present meaning;[94] (b) "adding the significances," or defining a word each time it occurs by the total accumulated meaning of all its etymological uses;[95] (c) "illegitimate identity transfer," or the semantic equation of two designations which, while not equal to each other, may at separate times be applied to the same object; and (d) "illegitimate totality transfer," or the definition of a word each time it occurs by the total accumulated meaning of all its contextual uses.[96]

Because the primary concern here is the meaning of the concept of slavery or servitude as explained in the context, the temptation to commit one of the etymologizing fallacies should not be problemmatic. The most potentially dangerous fallacy for this study is "illegitimate totality transfer." However, the purpose in investigating the slavery motif is not to show that one word (i.e., δοῦλος) can legitimately bear all possible meanings. Rather it is to collect the meanings of the various contexts to display the totality of meaning involved in the concept. Barr believes a proper procedure

> would be to group the words in groups each representing a related semantic field. . . . Within a general field thus loosely defined an attempt would be made to mark off the semantic oppositions between one word and another as precisely as possible; and from this to proceed to special contexts and word-combinations in which each word occurred--bringing in, of course, the words from outside the loosely defined field freely.[97]

Additionally, he believes that sentences more than individual words provide a more legitimate clue to accurate meaning.[98] These hints will be followed in this study. The primary words within the same semantic field of service and bondage will be used for discovering the contexts and then examined in light of the sentence and paragraph units in which they fall.

Divisions of the Study

In keeping with the purpose and procedure of the study, the slavery motif in the gospels will be discussed as follows: chapter two will investigate the imagery of slavery as it emerges in the Old Testament--

both in its institutional and in its figurative uses. Chapter three will discuss the cultural backgrounds of the era of Christ and the evangelists, demonstrating their awareness of the institution of slavery and discussing the slave systems of Rome, Greece, and Judaism as they might have bearing on the motif in the gospels. Chapter four will focus on the motif in the synoptics, isolating and elucidating the various passages. Chapter five will continue the biblical investigation of the slavery motif in the Fourth Gospel. Chapter six will conclude the dissertation by collating the "submotifs" or meanings derived.

Notes

^{1}Lewis Sperry Chafer, <u>Systematic Theology</u>, 8 vols., vol. 4: <u>Ecclesiology and Eschatology</u>, pp. 56-147, includes such figures as the shepherd and sheep, vine and branches, cornerstone and living stones, head and body, high priest and kingdom of priests, bridegroom and bride; other metaphors as "friends," "sons," and "new wineskins" further the point.

^{2}Chafer, for example, does not even list this figure in <u>Systematic Theology</u>, 8 vols., vol. 7: <u>Doctrinal Summarization</u>.

^{3}See C. H. Dodd, "Some Problems of New Testament Translation," <u>BiTr</u> 13 (July 1962):145-46.

^{4}See <u>NIDNTT</u>, s.v. "Slave," by Rudolf Tuente, 3 (1978):591, for the grouping of these three words under "subjugation."

^{5}BAG, 4th rev. ed., s.v. "θεράπων," p. 359.

^{6}<u>TDNT</u>, s.v. "διάκονος," by Hermann W. Beyer, 2 (1964):81.

^{7}Richard C. Trench, <u>Synonyms of the New Testament</u>, p. 31.

^{8}See C. Spicq, "Le Vocabulaire de l'Esclavage dans le Nouveau Testament," <u>RB</u> 85 (April 1978):216: ". . . le θεράπων a des relations d'intimité et de confiance avec son Maître; son poste de service implique une certain dignité et s'il sert son Créateur, c'est avec beaucoup plus de spontanéité et de zèle qu'un esclave proprement dit."

^{9}Robert Mounce, <u>The Book of Revelation</u>, NIC, pp. 380-81; Leon Morris, <u>The Revelation of St. John</u>, Tyn, p. 220.

^{10}Spicq, pp. 202-3.

^{11}This word is used in the LXX of Ruth and Esther.

^{12}Spicq, p. 217.

^{13}BAG, 4th ed., s.v. "δουλεία, δουλεύω, δοῦλος," pp. 204-5.

^{14}<u>TDNT</u>, s.v. "δοῦλος," by Karl H. Rengstorf, 2 (1964):261.

¹⁵BAG, 4th rev. ed., s.v. "δοῦλος," p. 205.   ¹⁶Trench, p. 30.

¹⁷NIDNTT, s.v. "slave," by Rudolf Tuente, 3 (1978):548.

¹⁸Though some of these uses are derived from a similar use in the Old Testament, Tuente may be right in suggesting that this sense of honor accompanying the apostolic description of "slave of God" may derive from the description of Christ taking the form of a servant (Phil. 2:7). Ibid., 3:596-97; also Spicq, pp. 209, 213.

¹⁹NIDNTT, s.v. "slave," by Rudolf Tuente, 3 (1978):589.

²⁰BAG, 4th rev. ed., s.v. "δέσμιος," p. 175.

²¹Ibid., s.v. "διακονέω, διακονία, διάκονος," p. 183.

²²Spicq does not include these words in his article on slavery vocabulary.

²³Trench, p. 32.

²⁴NIDNTT, s.v. "servant," by Klaus Hess, 3 (1978):544.

²⁵TDNT, s.v. "διάκονος," by Hermann Beyer 2 (1964):81.

²⁶Ibid.   ²⁷NIDNTT, s.v. "servant," by Klaus Hess, 3 (1978):546.

²⁸Ibid., p. 548.

²⁹BAG, 4th rev. ed., s.v. "ὑπηρέτης," p. 850; also TDNT, s.v. "διάκονος," by Hermann Beyer, 2 (1964):81.

³⁰Trench, p. 35.

³¹TDNT, s.v. "διάκονος," by Hermann Beyer, 2 (1964):81.

³²Trench, pp. 34-35.

³³Alan Richardson, ed., A Theological Wordbook of the Bible, s.v. "servant," by J. Y. Campbell, p. 223.

³⁴BAG, 4th rev. ed., s.v. "λειτουργός," p. 472.

³⁵TDNT, s.v. "διάκονος," by Hermann Beyer, 2 (1964):86. NIDNTT, s.v. "servant," by Klaus Hess, 3 (1978):544, denotes this as voluntary service to the *polis*, *cultus*, or the ἐκκλησία.

^{36}BAG, 4th rev. ed., s.v. "λατρεύω," p. 465. NIDNTT, s.v. "servant," by Klaus Hess, 3 (1978):550.

^{37}BAG, 4th rev. ed., s.v. "παῖς, παιδίσκη," pp. 609-10.

^{38}Spicq, p. 221. This is especially true when Christ is called Παῖς θεοῦ in Acts.

^{39}Ibid.; TDNT, s.v. "παῖς," by Oepke, 5:633.

^{40}BAG, 4th rev. ed., s.v. "οἰκέτης," p. 559.

^{41}Trench, p. 32.

^{42}TDNT, s.v. "δοῦλος," by Karl H. Rengstorf, 2 (1964):261.

^{43}Spicq, p. 218.

^{44}Oxford English Dictionary, compact ed., s.v. "motif," p. 1859.

^{45}Shemaryahu Talmon. "The Desert Motif," in Biblical Motifs: Origins and Transformations, ed. Alexander Altman, p. 38.

^{46}Anders Nygren, Agape and Eros, pp. x, 35.

^{47}P. L. Berger, "The Sociological Study of Sectarianism," Social Research 21 (1954):477.

^{48}Talmon, p. 39.

^{49}George W. Coates, "Conquest Traditions in the Wilderness Theme," JBL 95 (June 1976):179. Coates quotes from J. T. Shipley, ed., Dictionary of World Literature, p. 274.

^{50}See D. A. Knight, Rediscovering the Traditions of Israel: The Development of the Traditio-Historical Research of the Old Testament, with Special Consideration of Scandanavian Contributions, pp. 11-20.

^{51}Cf. the other articles in Biblical Motifs, most of which do not take the pains to make such precise definitions.

^{52}It must be agreed that the slavery imagery is a motif in the sense that it, as Coates puts it, "evoke(s) a similar mood, within a work, or in various works of a genre," p. 178. That it could do such in the mind of the reader of a gospel (or in the mind of a listener to Jesus) is fully understandable in light of the common cultural patterns of the day.

⁵³E.g., Curt Lindhagen's work, *The Servant Motif in the Old Testament*.

⁵⁴R. Grant Childs, "Editorial," *Interp* 23 (1969):78-80. For current studies about the methodology of Biblical Theology in contemporary practice, the reader should consult Gerhard Hasel, *Old Testament Theology: Basic Issues in the Current Debate*; B. S. Childs, *Biblical Theology in Crisis*; Krister Stendahl, s.v. "Biblical Theology, contemporary" *IDB*, 1:418-32. See the extensive bibliographies in Stendahl and in Ladd, p. 13.

⁵⁵James Barr, *The Semantics of Biblical Language*, pp. 273-74.

⁵⁶George E. Ladd, *A Theology of the New Testament*, p. 25. Other helpful definitions are found in: Chester K. Lehman, *Biblical Theology*, 2 vols., vol. 2: *Old Testament*, p. 26; Geerhardus Vos, *Biblical Theology: Old and New Testaments*, pp. 5-8; Charles C. Ryrie, *Biblical Theology of the New Testament*, p. 12.

⁵⁷The writer assumes that the sayings of Jesus as recorded in the gospels are authentic--an assumption by no means unanimously accepted by New Testament theologians.

⁵⁸Barr, p. 273.

⁵⁹*IDB*, s.v. "Biblical Theology, contemporary," by Krister Stendahl, 1:418-25.

⁶⁰Vos., p. 8, says: "biblical theology consists in its practical applicability."

⁶¹*BDictTh*, s.v. "Biblical Theology," by Geoffrey W. Bromiley, p. 96, says: "True biblical theology cannot be mere description. . . . It calls for the uncompromising commitment in those who pursue it."

⁶²Says Vos on the relationship of Biblical Theology to Systematics: "In Biblical Theology the principle is one of historical, in Systematic Theology it is one of logical construction. Biblical Theology draws a *line* of development. Systematic Theology draws a *circle*," p. 16. Ryrie adds: "Logically and chronologically Biblical Theology should take precedence over Systematic Theology, for the order of study ought to be introduction, exegesis, historical backgrounds, Biblical Theology, and finally Systematic Theology," p. 17.

⁶³Jurgen Moltmann, *Theology of Hope: On the Ground and Implications of a Christian Eschatology*; Dorothee Solle, *Political Theology*. See bibliography in Glenn R. Bucher, "Theology for the 'Oppressor,'" *JAAR* 44 (1976):519.

[64] James Cone, *A Black Theology of Liberation*; Cone, *God of the Oppressed*.

[65] Jacques Ngally, "Jesus Christ and Liberation in Africa," *ER* 27 (July 1975):212-19.

[66] Juan L. Segundo, *Liberation of Theology*; Gustavo Gutierrez, *A Theology of Liberation: History, Politics and Salvation*. See also George Plasterer, "A Bibliographic Essay," *AsbSem* 32 (July 1977):40-48.

[67] Robert M. Brown, "Who is this Jesus Christ Who Frees and Unites?" *ER* 28 (January 1976):11-12; Bucher, p. 521.

[68] Monika Hellwig, "Liberation Theology: An Emerging School," *SJTh* 30 (1977):141; Gutierrez, p. 153; Marten H. Woudstra, "A Critique of Liberation Theology by a Cross-Culturalized Calvinist," *JETS* 23 (March 1980):8.

[69] Hellwig, p. 143; J. van Wyk, "Latin American Protestant Theology of Liberation," *Missionalia* 5 (August 1977):87; John Goldingay, "The Man of War and the Suffering Servant: The Old Testament and the Theology of Liberation," *TynB* 27 (1976):87; Frederick Herzog, "Liberation and Imagination," *Interp* 32 (July 1978):230.

[70] Hugo Assman, *Theology for a Nomad Church*, p. 104.

[71] T. Howland Sanks and Brian H. Smith, "Liberation Ecclesiology: Praxis, Theory, Praxis," *TS* 38 (March 1977):15; van Wyk, p. 88.

[72] Van Wyk, p. 86; Hellwig, pp. 144-46; Robert T. Osborne, "Jesus and Liberation Theology," *CCen* 93 (March 1976):225-27.

[73] Hellwig, pp. 144-46; J. Robert Meyners, "Liberation 200 Years On," *CTSR* 66 (Fall 1976):39-41.

[74] Hellwig, p. 147.

[75] Meyners, pp. 39-41; Hellwig, p. 144.

[76] James Cone, "Revelation and Social Existence," *ThD* 23 (Autumn 1975):253.

[77] J. J. F. Durand, "Liberation for Reconciliation," *Missionalia* 5 (August 1977):115.

[78] Meyners, p. 39. "The Bible is the story of liberation starting with the Hebrew people's constant struggle to be free from external domination and the internal oppression of sin and faithlessness."

[79] Cone, "Revelation," p. 251. "As a history book, it begins with the Exodus in which the Israelites as slaves were led out of Egypt under the divine guidance of Yahweh."

[80] Gutierrez, p. 153.

[81] Michael Manley, "From the Shackles of Domination and Opression," ER 28 (January 1976):60-61; Brown, p. 15.

[82] Ferdinand Deist, "The Exodus Motif in the Old Testament and the Theology of Liberation," Missionalia 5 (August 1977):60.

[83] Dale Patrick, "The Moral Logic of Election," Encounter 37 (Spring 1978):198.

[84] John H. Stek observes with caution the trend of many theologians "to redefine the biblical message in terms of frames of reference borrowed from newly emerging conceptions of reality," in his "Salvation, Justice and Liberation in the Old Testament," CTJ 13 (November 1978):133.

[85] Goldingay, p. 87; also van Wyk, p. 89.

[86] Stek, pp. 146-47.

[87] Deist, p. 61. Cf. Woudstra, pp. 8-9, and Deist's evaluation of Luke 4:18, pp. 64-65.

[88] Christopher M. N. Sugden, "A Different Dream: Jesus and Revolution," TSFB 71 (Spring 1975):17.

[89] See van Wyk, pp. 89-91; Clark Pinnock, "Liberation Theology: The Gains, the Gaps," CT 15 (1976):13-15; Plasterer, pp. 46-48.

[90] Herzog, p. 237.

[91] John A. MacKay, "The Form of a Servant," ThTo 15 (October 1958):304, 307, 309.

[92] John R. W. Stott, The Preacher's Portrait, pp. 11-32, 100-124, deals with a preacher as a "steward" and "servant." Joseph C. Shenk, "Missionary Identity and Servanthood," Miss 1 (October 1973):505-15; Jack V. Reeve, "Preparing Professional Servants," LexTQ 13 (July 1978):96-98; Larry W. Hustado, "The Ministry as Servanthood," TriS 4 (Spring 1975):67-70; Ernest T. Campbell, "They Also Serve Who Lead," PSB 2 (1978):3-8; Bill Millikan, "Where Have All the Servants Gone?" FaW 88 (February 1975):32-33; Terence E. Fretheim, "On Being a Servant," PSB 66 (October 1973):59-64; J. A. Davidson, "Sacrament and Servanthood," NPulD 56 (January 1976):57-59; Gilbert J. Horn, "Servanthood vis-a-vis Sophistication," PSB 66 (Summer 1974):68-71, provide other examples.

[93] Lewis S. Mudge, "The Servant Lord and His Servant People," SJT 12 (1959):114-15.

[94] Barr, p. 109. [95] Ibid., pp. 144-47.

[96] Ibid., pp. 217-18. [97] Ibid., p. 235.

[98] Ibid., pp. 249, 263, 269.

CHAPTER II

OLD TESTAMENT BACKGROUNDS TO THE SLAVERY MOTIF

Introduction

Slavery, either in its institutional or metaphorical contexts, permeates all types of Old Testament literature; it is not restricted historically or literarily. Since there are concrete examples of New Testament writers alluding to Old Testament passages that contain the slavery theme (e.g., Luke 1:54, 69), it is both legitimate and necessary to seek to understand the conceptual framework in the Old Testament that underlies the slavery motif in the New.

It is the purpose of this chapter, therefore, to lay the biblical foundation of the meaning of the motif in the gospels by pursuing the following course: (1) to delineate the slavery motif by surveying its various lexical manifestations; (2) to investigate the non-religious slavery references to slavery in an effort to detect clues to the ethical meaning of the theme; and (3) to study the religious uses of slavery that could contribute most directly to a clearer understanding of being a slave of God.

Delineating the Slavery Motif

That there is a slavery motif in the Old Testament is not denied.

Curt Lindhagen's older but classic study entitled <u>The Servant Motif in the Old Testament</u>[1] and Walther Zimmerli's more recent work, <u>The Servant of God</u>, both assume the definability and legitimacy of such a motif.[2] Generally speaking, the motif is defined lexically with special emphasis placed upon the multifaceted uses of עבד.

Secondary Slavery Terms

There are several words in the Old Testament which are used to designate a slave. A frequently used term is אמה, or "handmaid." An example of its literal use is Hagar in Genesis 21:10, the "maid of her mistress." Figuratively it is used in address as a humble self-designation as with Ruth (Ruth 3:9) and with Hannah (1 Sam. 1:11); and it generally functions as the gender counterpart to עבד.

Another term for a female slave is שפחה which designates a female servant belonging to the mistress (Gen. 16:1), belonging to the master (Gen. 29:24), functioning as a concubine (Gen. 32:22), or functioning in a general sense as a performer of menial service (Exod. 11:5). It is used figuratively in polite address to denote deference but is never used in addressing God.[3]

Infrequent terms for servant or slaves are נער, נפש, and מקנת כסף. נער can mean either "boy" or "slave" and when used in the latter sense denotes either a literal slave who is a member of the household (e.g., Num 22:22) or a servant-follower of the king (e.g., 1 Sam. 25:5). The feminine form is used infrequently of female slaves and is always found in the plural (e.g., Gen. 24:61).[4] נפש, which can mean "person" in addition to its other uses, very infrequently denotes the slave (e.g., Gen. 12:5).[5] מקנה כסף, which means literally "one bought with money," is used primarily for foreign slaves acquired through purchases (e.g., Gen. 17:12, 13, 23, 27; Exod. 12:44). Exodus 12:44 contrasts the מקנה כסף with people born in the house.[6]

In their literal sense, these words stress the subordination of the slave to the master as expressed in ownership by the master or in service for him. It may not be inferred from these usages, however, that such subservience is oppressive in the sense evident in later slave systems. In fact, the handmaid also served as concubine (often with accrued legal rights); the slave of the house stood in contrast to the purchased slave; and the "man bought with money" was enjoined to become circumcised in order to partake of the religious functions of the cult. These instances suggest that a notably tight bond existed between master and slave.

The figurative uses of these same words (e.g., to denote a close relationship with the king or as a form of address either to God or to others of equal socio-economic status) do not frequently connote a negative relationship between the superior and inferior members. Thus it should not be surprising for Jesus and the gospel writers to depict the subordinate relationship that should exist between Christ and His followers in a similar way.

The Uses of עבד[7]

The function of עבד in the Old Testament--the most frequently used designation for slave—is a complex yet highly instructuve study. Because of the prominence of this particular term in the Old Testament, its various uses are outlined below and will provide the basic format for the considerations that follows:

    I. Non-religious uses

        A. Work in general
        B. Institutional slavery
        C. Political relationships
           1. Involuntary subjugation
           2. Voluntary service to one's king

    II. Religious uses

        A. Israel
        B. Righteous remnant
        C. Individuals
        D. Suffering Servant

Non-Religious Aspects of Slavery

The word עבד itself simply means "work" or "toil" and may refer either to a man's work on the earth (e.g., Gen. 2:5) or to God's work (e.g., of judgment, Isa. 28:21).[8] But the most frequent non-religious use of עבד designates service rendered out of compulsion for the benefit of another, i.e., the institutions of domestic or state slavery.

Institutional slavery in the Old Testament deserves study here for several reasons. First, the impact of Mosaic legislation and rabbinic Judaism on palestinian slave practices at the time of Christ makes it most probable that the patterns of Old Testament slavery would be highly influential on the New Testament patterns. Second, since institutional slavery in the Old Testament was governed by elaborate divine regulations, an inspection of this divinely ordered institution may yield insights into God's perspective of the master-slave relationship which may suggest spiritual implications that are carried into the New Testament. Third, the Jewish community's recognition of their own relationship to Yahweh as redeemed slaves has promising implications for the believer's relationship to the Father. Fourth, slavery to God implied a coordinate responsibility toward others in Israel's slave regulations (emerging in the constant distinction made between Israelite and non-Israelite slaves); and this surfaces in the gospels as well.

Institutional Slavery in the Old Testament

Roland de Vaux, in his discussion on the social institutions of ancient Israel, deals succinctly with the contention that real slavery was not a characteristic of Israel's society.[9] He points out that the distinction between slaves and freemen (or wage earners), the presumption of slavery logically inferred from the practice of manumission, and the mention of "purchased" individuals establish firmly that slavery as an institution did exist in Israel and in earlier periods.

Pre-Mosaic slavery

Although the institution of slavery is not thoroughly defined and explained in the Old Testament until Moses, a profile of institutional slavery surfaces in Genesis, Exodus 1-19, and Job.[10]

The causes of slavery

The causes of slavery inferred from this period are sixfold. (a) Some slaves (מקנה כסף) were acquired through purchase as shown by

Abraham (Gen. 17:21-22, etc.) and Joseph (Gen. 37:27-38).

(b) Some slaves were accumulated through birth. Such are designated as ילי בית and are associated with two characteristics: military proficiency and participation in the worship of the master's God when circumcised (Gen. 14:14; 17:12). Although יליד can mean "son" or "child," a contrast is made between ones born in the house and ones purchased by money--implying that the contrast is between two categories of slaves, not between slaves and freemen.[11]

(c) Slaves were acquired through war (e.g., Lot, Gen. 14:11-12).[12] (d) Freemen became slaves through indebtedness, a practice instituted in Egypt by Joseph (Gen. 47:20-26).[13] (e) Some became enslaved for punishment of theft, an implication from Joseph's promised "enslavement" of Benjamin (Gen. 44:1-17). (f) Finally, enforced slavery by royal fiat was the cause of Israel's slavery in Egypt (Exod. 1:10).

The value of slaves

The value of a slave is specified in Genesis 37:28, giving information not even found in the Mosaic Law. There Joseph--likely a lad--was sold for twenty pieces of silver.

The status and service of slaves

Male slaves in Abraham's household were melded into a crack fighting force (Gen. 14:14-15) or fulfilled significant administrative and emissarial functions (e.g., Eliezer of Damascus, Gen. 15:2; 24).[14] In that culture the master could designate a slave as his heir in the event he lacked progeny of his own (Gen. 15:3). Finally, Abraham's male slaves were allowed to enjoy a certain participation in the cultic observances of the household and were required to be circumcised (Gen. 17:12, 13, 23, 27).

There are numerous references to slaves who served kings (e.g., Pharoah, Gen. 47:25; 50:7; Abimelech, Gen. 21:25) although it is difficult to determine whether these refer to menial slaves or to court officials. Of greater significance is Joseph who, as a Hebrew slave, ascended from bondage to supreme political power--an indication that even among the segregationist Egyptians servile status was not an impassable barrier to upward social mobility.

The female slave engaged in menial toil for her mistress (Gen. 16:1, 6, 9); and her responsibility was to be submissive (Gen. 16:9). She was under the master's ownership (Gen. 12:16; 20:14; 24:35) and was the master's concubine (e.g., Hagar to Abraham, Gen. 16:3; Bilhah and Zilpah to Jacob, Gen. 30:4, 9). Though the female slave's position seems more restricted and exploited, her slave status is not totally stigmatized. Even the role of concubine represented potential advantage if, as in the case of Hagar, the concubine bore the master's heir.

Thus in sum, servile status for both male and female was not rigidly oppressive; rather, it afforded opportunities for mobility, mutuality, religious equality, and increased responsibility.

The attitudes toward slavery

Although one finds no impulse to abolish slavery, slavery did carry distinctly negative connotations (Gen. 9:25-27; 49:15; Job. 7:1-3).[15]

The greatest negative example of slavery is Israel's bondage to Pharoah (Gen. 15:13; Exod. 6:5); her liberation from Egypt was of pivotal importance to the formation of the nation and the covenant. It is so pervasive a theme in subsequent Old Testament literature that one might expect all metaphorical uses of slavery to be tainted against slavery. But this is precluded by two factors: (a) Some forms of slavery (e.g., through debt, thievery, or birth) are portrayed as legitimate; and even slavery through war is seen as a humanitarian alternative to the frequent practice of genocide. (b) God continued to designate His people as slaves who, though redeemed from Egypt, now were bonded to His service. The people who "serve" Pharaoh desire to depart into the wilderness to "serve" their God (Exod. 3:12; 4:23; 7:16; 8:1, 20; 9:1, 3; 10:3, 7, 26).

Thus, a tolerant attitude toward the institution is not surprising, particularly as it describes one's relationship to Yahweh. What has been said above about the potential personal benefits (e.g., of heirship, authority, political power) to a slave further substantiates this position. Furthermore, Job strongly suggests that the master-slave distinctions made by men are temporary and frail: that birth, death, and suffering are great divine equalizers between the classes (Job. 3:15, 19; 19:15-16); and that mistreatment may invoke God's wrath (Job. 31:13-14).

Mosaic legislation

The primary legislation regarding slavery is found in Exodus 21:1-

11, 20-27; Leviticus 25:1-55; and Deuteronomy 15:1-18; and two stark realities characterize it, which at first glance, suggest a certain inequity in the ordering of God's theocracy. The first is the very existence of slavery at all; the second is the preferential distinctions that are made between Hebrew and non-Hebrew slaves. The resolution of both of these issues lies outside the perspective of this study, and literature is replete with attempts to solve them.[16] It is sufficient at this juncture simply to note that the first issue is not unique to the Old Testament, as the New Testament's refusal to categorically ban the institution keeps the debate alive. The second issue is also peripheral here,[17] but a recognition of this Hebrew and non-Hebrew distinction (Lev. 25:35-55) provides an interpretive key for reconciling many divergent slave regulations,[18] and highlights the unique convenantal nature of the relationship of all the Israelites with God and with other members of the covenant community.

The reasons for enslavement

Of the non-Israelite.[19] According to the Pentateuch, a primary reason for the enslavement of non-Israelites was captivity in war--specifically as Israel executed Holy War in obedience to God. Deuteronomy 20:10-18, for example, explicates the procedure Israel was to follow in attacking, besieging, and capturing foreign cities. Canaanite cities and citizens were to be totally destroyed.[20]

Foreigners were also enslaved through purchase (Lev. 25:44-46), being acquired either from foreign nations or from alien sojourners.[21]

It is plain from this passage that the rules regarding Israelite enslavement were more stringent than those for foreign slaves; but even the acquisition of foreign slaves had certain regulations. For example, the Law deliberately rejected the practice of extradition of slaves (Deut. 23:15-16).[22] Further, Moses twice proscribed kidnapping for enslavement: in Deuteronomy 24:7, where the Israelite brother is definitely in mind, and in Exodus 21:16 where the more general prohibition would protect even foreigners from an illicit Israelite slave trade.

Enslavement by birth was another means by which foreigners were enslaved. Leviticus 25:45-46 implies that the offspring of foreign slaves also became a permanent part of the owner's household. It also suggests a final reason for foreign enslavement was bequest.

Of the Israelite. The causes for Israelite slavery were usually related to voluntary or involuntary sale. One form of voluntary sale involved the sale of a man's daughter as the buyer's wife or concubine (Exod. 21:7-11), thus providing marital security for her. The Exodus passages explain that she is to be accorded full rights as a wife (if the master himself took her) or daughter (if designated for the master's son); even in the event of polygamy this "slave" wife was either to be granted support (food, clothing, and conjugal rights) or was to be released without requiring payment. Why a man would sell his daughter is not expressed. While it may simply be to secure her marriage, it is more likely that the man sold her out of poverty or debt since this was by no means the customary way in which Hebrew marriages were transacted.

However, one valuable effect of this law was to prevent prostitution of the daughter and to preserve the marital relationship.

Voluntary self-sale due to poverty was perhaps the most frequent cause of slavery among the Israelites. Moses recognized that because of poverty some would sell themselves as slaves to other Israelites (Lev. 25:39), some would be sold by Israelites to other Israelites (Deut. 15:12), and some would even sell themselves to non-Israelite sojourners (Lev. 25:47).

The Law also allowed for intances of involuntary sale.[23] Basic to this regulation was the principle of restitution; the one who borrowed was to repay what was lent (without usurious interest to a Hebrew, Exod. 22:14-15); and a thief was to make restitution for what he had taken and to pay an additional indemnity (Exod. 22:1-4). Slavery was effected only for the thief who owned nothing and was sold to pay the restitution (Exod. 22:3). While this doubtless served as a form of punishment, this was not the primary intention of the law.[24]

Birth by enslaved Israelite parents was also a reason for enslavement on the premise that the offspring of a slave automatically belonged to the master. Unlike non-Hebrew slaves born in the house, however, children of Israelite slaves could gain their freedom at the year of jubilee (Lev. 25:54).

The treatment of slaves

The treatment of slaves was rather tightly regulated and, as Zimmerli points out, reflected the tendency to humanize--though not eliminate--the instituion of slavery.[25]

Universal practices. Israel did not practice the custom of branding slaves. A slave, out of love for his mater, could voluntarily have his ear pierced with an awl to signify perpetual servitude (Exod. 21:5-6; Deut. 15:16-17). But while this would thus become a sign of possession, it equally signified mutual affection.[26]

The discipline and punishment of slaves was practiced[27] but restricted.[28] Exodus 21:20-21 provided for the master's punishment if he directly killed a slave, but allowed the lost value of the slave to be sufficient penalty if the slave died later.[29] De Vaux observes that the protection of the master's property was thus balanced with the protection of the slave's humanity.[30]

Also, if the slave was maimed in any way, he could be freed (Exod. 21:26-27). This applied not only to the loss of an eye (a great loss to the slave which would limit his effectiveness in the master's service) but also to the loss of a tooth (by comparison a less significant loss). This regulation preserved the humanity of the slave, although the master himself was not to be maimed on account of the slave (Exod. 21:22-25).

Both Hebrew and non-Hebrew slaves could participate to some degree in religious worship.[31] For example, all circumcised male slaves were allowed to eat of the Passover; all slaves were to be exempt from work on the Sabbath (Exod. 20:10; 23:12). A priest and his slave could partake of the holy portion of the offering (Lev. 22:10-12), which was denied other Israelites, suggesting a close domestic bond that existed in the household and which extended certain privileges to all its members, whether slave or free. Finally, slaves could participate in religious celebrations: the bringing of burnt offerings (Deut. 12:12), the enjoyment of the feast of weeks (Deut. 16:11), and the feast of booths (Deut. 16:14).

Practices regarding female slaves.[32] Since Exodus 21:4 suggests the female slave served to produce children, one might be tempted to conclude that she was diminished to a sexual commodity. Additionally, in Exodus 21:7-11 she is denied the right of sabbatical manumission accorded to men, a right given to her in Deuteronomy 21:10-14.[33] But, while the progenitor function is prominent in the regulations regarding female slaves, it is closely hedged by marital stipulations that prevent unchecked promiscuity.[34] Leviticus 19:20 also enhances the treatment of the female slave by specifying a guilt offering be submitted by the violator of a bethrothed slave girl.[35]

Practices regarding Israelite slaves. The Law made a most outstanding differentiation between Hebrews and non-Hebrews, as outlined primarily in Leviticus 25.[36] Only the enslaved Israelite could be redeemed by a blood relative (Lev. 25:47-55), and only the Israelite had the right of self-redemption with the concomitant ability to accumulate his own property while enslaved. Obviously, in the case of the self-sale, the new slave would have the exclusive possession over his own sale revenue (which likely would be used to pay debt or to provide for needs).

However, Leviticus 25:49 implies that the Israelite slave had the right to a *peculium* from which he could then redeem himself.[37]

Furthermore, the Israelite slave was not to be subjected to "slave's service" but to be treated as a hired man (Lev. 25:39-49; 25:53). Finally, the Hebrew slave was not merely to be freed on the sabbatical year, but also to be sent forth with ample provisions (Deut. 15:12-15) as a reminder of Yahweh's generous redemption of the nation from Egypt.[38]

The manumission of slaves

In addition to previously mentioned causes for release (denial of a female slave's rights, maiming, and redemption), two primary means of manumission for the Israelite slave involved expired terms of service on the sabbatical year and on the year of jubilee.

The sabbatical year (Exod. 21:2-6; Deut. 15:12-18) refers to the seventh year which followed six years of service. Six years was the limitation for Israelite servitude and the seventh was to be a time of rest and freedom (on the analogy of the sabbath of days). The scope of this regulation included at least all male and female Israelite slaves (Deut. 15:12-18).[39]

The year of jubilee is explained only in Leviticus 25 and 27.[40] It provided for the automatic freeing of all Israelite slaves after the forty-ninth year. It is not clear from this passage whether female slaves were included (although the comprehensive changes effected by the coming of jubilee virtually affirm their inclusion), but non-Hebrew slaves were not included in the reshuffling (Lev. 25:46). The possible economic implications of selling a slave just before jubilee were anticipated and specified (Lev. 25:50-52).

Post-Mosaic slavery

Mendelsohn accurately observes that Palestine, like most other ancient civilizations, had three kinds of slavery: domestic, temple, and state.[41] Mosaic legislation concerned itself almost exclusively with domestic slavery. The subsequent history of the Israelites demonstrates that forms of state slavery and temple slavery also emerged. Domestic slavery of course endured (e.g., 2 Kings 4:1-7; Prov. 17:2; 1 Chron. 2:34-35; Isa. 50:1; Neh. 5:1-5), although the regulations were not consistently obeyed (Jer. 34:8-17).

State slavery

State slavery may be strictly defined as the ownership and utilization of slaves by an organized state or crown.[42] As such, it did not exist until the period of the monarchy. During the theocracy, however, the deceptive Gibeonites and certain of the Canaanites were enslaved, not exterminated as God commanded. The Gibeonites in particular served as menials for the tabernacle (Josh. 9:3-27; 16:10; 17:13).[43]

Saul did little to perpetuate state slavery. David, in his expansion of the nation's borders, enslaved the Ammonites (2 Sam. 12:31) and apparently was the first to give the Levites the Nethinim to assist them in the temple (Ezra 8:20).

It was under king Solomon, however, that state slavery, temple slavery and the corvée become fully realized. In building the temple (1 Kings 5:13-14), Solomon enlisted Israelite laborers (מס)--a group of about 30,000--to work in rotating relays of 10,000 each. That these were Israelites is a logical inference drawn from the context and from similar new Eastern practices.

Solomon, however, also enslaved non-Israelites: the Amorites, Hittites, Perizzites, Hivites, and Jebusites (1 Kings 9:20-21). These slaves fulfilled a variety of functions in the kings court (and perhaps around the temple after it was completed); and they probably constituted the work force for the ships sent to Ophir and for the mines of Eloth and the Arabah (1 Kings 9:26-28).[44]

Temple slaves

The Nethinim (literally, "those who are given") were temple workers from Israel, the priests, and the Levites (1 Chron. 9:2; Neh. 11:3). They originated in the time of David (Ezra 8:20), and while their actual identity is a matter of debate,[45] it is more probable they were descendants of the earlier Gibeonites who served in the temple but who, by the post-exilic period, were now depicted not by their race but by their function. The other group of temple slaves were the "sons of Solomon's servants." The geneologies in Ezra and Nehemiah (Ezra 2:43-58; Neh. 7:46-60) show clearly that they were neither Israelites nor Nethinim.

Both Haran[46] and Mendelsohn[47] understand these two groups to be descendants of Canaanites forced into royal slavery at the time of

Solomon or David. By the post-exilic period they seemed to have lost
both their servile status (since Israel no longer enslaved or utilized
slaves for royal service), and the past stigma often attached to the
Canaanite peoples (likely because these descendants themselves became
followers of Yahweh, Neh. 10:28; 11:3).

Theological presuppositions underlying institutional slavery

A theology of creation

One theological principle foundational to the Old Testament
institution of slavery is God as Creator of all men. This "theology of
creation"[48] affirms a certain equality of both slave and free because
of their common origin (Exod. 21:20; Job. 31:13-15). Thus, it is not
difficult to see why the Israelite attitude toward the treatment of
domestic slaves was, by contrast, more humanitarian than the attitudes
and practices of their contemporaries. This application to God as
Creator is frequent in New Testament theology,[49] as illustrated in Paul's
admonition to masters and slaves to behave in light of their mutual
relationship to their heavenly Master (Col. 4:1) who is the Creator of
all things (Col. 1:15-17).

A theology of redemption

Also fundamental to Israel's conception of slavery was the historical reality of her own bondage in Egypt, her redemption from oppression, and her consequent new status as the slaves of her Redeemer,
Yahweh (Lev. 25:42; Deut. 15:13-14).[50] This predominant Old Testament theme

is explicit in Paul (e.g., Rom. 6) and implicit in the parables and proverbs of Christ.

A major implication of this is that the Israelites were therefore brothers to one another.[51] This might explain the preferential treatment Israelite slaves were to receive. Of course, the strong sense of national brotherhood might simply have arisen from the common experience of the Exodus itself, but likely the relationship between parties in a covenant was not that dissimilar from the relationship between master and slave. But whatever the cause, it is more than coincidental that the sense of brotherhood among fellow-slaves is one tangible feature of the slavery motif in the gospels.[52]

Political Service and Subservience
in the Old Testament

The Old Testament also uses עבד to speak of political service of either voluntary or involuntary character. These political and military uses confirm, on the one hand, the emphasis on allegience and abasement that emerges in the institutional uses. On the other hand, they give expression to some new implications of ambassadorship and representation that arise from the voluntary aspects of political service.

The negative emphasis: political subjugation[53]

In 1 Samuel 8:4-22, where the nation is warned against the evils of a monarchy, the language of slavery is used to describe the king-subject relationship. עבד denotes, in one instance, domestic slaves (or chattel) that the king would possess (vs. 16). In verses 14-15, עבד

depicts the king's courtiers and inner-circle advisors who stand to receive for their faithful service a reward drawn from the people's possessions. Finally, עבד is used to describe a form of conscripted service (vs. 17) in which free citizens were enlisted to perform tasks at the behest of the monarch.

The two primary examples of a conscripted free citizenry in Israel were military conscription and the corvée. Saul exercised his royal perogative in building an army to fight the Philistines. David and Solomon surrounded themselves with a multitude of royal officials designated as "slaves," and Solomon instituted the corvée for his building projects. However, both practices were mitigated in their severity. Military service had its compensations of rank and its rewards of spoil (1 Sam. 22:7) and, as Zimmerli points out, was motivated by a national allegiance which "superceded previous relationships."[54] The corvée too had its compensatory elements. It was temporary, it operated on the rotational system, and it contributed to the national goal of constructing the temple of Yahweh. Thus, these national examples of subjugation would not have totally negative connotations to the Israelites. Even here the notion of עבד contains a dual implication of allegiance and abasement.

Internationally, political subservience not only took the form of the institutional enslavement of foreigners but also included the submission of vassals to their suzerain lords (e.g., 2 Sam. 10:19). While the vassal-suzerain relationship denoted an unequal and often subservient relationship, it was not always negative, for the vassal

sustained a relationship with his suzerain that included both protection
and responsible service.

The positive emphasis: royal service [55]

The prevalence of royal servants extended from the reigns of Saul
to Josiah, and they illustrate a variety of relationships with their
masters.[56] Some of the kings' slaves (עבד המלך) served outside the court
(1 Sam. 21:7; 1 Kings 16:9), functioning in both menial and military
capacities but with significant responsibility and considerable access
to the king. Most occupied roles in the court: in roles undefined (2 Sam.
9:2) yet suggesting constant access to their master; as royal ambassadors (2 Sam. 10:204) whose mistreatment evoked full royal retaliation;
as advisors and counselors, suggesting a mutuality of respect and
dependence between sovereign and servant (1 Sam. 16:15) which could be
raised to the level of friendship (2 Sam. 15:34, 37) or spiritual
dependence (2 Kings 22:12).[57]

The parallel between the ruler-subject and the master-slave
relationships make it tempting to suggest that such relationships may
provide an interpretative background for the slavery motif in the gospels.
Since Christ is recognized as the King of the Jews, and the Son of David,
it is not farfetched to suppose that Jesus' relationship to His disciples
would reflect in many ways the relationship of a king to his royal
officials in matters of representation, reward, close intimacy, and
delegated authority.

Religious Aspects of the Slavery Motif

The more metaphorical or religious applications of the motif shall be considered as it relates to four spheres: (a) the nation as a whole; (b) the righteous remnant within the nation; (c) individuals; and (d) the Suffering Servant.

Designating the Nation as a Whole[58]

While Isaiah 41:8 denotes the nation as a spiritual servant of Yahweh in a context of covenantal blessing and sovereign election, this emphasis is unfolded throughout the entire Old Testament. One finds a twofold outworking of the nation's role: (a) in the practice of the cult and (b) in the ethical relationship of Yahweh in the covenant.

Cultic uses

Although עבד itself is rarely used of cultic ministers (cf. Ps. 134:1; 135:1),[59] the biblical writers do utilize עבד and עבדה to describe the cultic forms as they existed historically in the tabernacle (e.g., Exod. 35; Num. 3-4); in the two temples (1 Chron. 23; Ezra 6:8); and prophetically in the future temple (Ezek. 44:14). In these cultic contexts the words combine the ideas of compulsory service and high honor.

The use of עבד designates general cultic practice (rendered frequently as the "work of service," 1 Chron. 9:13). It describes the officials of the cult (including the three Levitical families who maintained and moved the tabernacle, Num. 3:21-37; 4:1-33); the objects of the cult (2 Chron. 8:14; and including the tabernacle, Exod. 27:19; 1 Chron. 23:32; and its utensils, 1 Chron. 23:26); the non-Levitical "work of service" in constructing the temple (1 Chron. 28:20); the liturgy of worship (e.g., the ministry of music, 1 Chron. 25:1); the responsibilities of a priest or Levite (2 Chron. 31:2); and the sacrificial ritual itself (2 Chron. 35:10).

Theological uses

The book of Exodus recounts the historical liberation of the nation from the womb of Egypt. But theologically, service is used in Exodus to define the nation's new relationship to Yahweh in terms of the already familiar concept of bondage. While the earlier chapters stress Israel's servitude in Egypt (1:13, 14; 14:15, etc.), Moses appealed to Pharaoh to let the people go into the wilderness so they could "serve" Yahweh (Exod. 3:12; 7:16; et al.) by which he meant cultic activity (3:18; 10:9). Thus, by a subtle wordplay, the theme of bondage and service functioned as an analogy for Israel's future relationship to Yahweh. There is never a hint that the nation would experience complete freedom or unrestraint; rather her redemption from Egypt merely signaled a change of masters (Exod. 6:6-7).

The reality of this redemption is reinforced by the ransom price demanded by Yahweh--the setting apart of one tribe in lieu of the nation's firstborn and the payment of a five shekel fee for each Israelite over the total number of Levites. Their perpetual service to the divine Redeemer illustrates not only the costliness of their new relationship of God but also its permanence (Num. 3:40-48).

Ethical uses

Serving God not only pertained to physical ritual but also to the heartfelt attitude toward the divine Master. Deuteronomy 10:12, for example, juxtaposes the commands to "fear God," "walk in His ways," and "love Him" with the admonition to voluntarily serve Him with one's total being. Thus, there is a congruence between attitude (love) and action (service).[60]

While the initial basis of the nation's relationship to God is found in His redemption of them, the heightened expression of their ethical obligation is found in the Mosaic covenant. It created new implications: the possibility of greater penalty for disobedience and the promise of expanded blessing for obedience.

The negative thrust of the covenant can be summarized in God's proscription against serving other gods. It finds its rationale in the exclusiveness of Yahweh's demands for worship and it is consistent with His work of electing one nation for His purposes. A constant contrast is sustained between serving other gods and serving the true God (especially in Deut. 4; Josh. 24),[61] where both a cultic and ethical nuance exists (cf. Jer. 22:9 where service equals worship). And severe is the punishment for violation! One notices, interestingly, that serving other gods is both something to be punished (Deut. 11:16, 17) and a punishment (Deut. 4:28; 28:24, 36).

The severity of the prohibiton against serving other gods is balanced, however, by the immensity of the blessing that would come from unstinted allegiance to Yahweh. Many of the blessings were conditioned upon this obedience, especially as they related to material prosperity in the land (Deut. 4). Lindhagen rightly points out, however, that unconditional benefits do exist: the guarantee of a preserved remnant, restoration of the remnant after the deportation, and a future exaltation of the nation.[62]

Designating the Righteous Remnant

The passages in which a righteous religions remnant are called God's servants are relatively few (Ps. 34; 1 Kings 9:7; Dan. 3:26, 28; and Isa. 65), but they do present some predicates of spiritual slavery. Psalm 34, in contrasting the righteous and the wicked (vv. 15-19) reaches a climax when these righteous ones are called "His slaves" (vv. 21-22). The title of slave is most probably associated with those true to the theocratic purpose of God (in this case, the Israelites, not the Philistines).[63] These righteous slaves are identified with God because they sought God's face, not because they were born into the select nation.

In 1 Kings 9:7, where the Lord commanded Jehu to avenge the blood of "My servants the prophets," it is clear that to be a slave of God one had to be totally identified with God's cause as manifested in a refusal to bow the knee to other gods even if such refusal meant death. As such it was a designation of honor. Similarly, the three Hebrews in Babylon's fiery furnace (Dan. 3:26, 28) also were identified with Yahweh's cause, refusing to compromise that devotion by practicing idolatry.[64]

Isaiah 65 uses the word slaves to contrast the righteous remnant of Israel with the entire nation in an eschatological setting. These servants are not only elect but actively seeking the Lord (65:10); they are juxtaposed with the rest of the nation who had forsaken the ways of Yahweh; and they will enjoy the blessings of occupation in the land: food and drink, joy, and a new name (Isa. 65:9, 13, 15).

Thus, the word slave was used to denote the righteous remnant of Israel. Their relationship with their divine Master was intensified because of their refusal to worship strange gods, their devotion to His character, and their reception of His special millennial favor. Here the honor and exaltation that accompanies obedient slave service to God becomes evident again.

Designating Righteous Individuals[65]

Specific individuals

A person could designate himself as God's slave, be so described from the mouth (or pen) of another, or be called a slave by God Himself.

The patriarchs

Abraham and Jacob refer to themselves as "Thy slave" in speaking to God (Gen. 18:3; 32:11), Isaac is called God's slave in the prayer of Abraham's wife-seeking messenger (Gen. 24:14), and all three patriarchs are corporately called the slaves of God by Moses (Exod. 32:13; Deut. 9:27). Nowhere in the Old Testament does God denote the patriarchs as His slaves.[66]

The kings

David is the most frequent royal bearer of the title. In the historical literature, David addresses God as "Thy slave" (2 Sam. 7:25-29), others in prayer refer to David as "Thy slave" (1 Kings 3:6-7), and God Himself describes David as His slave. When God initiates the Davidic covenant in 2 Samuel 7, it is quite significant that David, the recipient of this blessing, is called "My slave" (2 Sam. 7:8) by Yahweh. The slave relationship David sustained combines the elements of election, responsibility, intimate relationship, exaltation, and favor that God granted only to a select few. In the Psalter, David uses "Thy slave" as a self-designation in worship of Yahweh. While David's use of this phrase may simply be a substitute for the personal pronoun, the expression of slavery to Yahweh more likely reveals the spiritual unity of purpose that the worshipper seeks with his Master, or the fear he may have if separated from his Lord.[67] Additionally, it suggests total dependence and humble obedience when used in covenantal contexts (Ps. 143:12, where the "slave" appeals to God's חסד).

Other kings beside David hold this title. Hezekiah is called "His slave" (2 Chron. 32:16) in an ironic contrast between himself and Sennacherib's royal slaves that suggests the representative function of the slave for the master. Zerubbabel[68] is called "My slave" by the Lord (Hag. 2:23) in a context that suggests sovereign election and designated authority.

The prophets

Collectively, the prophets are repeatedly being called "My slaves" by God when their responsibility to communicate God's revelation is keenly emphasized (e.g., 2 Kings 21:10) and God would avenge their faithful service if they met hostility, persecution, or death (e.g., 2 Kings 9:7).

Individual prophets who are called slaves of Yahweh include: Elijah (2 Kings 10:10); Ahijah of Shiloh (1 Kings 14:18); Jonah (2 Kings 14:25); and Isaiah (Isa. 20:3). Often these designation occur when the evidence of their prophetic service is seen; and of these only Isaiah is directly denominated by God as "My slave."

Persons of "theocratic" significance

The supreme figure here is Moses of whom the title is used most frequently (e.g., of himself, Exod. 4:10; by others, Neh. 1:7; and by God, 2 Kings 21:8), and of whom references are found in all divisions of the Old Testament. Because of Moses' crucial place in the theocracy, this title not only denotes humble obedience to God's commands, but, as it is used both by an admiring nation and by Yahweh Himself, is also the title of honor for a man faithful to God and favored by Him.

The only other persons important to Israel's history which are given the slave description are Joshua (Josh. 24:29), Caleb (Num. 14:24, in a context where the loyalty of heart, unremitting obedience, and the promise of blessing are the concommitant factors with slavery to God), Eliakim, slave of Hezekiah (Isa. 22:20, where God's use of "My slave" here suggests the traits of sovereign election, authority, and exaltation that have been previously associated with this title). Samson, Samuel, Nehemiah, and Daniel all use slave as a self-designation of their relationship to God. Thus, both emphases of humility and honor emerge with this single description.

Non-Israelites

The earliest representative of this group is Job (Job. 1:8; 42:7-8). What makes Job the slave of God in these contexts is his unswerving loyalty to the righteous character of his Master even in suffering. Whereas the prophets vindicated God's message by being slaves who accurately and unabashedly communicated the prophecies, Job vindicates God's character by reflecting in his life the claim that God made about him.

A non-Israelite "slave"[69] of a starkly contrasting character is Nebuchadnezzar (Jer. 25:9; 27:6; 43:10). The prominent theme of this usage is God's sovereign choice of a human instrument to accomplish His purpose. The spiritual character of the Babylonian king was not a requirement for his fulfilling God's purpose, and even performing the intended task would not exempt that individual from God's harshest judgment (Jer. 25:12-14).

Implications

From God's perspective, being His slave implies several things. (1) The slave had been sovereignly chosen for his task. (2) God granted special authority to act as His representative. The prophets, for example, were God's mouthpieces for revelation;[70] the kings, too, had special responsibilities to keep the law, to exercise leadership, and to demonstrate moral behavior as a theocratic figure. (3) God took the initiative to protect or avenge His faithful slaves when they encountered persecution or death, or to remove His blessing or protection from any disobedient slave. (4) God did elevate the status of some individual "slaves" to a position not only of great authority but to a position of heightened intimacy with Himself (e.g., David, Moses, Job).

From the slave's perspective, being a slave of God also connotes several ideas. (1) It signifies obedience to a task—whether to speak God's Word, to rule God's people, or to serve God faithfully in the cult. Never in the Old Testament does the idea of possession by the Master totally disappear from the purview of Scripture. (2) It contains the idea of humility, particularly in the way men use "Thy slave" in addressing God. (3) It does not exclude suffering and persecution, which may come precisely because the slave is being faithful in the discharging of his tasks or in righteous living. (4) It may denote special honor or exaltation from His Master for faithful service.

Designating the Suffering Servant

עבד is used, finally, of the Suffering Servant in four distinctive passages in Isaiah. Most scholars today agree with the delineation of the passages as follows:[71] Isaiah 42:1-4;[72] 49:1-6; 50:4-9; and 52:13-12.[73] This delineation is substantiated in the first three passages by the formula, "Thus says the Lord," which immediately follows the Servant songs. While the formula is absent after Isaiah 53:12, the content of the passage puts that segment into a unique category. Also, although there is wide disagreement over the actual date of the songs,[74] most agree that they must be considered in close relationship to their surrounding contexts.[75] As I. Engell says, "The very difficulties in the attempts at distinguishing the songs as literary units and the very different results should be sufficient evidence for the fact that they are from the first at home in their environments."[76]

The identity of the Suffering Servant

There are numerous questions concerning the Suffering Servant around which voluminous scholarly debate rages. These include questions about the origin of the idea: whether Isaiah drew the concept from older biblical ideas[77] or from non-biblical analogies,[78] or whether the idea originated with the author. The most frequently discussed question, however, relates to the identity of the Servant.[79] The confusion is well-stated by Leland Wilshire: "The prevalent interpretation at the present time is some sort of 'fluid,' oscillating or linear concept that takes in Israel, some political, spiritual or ideal portion of Israel and/or some individual either in Israel's past, present or future."[80] The most usual approaches include the collective view[81] (usually Israel, with its corollary interpretation of "collective personality"[82]), the individual view (in which the Servant may be seen as either an historical figure,[83] as autobiographical of Isaiah,[84] or as an idealized figure[85]), and the messianic view[86] (a form of the individual view which makes the reference specific to Jesus Christ as the Messiah).

It is the position of this writer that even while acknowledging the various difficulties the evidence suggests that the Suffering Servant is to be identified with the Messiah who is Jesus. The primary reasons for this include: the interpretation of early Judaism inclined toward the messianic view (as seen in the ways the Septuagint and the Targum handle the text);[87] the songs themselves include traits of the Servant which transcend mere human attributes;[88] and the New Testament's interpretation of Isaiah 53 in Acts 8:30-35 makes the application to Jesus explicit.[89] As D. F. Payne observed: ". . . recent linguistic and textual contributions to the study of Isa. 52f. . . do not seem when in perspective in any way to have undermined the New Testament and Christian application of the prophet's words to Jesus of Nazareth."[90]

In one sense, the resolution of the issue of the identity of the Suffering Servant is secondary to this background study, for whichever interpretation is taken, the point that the word slave is used in both a sense of humiliation and exaltation cannot be denied. On the other hand, if the Servant is identified with Jesus Christ, then the use of the slavery motif in the gospels takes on added significance: the believer is to maintain a "slave" relationship to One who Himself provides the supreme example of slavery to God.

The traits of the Suffering Servant

The relationship of the Suffering Servant to the Lord is characterized by several factors which were true of other master-slave relationships in the Old Testament. First, the Servant is elected by God to His task (Isa. 42:1), thus he stands in a unique relationship with His Master, implying the great responsibility that He has to that task. Second, the Servant is upheld by God (Isa. 42:1) throughout the successful accomplishing of the mission. Third, the Servant can expect God's reward (Isa. 49:4) and exaltation (Isa. 52:13-14) for His faithfulness. Although the particular exaltation of the Servant is unique, the promise of reward and exaltation is a theme to be developed in New Testament references to slavery.

The Servant's mission is essentially soteriological in nature. He is to establish justice and to inaugurate salvation (Isa. 42:1, 3-4). Yet it is the Servant's commitment to His mission that is exemplary.[91] Despite the extreme hazards and costly sacrifice (Isa. 50:6; 53:3-12), He is in no way deterred from carrying out His task completely and successfully (Isa. 50:7), a task in which the suffering was not only the consequence of His mission but also the means by which it would be accomplished.[92]

His personal character also provides an example for other "slaves." The Servant is gentle (Isa. 42:2-3); His coming was not accompanied with loud clamoring nor was He of a violent nature. The Servant has compassion not only for a lost nation but for the weary

(Isa. 50:4), having a ministry not only to a perverse people but also with fellow slaves. Thus, the Servant epitomizes the perfect slave in obediently facing the worst of persecution, even to the death. He is more concerned to accomplish the Master's task than to protect Himself from adverse consequences because he possesses an unshakable confidence in His Master's care (Isa. 50:7-10).

Conclusion and Summary

The rich and varied uses of the slavery motif in the Old Testament have three important connections with the present investigation of the slavery motif in the gospels. (1) The Old Testament provides some important theological bases for the existence and nature of the master-slave relationship. (2) The individual occurrences of the motif suggest several specific predicates of slavery to God. (3) The idea of slavery to God has two seemingly opposite nuances: of humble servitude rendered to a superior, on the one hand, and honorable, exalted privilege in relationship to that superior, on the other.

Theological Bases for the Master-Slave Relationship

God as Creator

That God is the creator of all people, nations, and things is a universal basis for establishing man's spiritual slavery to God. It follows there is therefore an obligation to that Creator that is similar to the master-slave relationship because man is "owned" by God by virtue of creation.

God as Redeemer

God's salvation of Israel from literal slavery in Egypt is frequently depicted in slavemarket language. He is the Redeemer of the nation and thus has an additional claim on them for their service and worship. The contrast between servitude to Egypt and service to Yahweh is great indeed; but while the nation's new relationship with God differs from their subjugation to Pharaoh, they are still owned by the One who redeemed them.

God as Covenant-maker

Israel's relationship to Yahweh is intensified by the Mosaic covenant which stipulated bilateral responsibilities and privileges. Yet, by virtue of the position of the divine Covenant-maker, the covenant (like a suzerainty treaty) displays similarities to a master-slave relationship. God bestows benefits; the nation renders service.

God as Elector

God is the initiator in any relationship with men, and He chooses nations and individuals to do His bidding. As such, God's role as elector is a basis for the master-slave relationship. Election lies at the heart not only of Isreal's status as a slave of God but also of the function of individuals (including the Suffering Servant) whom God has raised up for His mission.

The Suffering Servant as example

The Suffering Servant, no matter how His identity is taken,

presents a vivid picture of an ideal master-servant relationship with God. That relationship is one characterized by mutual trust and reciprocity of performance. When the Servant is identified with the Christ of the gospels, then the portrait of the Servant is an example of immense significance which the follower of Christ should emulate.

Predicates of Slavery to God

Those implying humble service

Ownership

This basic meaning attached to institutional slavery (and freely implied in the religious and ethical use of the term) suggests that the energy and time of God's slave belong not to himself but to his master.

Compulsory service

Slavery implies not simply a relationship but the manifestation of that relationship into the performance of the master's bidding.

Exclusiveness

As shown by the covenantal definitions of Israel's service to God, spiritual slavery allows no deviation from a total commitment to the Lord.

Obedience

The essence of compulsory service is obedience to the owner's demands. Examples of spiritual slavery show that this obedience must be both behavioral and attitudinal.

Responsibility

Whether the relationship is one of king to God, worshipper to deity, subject to ruler, or slave to master, the inferior element inevitably has specific responsibility placed upon it. It may take the form of a menial task, cultic ritual, official representation, or spiritual leadership.

Suffering

Suffering, a frequent but not inevitable element of slavery, can refer not merely to the oppression of domestic slavery but also to the persecution or hostility that the slave can bear from others in the faithful discharging of his responsibilities.

Faithful devotion

Scripture's best examples of loyal slaves of Yahweh are those who are faithful to God not only in the execution of their task but in their commitment to God's character and purpose. The true slave of God makes God's purposes his purposes. He is, like David, "a man after God's own heart."

Those implying exalted status

Authority

Slaves often carry the full authority of the master as they perform his bidding. As such they are the master's legal representatives with all his resources and influence.

Official status

Slavery, in royal contexts, depicts an official status that implies benefit, prestige, and personal authority. Slavery to the divine Monarch suggests certain parallels to the office of royal slave.

Exaltation

The Suffering Servant uniquely receives God's exaltation and reward. Yet, the title "My servant" when used of other faithful individuals (e.g., Moses, David, Job, and Zerubbabel) also indicates special exaltation and relationship to God.

The Dual Nuance of Slavery

Humble servitude and honorable privilege occur with differing emphases throughout the Old Testament, but is nevertheless present in all major categories. Even among the institutional references, where the idea of ownership and subservience is strongest, dignity, fellowship, and even special privilege with the master is often implied. The balance between service and privilege is clearly maintained, both in political contexts and in the religious designations.[93]

It is from this perspective that the slavery motif in the gospels will be investigated. That believers would be called "slaves" (when they are also called "friends" and "sons") makes perfect sense only when this dual emphasis is maintained. How the gospels expand upon this is the burden of chapters four and five.

Notes

[1] Curt Lindhagen, The Servant Motif in the Old Testament.

[2] TDNT, s.v. "Παῖς θεοῦ," by Walther Zimmerli and Joachim Jeremias, 5 (1967):654-717. See also Zimmerli, "The Theme of the Servant of Yahweh in Primitive Christian Soteriology and its Tranposition by St. Paul," CBQ 16 (1954):385-425.

[3] BDB, s.v. "שפחה," p. 1046. [4] Ibid., s.v. "נער," pp. 654-55.

[5] Cf. ZPBE, s.v. "slave, slavery," by Arthur A. Rupprecht, 5:454.

[6] BDB, s.v. "כסף," p. 494.

[7] For detailed discussions of the uses of עבד, see Lindhagen; Zimmerli; BDB, s.v. "עבד," pp. 712-13; s.v. "עבד," pp. 713-14; and K-B, s.v. "עבד, עבד," pp. 670-72.

[8] These senses are evident only in the verbal form and fall outside the category of compulsory service, BDB, s.v. "עבד," p. 713.

[9] Roland de Vaux, Ancient Israel, 2 vols., vol. 1: Social Institutions, p. 80. See also Edwin Yamauchi, "Slaves of God," BETS 9 (Winter 1966):31, who argues against the contention of Yehezekel Kaufmann that Israel had done away with bondage.

[10] Many conservative scholars agree that the historical background for Job fits best in the patriarchal period, ZPBE, s.v. "Job," by Elmer Smick, 3:602; see also James B. Pritchard, Ancient Near Eastern Texts, 3rd ed., pp. 405-7, 434-38. Cf. Robert Gordis, The Book of God and Man, pp. 209-18, who suggests a post-exilic date.

[11] Gen. 17:23 alludes to three groups of males: kin (Ishmael), those born in the house, and those purchased. Folker Willesen, "The Yalid in Hebrew Society," StTh 12 (1958):192-210, concludes that יליד בית refers to slaves ritually freed by becoming "enslaved" to the house gods.

[12] The Code of Hammaurabi (32. 133-35) regulates the ransom of captives and the remarriage of wives and captured warriors. See IDB, s.v. "slavery," by I. Mendelsohn, 4:384; Pritchard, pp. 167, 171.

[13] Note the parallel between the Egyptians who accepted a tax as recognition of their slavery to Pharaoh and the liberated Israelites who paid money, in lieu of the firstborn son, to Yahweh.

[14] Although this probably is Eliezer, the slave is unnamed. Zimmerli, TDNT, 5:657, suggests this anonymity is deliberate, implying the slave's total ownership by and devotion to his master Abraham.

[15] For commentators who so interpret Jacob's benediction, see C. F. Keil, in K&D (10 volume reprint set), 1:403; and H. C. Leupold, Exposition of Genesis, 2 vols. 2:1187-88.

[16] For a classic treatment of institutional slavery from an "abolitionist" viewpoint, see Albert Barnes, An Inquiry into the Scriptural View of Slavery. Two works giving biblical defenses of the institution of slavery are: Robert L. Dabney, Discussions, ed. C. R. Vaughn, vol. 3: Philosophical; James H. Thornwell, The Collected Works of James Henley Thornwell, vol. 4: Ecclesiastical.

[17] Harmonizing this apparent inequity includes recognizing: (a) that God's election of the nation was itself based not on "equity" but on divine perogative; (b) that in the ANE slavery was an act of beneficance on the part of a captor who saved a life; (c) that the Mosaic covenant united all Israelites to one another uniquely because of their relationship to Yahweh.

[18] Contemporary source critics interpret these differences by denying their unity of authorship. Rather, the present writer agrees with Umberto Cassuto, The Documentary Hypothesis, trans. Israel Abrahams, in his cogent rejection of source criticism. Mosaic authorship of the Pentateuch is affirmed. See also Gleason Archer, A Survey of Old Testament Introduction, pp. 96-109; K. A. Kitchen, Ancient Orient and Old Testament, pp. 112-29.

[19] A distinction between Hebrew and non-Hebrew slaves is made in Exod. 21:2-6 where the term "Hebrew slave" is used. Cf. with Lev. 25:39-43 where the term is not used. E. L. Ellison, "The Hebrew Slave: A Study in Early Israelite Society," EQ 45 (1973):30-35, argues that the phrase originally denoted any group of people without citizenship, status, and land, and later designated Israelites. Lev. 25 does not use this phrase because it speaks of "true" Israelites who were only "semi-slaves" as they maintained control over family, inheritance, etc. However, the absence of the phrase "Hebrew Slave" in Leviticus 25 is not contradictory because the sustained distinction between Hebrew and non-Hebrew slaves is made repeatedly with other phrases. For other ideas see N. B. Lemche, "The 'Hebrew Slave': Comments on the Slave Law," Exod. 21:2-11," VT 25 (1975):129-44; and Lemche, "Manumission of Slaves," VT 26 (January 1976): 38-59.

²⁰Even in the event of divorce, she must be neither mistreated nor sold. See de Vaux, 1:81; also see Mendelsohn's comparison of this regulation with the Code of Hammaurabi, IDB 4:384.

²¹IDB, 4:389.

²²De Vaux, 1:87, argues that the regulations applying only to Israelite slaves (such as the right of redemption by kin or self) and the restriction on Isrel masters against mistreating their own brothers make the extradition law extraneous if only Israelites are in view. Thus, Moses here refers to the fleeing of foreign slaves to the sanctuary of Israel.

²³Ibid., 1:83.   ²⁴IDB, 4:385.

²⁵Ibid., suppl., s.v. "slavery in the Old Testament," by Walther Zimmerli, p. 829.

²⁶Ibid., 4:385; de Vaux, 1:84. Some contend the ritual violated God's intended purpose for each member of the nation to remain the slave of God, Ellison, p. 35; S. Scott Bartchy III, Μᾶλλον Χρῆσαι: First-Century Slavery and the Interpretation of 1 Corinthians 7:21, p. 53. But there is little in the text which censures the slave's choice.

²⁷Hans Walter Wolff, The Anthropology of the Old Testament, trans. Margaret Kohl, p. 200. Also "Masters and Slaves: On Overcoming Class Struggle in the Old Testament," Interp 27 (July 1973):259-72.

²⁸IDB, 4:387.

²⁹This does not deny the sacredness of life. These regulations only strive to determine the intent of the master's discipline.

³⁰De Vaux, 1:85.

³¹NBDict, s.v. "slave, slavery," by Kenneth A. Kitchen and E. A. Tudge, p. 1196.

³²De Vaux, 1:86, argues male and female slaves merit separate consideration.

³³Exod. 21:7-11 and Deut. 21:10-14 seem in apparent contradiction. In Exod. 21:7, female slaves are not to be freed on the sabbatical year. Some theorize that Deut. 21 reflects a later, more humanitarian spirit; DB(H), s.v. "servant, slave, slavery," by Owen C. Whitehouse, 4:464. I. Mendelsohn, "The Conditional Sale into Slavery of Free-Born Daughters in Nuzi and the Law of Exodus 21:7-11," JAOS 55 (1935):190-95, however, argues convincingly from Nuzi parallels that in Exod. 21:7-11, אמה refers

to "bride" and that the entire transaction refers to a "brideship sale"--
a special but not contradictory exception to the Deuteronomic stipulation.

[34]Mendelsohn, "Conditional Sale," pp. 192-93.

[35]Deut. 22:23-27 stipulates death to the violator of a free
betrothed girl. This difference need not imply that the slave girl is
less human but that her slave status before the law differs.

[36]That such a non-egalitarian emphasis is made in the Holiness
Code, which source critics tend to date later, tends to confirm Mosaic
authorship of this section of Leviticus.

[37]IDB, 4:387.   [38]Wolff, Anthropology, p. 201.

[39]Since the sabbath rest of Exod. 23:12 is all-inclusive, it
seems sounder to conclude that the sabbatical applied to non-Israelites
as well. Interestingly, this six year tenure was longer than that pre-
scribed in the Code of Hammaurabi (Hamm. 117; Pritchard, pp. 170-71),
IDB, 4:387.

[40]Its absence elsewhere has led some to affirm this is a post-
exilic regulation, de Vaux, 1:82. This is unlikely by the source
critic's own premise, since jubilee, a more "idealistic" regulation,
would be an unlikely later improvement for an ignored sabbatical regulation.

[41]I. Mendelsohn, "State Slavery in Ancient Palestine," BASOR 85
(February 1942):14.

[42]Ibid.

[43]Menham Haran, "The Gibeonites, The Nethinim, and the Sons of
Solomon's Servants," VT 11 (1961):163, n. 2, argues strongly for this
form of state slavery against Mendelsohn's contention that the Canaanites
were simply forced to pay tribute.

[44]Ibid., p. 162. This passage is often considered to be contradictory to 1 Kings 5:13-14 because 1 Kings 9:21 explicitly denies
Solomon's enslavement of Israelites, e.g., J. A. Montgomery, A Critical
and Exegetical Commentary on the Book of Kings, ICC, pp. 209-19. Haran
gives a plausible solution by distinguishing between מס (5:13) which
implies only temporary forced labor (i.e., the corvée), and מס-עבד (9:21)
which denotes total, permanent enslavement of the Canaanites. A third
level of "state slavery" is "the people that wrought in the work," (5:16).
Haran refines and refutes the position of Mendelsohn, "State Slavery,"
p. 17, who feels מס could mean total enslavement.

⁴⁵ZPBE, s.v. "Nethinim," by Wilber B. Wallis, 4:414.

⁴⁶Haran, pp. 165, 167, believes "Nethinim" suggests only a functional entity, while "Gibeonite" refers to a specific ethno-geographic unit.

⁴⁷Mendelsohn, "State Slavery," p. 17.

⁴⁸IDB, suppl., p. 829; Wolff, p. 204.

⁴⁹See, e.g., Herman Ridderbos, Paul: An Outline of His Theology, trans. John R. DeWitt, pp. 82-83, 105; C. C. Ryrie, Biblical Theology of the New Testament, p. 108.

⁵⁰IDB, suppl., p. 829; Wolff, p. 192, suggests that Israel's history is unique in that it is rooted not in cosmic monarchy but in liberation from slavery.

⁵¹IDB, suppl., p. 827.

⁵²Consult Wolff, pp. 204-5, for additional theological implications relevant to the large issue of institutional slavery.

⁵³Wolff, Anthropology, pp. 192-98, explores the theological bases for the monarchy by elucidating the Mosaic regulations for a king (Deut. 17:14-20), by tracing Abimelech's early impetus for kingship (Judges 9:1-57), and by describing Israel's official request for a king (1 Sam. 8:4-22).

⁵⁴TDNT, s.v. "Παῖς θεοῦ," by Walther Zimmerli, 5 (1967):657.

⁵⁵Lindhagen, p. 78.

⁵⁶Zimmerli categorizes these uses into three groups: army professionals, officials dependent upon the king, and bearers of an important individual office at court, TDNT, s.v. "Παῖς θεοῦ," 5:657.

⁵⁷Lindhagen, p. 80, concludes that the use of עבד here is highly reminiscent of the covenantal relationship, a point he later develops in the religious uses of עבד. Zimmerli, TDNT, s.v. "Παῖς θεοῦ," 5:658, n. 13, takes serious exception to this concept.

⁵⁸A discussion of this designation occupies some 50 pages in Lindhagen's treatise, and is contested by Zimmerli, TDNT, 5:662-67, n. 41, who believes Lindhagen overemphasizes the use of עבד for the nation, implying the national use of עבד is seminal for the individual use when in fact the reverse is true.

⁵⁹Marcos Treves, "Isaiah LIII," VT 24 (January 1974):99, cites several passages with questionable accuracy: Psalm 86:16; 113:1; 116:16.

⁶⁰Whitehouse, DB(H), 4:469, discusses the Old Testament use of servant as a worshipper, comparing this to numerous ANE parallels. See also Yamauchi, pp. 31-35.

⁶¹See Lindhagen, p. 231.   ⁶²Ibid., p. 230.   ⁶³Ibid., p. 238.

⁶⁴Ibid., pp. 261-62. He believes the story is a propaganda piece to instill inner strength during difficult times. Yet, he sees the main point as being "adherence to the worship of a certain God (the service of Yahweh) as distinct from other cults," p. 238.

⁶⁵Passing mention should be made here of certain proper names which contain a morpheme meaning "slave of Yahweh" (e.g., Obadiah), a practice not unique to Israel (cf. Yamauchi, pp. 31-34). Most designate such cultic officials as Levites, priests, or prophets (Lindhagen, pp. 276-77), and few see much theological significance in them. But cf. Yamauchi, p. 33.

⁶⁶It may be that the designation "My Slave" is used of leaders (e.g. Moses and David) who had more direct theocratic responsibilities. God's special designation for Abraham is "My friend" (Isa. 41:8; James 2:23). While God refers to Jacob as "My servant" in the prophetic literature (e.g., Isa. 44:1-2; Jer. 46:27-28; Ezk. 28:25; 37:25) it is probable that Jacob means Israel (as in Isa. 41:8).

⁶⁷Ibid., pp. 207-71, 275.

⁶⁸Zimmerli thinks "My servant the Branch" (Zech 3:8) refers to Zerubbabel, TDNT, 5:664. It more likely refers to the Messiah (Isa. 11:1).

⁶⁹Another pagan ruler, Cyrus, was clearly a divine instrument of God. However, while he was called the shepherd (Isa. 44:28) and anointed (Isa. 45:1), he was never called God's slave.

⁷⁰Lindhagen, p. 278, sees the prophetic role emphasized by God's determination not to judge unless the nation was first warned by his servant spokesmen.

⁷¹Such diverse scholars as W. M. W. Roth, "The Anonymity of the Suffering Servant" JBL 83 (1964):171; Zimmerli, TDNT, 5:654-66; H. H. Rowley, "The Servant Mission: The Servant Songs and Evangelism," Interp 8 (1954):259; and Edward J. Young, "Of Whom Speaketh the Prophet Thus?," WThJ (1949):141-49, accept these four passages as the distinct Servant songs.

⁷²Leland E. Wilshire, "The Servant-City: A New Interpretation of the 'Servant of the Lord' in the Servant Songs of Deutero-Isaiah," JBL 94 (1975):357, n. 8, follows the delineation of Isa. 42:1-7.

⁷³H. M. Orlinsky, detaches 52:13-15 from Isa. 53 in "The So-called 'Suffering Servant' in Isaiah 53," Interpreting the Prophetic Tradition, ed. H. M. Orlinsky, pp. 229-32.

⁷⁴Treves, e.g., dates most of Deutero-Isaiah in the Maccabean Age, "Isaiah LIII," p. 100.

⁷⁵TDNT 5:666; Treves, p. 98. Cf. Young, "Of Whom Speaketh?," p. 142.

⁷⁶Ivan Engnell, "The 'Ebed-Yahweh Song and the Suffering Messiah in 'Deutero-Isaiah,'" BJRL 31 (1948):62.

⁷⁷J. Philip Hyatt, "The Sources of the Suffering Servant Idea," JNES 3 (1944):79-84, sees the sacrificial system, corporate personality, and the concept of prophet as seminal ideas; A. S. Kapelrud, "The Identity of the Suffering Servant," in Near Eastern Studies: In Honor of William Foxwell Albright, ed. H. Goedike, pp. 305-14, believes the Hebrew King was influential in the concept.

⁷⁸G. Pidoux, "Le Serviteur souffrant d'Isaïe 53," RTP 7 (1956): 36-46 (the Baal dying and rising myth); J. Scharbert, "Stellvertretendes Sühnleiden in dem Ebed-Yahweh Liedern und in altorientalischen Ritual Texten," BZ 2 (1956):190-213 (the Tammuz liturgy and the šar-puhi text of substitute enthronement). Edward J. Young, "The Origin of the Suffering Servant Idea," WThJ (1950):22-23, refutes the Baal myth; Scharbert, pp. 190-213, admits vicarious suffering has no ANE ritual analogs; and North, p. 201, criticizes the "mythological" interpretation for its inability to explain the soteriological purpose of the Servant.

⁷⁹See Christopher R. North, The Suffering Servant in Deutero-Isaiah: An Historical and Critical Study, pp. 192-210, for one of the authoritative studies on the history of interpretations. Also see TDNT, 5:668; and Colin G. Kruse, "The Servant Songs: Interpretative Trends since C. R. North," SBTh 8 (April 1978):13-27. For a specialized study on the Jewish interpretations of Isa. 53 since the rabbinic period, see Jack Meadows,"A History of the Jewish Interpretation of the Suffering Servant of Isaiah 52:13-53:12," (Th. M. thesis, Dallas Theological Seminary, 1967).

⁸⁰Wilshire, p. 356. See also Young, "Origin," p. 19; Roth, p. 171.

[81] This view is neither the oldest (Meadows, p. 40; W. Zimmerli and J. Jeremias, The Servant of God, p. 41; and North, p. 18) nor the most popular today (Kruse, p. 24). See Treves, p. 101; Rowley, pp. 259-72; and North, pp. 202, 205-7 for refutation. J. Guillet, "La Polemique contre les idols et le Serviteur de Yahve," Bib 40 (1959):428-34, still holds the view. Scholars who hold a "righteous remnant" view include Kapelrud, p. 311, and H. L. Ginsberg, "The Oldest Interpretation of the Suffering Servant," VT (1954):400-4, in which the "enlighteners" of Dan. 11:33—12:20 are the Servant who "justifies the many."

[82] Otto Eissfeldt, "The Ebed-Jahwe in Isaiah XL-LV in the Light of the Israelite Conception of the Community and the Individual, the Ideal and the Real," trans. A.R. Johnson, ET 44 (January 1933):261-68. Young, "Of Whom Speaketh?," pp. 137-41, and North, p. 110, refute this interpretation.

[83] Such biblical characters as Uzziah, Hezekiah, Josiah, Jeremiah, Ezekiel, Job, Moses, Jeoiachin, Cyrus, Sheshbazzar, Zerubbabel, Meshullam, Nehemiah, and Eleazar have been suggested. North, pp. 192-94. A recent suggestion is the high priest, Onias, by Treves, pp. 101-8. J. Morgenstern, "The Suffering Servant—A New Solution," VT 11 (1961):292-320, 406-31, sees him as an anonymous King. North, pp. 194-95, sees him as an anonymous contemporary of Isaiah thought to be Messiah.

[84] This old view (Jerome, Patrologiae Latinae 24. 496), is maintained by Ernest Sellin, "Die Lösung des deuterojesajanischen Gottesknechtsträtsels," ZAW 14 (1937):178-91, n. 1, and Orlinsky, pp. 253-54, despite the problem of the Servant's dying and rising in the fourth song. Cf. Young, "Of Whom Speaketh?," pp. 140, 146, 159-64.

[85] This popular view can be subdivided. Some take an ideal individual approach: Roth, p. 172; Kapelrud, p. 313; Pidoux, pp. 45-46; R. L. Tourney, "Les Chants du Serviteur dans la seconde partie d'Isaie," RB 59 (1952):509; C. Chavasse, "The Suffering Servant and Moses," CBQ 165 (1964):152; and R. A. Rosenberg, "Jesus, Isaac, and the Suffering Servant," JBL (1964):385. Others see the Servant as a prototypical office: Claus Westermann, Isaiah 40:66: A Commentary, p. 211; J. M. Ward, "The Servant Songs in Isaiah," $\underline{\text{RExp}}$ 65 (1968): 441-42; Roth, p. 130. Some, like Rowley, "The Servant Mission," p. 267, take an "oscillating" view that combines the collective and the ideal. Wilshire, p. 367, says the Servant is the cultic-center city of Zion-Jerusalem.

[86] North, pp. 206-8, differentiates between two kinds of messianic interpretations: the "idealistic" (in which the Servant songs are "pre-written history" which Jesus completely fulfills) and the "realistic" (in which the prophet, drawing from contemporary material, alludes to a messiah figure that Jesus best fulfills). North chooses the latter approach, p. 208.

[87] See Zimmerli's comprehensive treatment of the nature and antiquity of this view, Servant of God, p. 41 (the LXX translation supports a future messianic view), p. 67 (the rabbinic Targums apply some of the songs to the Messiah), and p. 75 (how the more recent collective approach in Jewish interpretation was a reaction to early Christian apologists). See also Meadows, pp. 12, 14, 40.

[88] Young, "Of Whom Speaketh?," p. 154. Also see D. F. Payne's good discussion on the controversial phrases "length of days" and "light" in "The Servant of the Lord: Language and Interpretation," EvQ 43 (July 1971):138-40.

[89] Young, "Of Whom Speaketh?," pp. 133-35. M. D. Hooker, Jesus and the Servant, is a notable exception whose thesis is rejected by most.

[90] Payne, p. 143.

[91] Rowley elucidates the relationship of the Servant's mission to the evangelistic mission of the church, pp. 271-72.

[92] Ibid., p. 261.

[93] Gerhard Sass, "Zur Bedeutung von δουλος bei Paulus," ZNW 40 (1941 Juni):25-27. He argues strongly that in the Old Testament the phrase is עבד יהוה became a title of honor.

CHAPTER III

CULTURAL BACKGROUNDS TO THE SLAVERY MOTIF

Introduction

The slavery motif in the Old Testament, though rich in implications, is several centuries removed from the events recorded in the gospels. Thus, it is essential to investigate the slave practices as they existed in Palestine during the time of Christ to discover what differences from the Old Testament economy and ideology might have existed and perhaps influenced the New Testament slavery motif.

Because of the central importance of Judaism in Palestine, the discussion must begin with the Jewish practices and attitudes relating to slavery since the closing of the Old Testament Canon. However, the task is complicated by the presence of two other cultures--Rome[1] and Greece[2]--whose intricate legal, social, economic, and political customs regarding slavery may also have had an impact on the gospel narratives. For that reason, these two systems will be briefly described, differentiated, and evaluated as to their importance to the slavery motif in the gospels.

Slavery in Judaism

The Reality of Jewish Slavery in the
Second Commonwealth

Although some agree that slavery had ceased in the period

following the second temple (since the Talmud limits slavery to the custom of jubilee and jubilee had ceased),[3] there is stronger evidence that slavery did exist: F. Josephus mentions slaves that were owned by the high priestly family,[4] some Talmudic tractates defend the legal position of slavery,[5] numerous other examples of the existence and regulation of slavery exist.[6] It may have been the enslavement of Jews by other Jews which ceased with jubilee, while the enslavement of Gentiles continued;[7] but Solomon Zeitlin offers a more realistic suggestion: the slavery that ended at jubilee was enslavement of a debtor; other practices of Jewish slavery continued.[8]

Slavery was practiced quite openly in Jerusalem, male and female slaves being sold at a stone in the center of the city.[9] In Palestine there were more slaves in the urban than in the rural areas, there were more freedmen than slaves (an indication of the frequency of manumission), and there were more day-labourers than slaves (indicating that Palestine was not strictly a slave economy).[10]

The Institutional Practice of Slavery

The Hebrew slave

There was an unquestionable double standard by which Jewish masters treated Jewish and Gentile slaves which stemmed from pentateuchal legislation in which the duration and kind of service for a Hebrew was limited.[11] With a few exceptions, Hebrew slaves were treated in a very humane way; consequently, Jews enslaved to Jews had less market value and were in less quantity.[12] The proverb, "Acquire a slave, acquire a master" aptly is summarized in this treatment.[13]

Entrance into slavery

A Jewish male could become a slave through the court-ordered sale if he was a thief unable to pay what was due. On the basis of Exodus 22:2, any man at the time of Jesus who could not repay the amount that was stolen could be sold into slavery.[14] Also, according to Leviticus 25:39-43, persons in poverty could sell themselves into slavery voluntarily. This practice was restricted to male adults under the most extreme poverty, and only rarely were they sold to Gentile masters (since relatives were responsible to redeem them immediately).[15] Slavery for indebtedness existed among Jews in the Old Testament (2 Kings 4:1), but by the time of Christ only a person's property was seized to pay a debt. Zeitlin suggests that slavery for indebtedness was abolished when jubilee ceased;[16] thus it follows that such a practice (as implied in Jesus' parable of the unmerciful slave) was not primarily a Jewish but a Gentile (or more specifically, Herodian) practice.

The enslavement of Hebrew female slaves was even more tightly regulated. They could not sell themselves into slavery;[17] they could not be sold into slavery as thieves; their ears could not be pierced for perpetual servitude.[18] In fact, the only way a female could be enslaved was for her, as a minor under twelve, to be sold by her father to another Jew. The strangeness of this stipulation is understood in light of the regulation in Exodus 21:7, in which such sale had as its ultimate goal the safe marriage of the daughter to the master or his son.[19]

Status and treatment of slaves

The Hebrew slave was to be treated according to Leviticus 25:40: "He shall be with you as a hired man." Legally, he was in a position equal to that of the eldest son in the household;[20] and there were even certain tasks--such as footwashing and putting on of shoes--that were not required of him.[21] The intensity of the slave's work was regulated by the interpretation of Deuteronomy 15:18, "for he has given you six years with double the service of a hired man." Some interpreted this as meaning twice the work (i.e., working day and night),[22] but the Talmud said this granted the master the right to give the slave a bondwoman in order to begat other slaves, thus doubling his effectiveness.[23] In this regard, the master, on the basis of Exodus 21:4, could force the slave to marry a Gentile wife for childbearing purposes.[24]

The Hebrew male slave enjoyed certain protections and rights. He was not held responsible for his torts until he came again into property;[25] and he had the right to stay in Israel and to be sold only to a Jew.[26] He had the right to hold and own property (though not the right to dispose of it by will);[27] and he had the hope of temporary service: a six year maximum tenure with earlier redemption.[28] The more severe forms of mistreatment and maiming (for which the Jewish slaves had full recourse before the law) were restricted; and the Mishna provided that a person could be liable for inflicting injury, pain, wounds needing healing, loss of time, and indignity on a Jewish slave.[29]

There were numerous other regulations, but one relevant to the slavery motif is the possibility that a slave could be owned by two masters or could be considered half slave and half free.[30] This makes Jesus' remarks about the impossibility of serving two masters even more striking.

Manumission from slavery

The normal means of manumission for male slaves was automatic freedom after six years of service. Even the service of the slave who had his ear bored for perpetual service ended at the death of the master.[31] Additionally, redemption was a primary means of manumission before the full six years elapsed. Of course, the master could free the slave by a deed of release;[32] and, while jubilee no longer applied, a slave could be freed upon the death of the master if all the goods of the master were deeded to the slave.[33]

Automatic freedom before the law resulted in two other circumstances: if a Jew was sold to a Gentile or taken outside the land.[34] As to why this was promulgated and how could it be effected, Zeitlin suggests that, due to the Herodian tightening of slave of laws for housebreakers and thieves, the Jewish community accepted these forms of release to encourage redemption of the slave by other Jews.[35]

While many of the same manumission privileges applied to females, there were some distinctives which specifically pertained to her relationship to the master, since a primary purpose for which a female legitimately entered slavery was security through marriage. Thus, if at puberty she was not freed and given in marriage, or if the master died, then manumission was automatic.[36]

The Gentile slave

Entrance into slavery

The enslavement of Gentile slaves was more reminiscent of such procedures in Greece and Rome. While some slaves were born in the house, the primary means of enslavement were through purchase (either by money or by writ) and through usucaption (or possession) of three years.[37] Phonecian traders (2 Macc. 8:11) and Arabian merchants were primary sources of slaves;[38] and Tyre was one of the slave trading centers.[39] The Talmud affirms that barter, war, and physical seizure were later means of gaining slaves.[40]

Status and treatment of slaves

Legally the Gentile slave was considered to be property or chattel.[41] They were owned by their master and could be traded, sold, pledged, or deeded as other property.[42] In the tannaitic literature this is never questioned; there is only debate over whether they should be classed as movable or immovable property.[43]

Despite this, however, there were provisions which tended to soften the austerity of chattel-status. For one thing, there was a debate over the culpability of a slave's wrongdoing. While the Sadducees put the responsibility on the master, the prevailing view was held by the Pharisees who made the slave culpable, thus ascribing to him understanding and genuine humanity.[44] Additionally, the slave was considered as a reliable witness in some, though not all, instances, thus affirming an intrinsic understanding of the humanness of the Gentile slave.[45]

Of the social plight of Gentile slaves Jeremias says: "This abysmal social position . . . made the word 'slave' one of the worse insults and punishable by anathema."[46] He substantiates this in part by his understanding of their place in the Jewish social order: priest, Levite, Israelite, bastard, Nethinim (Gibeonite), proselyte, and freed slave.[47] Female slaves had an even more severe social stigma, for "every freed woman slave was regarded *ipso facto* as a harlot!"[48] Nevertheless, Jewish masters came to care for and love their slaves as beloved brothers.[49]

Certain religious rights and privileges were accorded the Gentile slave, providing that the slave became a proselyte (i.e., female slaves to be baptized; male slaves to be baptized and circumcized)[50] and that his religious privilege did not conflict with his responsibility to his master.

Specifically, his religious duties were "governed by the principle that he should perform only those which were not related to any particular moment, since he was not the master of his own time."[51] For example, slaves were not to wear philacteries or to recite the Shema,[52] nor were they required to attend the pilgrim feasts (especially tabernacles).[53] They could take the Nazarite vow, but whether the master could force the slave to break it was debated.[54]

On the other hand, they were entitled to the Sabbath rest (cf. Exod. 20:10; Deut. 5:14), were guaranteed not to be sold to Gentiles against their will,[55] were allowed to recite the benediction, and could partake of the Passover (Exod. 12:24).[56]

A primary factor that tended to make treatment of slaves more humane was the regulation regarding injury, as most of the rabbis extended the Mosaic legislation (Exod. 21:20-21 and 26-27) to Gentile slaves.[57] Thus, premeditated death of the slave was a capital offense and mutilation warranted release.[58] However, the owner's culpability for injuring the Gentile slave was different than for a Jewish slave. So, for example, while an owner was guilty if he maimed or killed his slave,[59] he was not similarly responsible if his ox did it to a Gentile slave.[60]

The five counts for which a non-owner could be liable for striking a Hebrew slave (injury, pain, healing, loss of time, and indignity) were also maintained for the Gentile slave (with the possible exception, according to some rabbis, of indignity).[61] Yet, the owner himself could commit any of these indignities to his slave without fear of redress.

Manumission from slavery

Manumission of Gentile slaves occurred frequently and in a variety of ways,[62] despite a debate over whether Leviticus 25:46 taught that enslavement of Gentile slaves was obligatory.[63] These included: (1) permanent injury or maimimg (provided there were witnesses that such injury was intentional on the part of the master);[64] (2) redemption only through a third party (because the propertyless Gentile could not redeem himself);[65] (3) the decision of the master to release his slave (through a writ of manumission,[66] through a will if the master left all his goods to his slave,[67] or if he died without heirs[68]); (4) forms of *de facto* release (e.g., allowing a slave to perform before witnesses things only a free man could do--such as wearing phalacteries or reading the Torah in public[69]- or permitting a slave to marry an Israelite with the master's consent[70]).

Manumission gives an insight into the attitude with which slaves were regarded. Thus, the variety of options for manumission, including the acceptance of a freed Gentile slave as a full proselyte and even son-in-law, somewhat qualifies Jeremias' appraisal of the slave's social position as "abysmal."

Religious Uses of Slavery
As reflected in the Septuagint

The Septuagint reveals the development in the Jewish understanding of the religious idea of slavery in the way it renders the very general word עבד into one of the more precise Greek equivalents: παῖς, δοῦλος, οἰκέτης, θεράπων, υἱος, and ὑπηρέτης.[71]

The interplay of παῖς and δοῦλος as equivalents for עבד is especially illuminating. In the Pentateuch, for example, παῖς is used of house-born slaves ("slave from the first"[72]), while δοῦλος is employed to describe unlawful or unreasonable service. Δοῦλος is not used in the Mosaic legislation regarding slaves,[73] but derivatives of δουλεύω are used in later books to describe the state of subjugation of one people to another (Judg. 3:8; 1 Sam. 17:9). Similarly, in the king-subject contexts, παῖς tends to nominate soldiers, ministers, and other officials who entered the service of the king freely, while δοῦλος tends to designate forced or restricted service (2 Kings 10:19) or is used as an official's self-designation in courtly speech spoken in addressing the king.[74]

Δουλεύω is often used of עבד to describe loyalty and service to God, and "the term always implies the exclusive nature of the relationship, whether we think of the Hebrew equivalent עבד or of the Greek δοῦλος."[75] In contrast to the Greeks, the Jews worshipped a God of "unconditional majesty and absolute superiority to man."[76] Δοῦλος aptly captures that relationship.

The men in the Old Testament called "slaves of God" or "My slaves" are often designated in the Septuagint by the word δοῦλος (Josh. 24:29; 2 Kings 17:23; Isa. 48:20). The Pentateuch seems to be a major exception to this rule in that other terms than δοῦλος are used of certain notables either in their addresses to God (Jacob, παῖς, Gen. 32:10; Moses, θεράπων, Exod. 4:10; the patriarchs, οἰκέται, Exod. 32:13) or in God's reference to them (Caleb, παῖς, Num. 14:24).[77] Another exception is the rendering of the Suffering Servant as παῖς θεοῦ, a phrase used only once of Christ in the gospels. Rengstorf believes: "The basis of this rendering is the recognition by the translator of the fact that the עבד יהוה does not render his service within the framework of a relationship to his master which is established for the purpose, but on the basis of an essential position of his οἶκος."[78]

As reflected in later Jewish intertestamental literature

After 100 B.C., the use of עבד יהוה in the Greek versions was rendered with a variety of Greek phrases.[79] Παῖς θεοῦ could mean either "child of God" or "slave of God," but after 100 B.C., it was used less frequently.[80] The more prominent phrase during the period was δοῦλος θεοῦ which was used in a suppliant's prayers to refer to himself.[81] It was employed in a plural sense to designate people who enjoyed a master-slave relationship with God (including Israelites, prophets, the righteous, priests, proselytes, parents, and angels);[82] and was utilized less frequently as a title of honor for such men as Moses and David. By the close of this period only παῖς θεοῦ was used of the Suffering Servant, which likely explains the absence of δοῦλος θεοῦ in the gospels.[83]

Implications

In sum, at least some translators of the Septuagint distinguished two nuances of עבד using δοῦλος to render the harsher connotation of submissive, dependent servitude and introducing παῖς to depict more voluntary submission.[84] This was not strictly maintained, however; thus, both the harsher δοῦλος and the more moderating words were used to describe the important patriarchs and kings who were designated as slaves of God. By the first century before Christ, there was an increased tendency to designate one's relationship to God in the harsher term of δοῦλος (as seen by the less frequent use of παῖς θεοῦ).

The differentiation between παῖς and θεοῦ (especially in the pentateuch of the LXX) may reflect a certain Hellenistic bias on the part of some Alexandrian Jews who wished to moderate the harshness of the Old Testament slavery motif to more acceptable Greek modes of thought.[85] More likely, this change represents a shift in Judaism's understanding of the person of God and Israel's relationship to Him. Thus, the Septuagint would illustrate a more immanent view of God and a more familial (i.e., covenantal) relationship to God as their master, while the later literature would picture God in His transcendence, stressing a greater sense of distance from God.[86]

Implications of Jewish Slavery for the Slavery Motif in the Gospels

The practices and attitudes of Palestinian Judiasm regarding slavery help place the slavery motif in the gospels into perspective in several ways.

First, there is great consistency with Old Testament institutional practices and attitudes. The differentiation between Jewish and Gentile slaves, the humane treatment of Jewish slaves, and religions participation of Gentile slaves all comport fairly well with Old Testament regulations. The differences noted in the previous discussion often resulted from varying rabbinical interpretations of the standard Old Testament texts, not from attempts to establish an entirely new foundation. Thus, it may be presumed that the Old Testament, albeit with Judaism's later interpretations, still is highly influential on the gospel's slavery motif.

Second, where practices of institutional slavery do differ with the Old Testament, the general tendency is to follow a more humane treatment of the slave, whether Jew or Gentile. This is helpful in understanding the freedom with which the evangelists and Jesus use the slavery imagery, because the "slave as chattel" definition is too simplistic whether one is describing Jewish slaves or describing disciples of Jesus. The humanness of slaves in Judaism is never questioned; and this helps avoid a one-dimensional perspective of what the gospels mean by slavery to God.

Third, slavery practices in Judaism do illuminate the meaning of some specific gospel references. For example, it was possible, legally, for a slave to serve two masters. Thus, Jesus' maxim must be interpreted in light of that reality. Similarly, the Jewish attitudes toward slaves as a class (and the "anathema" placed by some rabbis upon Gentile slaves) gives insight into the hostile reaction of the Jews to Jesus' indication they were not really free (John 8:32-35). On the other hand, the decline of debt as a cause of slavery among Jews in this period may indicate that some gospel references (e.g., the parable of the unmerciful slave) draw more from a Hellenistic rather than a Judaistic understanding of slavery.

Finally, the religious idea of slavery to God found in the Old Testament is continued in Judaism, not simply as a reference to past heroes but also as a description of one's present relationship to God. A different emphasis does exist in that יהוה עבד is translated more frequently with δοῦλος θεοῦ, a phrase that suggests severity of service rather than privilege of relationship. Yet this does not mean that the dual nuance of slavery noted in the Old Testament (of subjugation and exaltation) is lost. In fact, since the ones Jesus designates as slaves in the gospel are also nominated as sons and friends, it may be inferred that Jesus is trying to restore and expand upon an Old Testament nuance that Judaism itself had begun to lose.

Slavery in Greece and Rome

That Greek and Roman slave practices influenced the province of Palestine, and thereby the events of the gospels and the teachings of Jesus, cannot simply be assumed because the evidence can lead to opposite conclusions.

There is indirect evidence, on the one hand, that the laws and customs of Hellenism and Rome pertaining to slavery would have been known. Certainly Jesus was aware of Hellenistic culture in general. It is possible he spoke Koine Greek[87] and this *lingua franca* was a primary vehicle for the transmission of Greek culture;[88] He referred to Greek and Roman coinage in His parables (e.g., the τάλαντον, the δηράριον, and the μνᾶ);[89] and He had several political contacts with the Herod Antipas[90] whose court was "entirely dominated by the Spirit of Hellenism."[91]

Jesus also had extensive contact with cities in Galilee (e.g., Capernaum,[92] Bethsaida,[93] and Tiberias[94]), in Samaria,[95] in northern Palestine (e.g., Tyre and Sidon,[96] Caesarea Philippi[97]), in the Decapolis (Mark 5:10; 7:31), and in Judea (Jericho[98] and Jerusalem). Each of these cities manifested distinctly Hellenistic traits ranging from architectural accouterments to political government.

Furthermore, Jesus was exposed to Roman rule, although to a lesser extent, because, as Jeremias observes, culturally Greece had a greater impact on Palestine than Rome[99] and because He spent most of His time in Galilee. There was a military presence in Palestine (Luke 23:47) and Roman law was often transmitted by these soldiers,[100] particularly as it related to the imposing and collecting of taxes. Jesus' association with taxgatherers (Matt. 9:9; Luke 15:1-2; 19:1-10) may have given Him greater awareness of Roman laws and customs since the slave trade itself was subject to a variety of taxes throughout the empire.[101] And of course Jesus was tried by Pilate, a Roman prefect.

    The above contacts are quite circumstantial and do little more than render Jesus' awareness of non-Jewish slave practices possible. However, there is concrete evidence that Jerusalem—the Jewish political and religious capitol—practiced a slave trade[102] in which both male and female slaves, likely acquired through Tyre,[103] were sold as merchandise.[104] Josephus reports that slavery as a punishment for housebreaking was enacted into law under Herod the Great;[105] and this precedent may have encouraged what was essentially a non-Jewish practice to flourish by the time of Jesus' ministry. Furthermore, the allusion to the libertines (or "freedmen," Acts 6:9) substantiates the prevalence of manumission in the city. This, coupled with the fact that Jesus repeatedly visited Jerusalem, supports the presumption that He could have observed the trading of slaves and been aware of the laws and attitudes affecting them.

    Furthermore, some references to slaves in Christ's encounters and teaching contain elements which do not easily fit a Judaistic pattern: the slave of the centurion (Luke 7:1-10; Matt. 8:5-13);[106] the proverbs that enjoin slavery as the path to greatness in contrast with the Gentiles (e.g., Mark 10:35-45); the parable of the unmerciful slave's harsh punishment (Matt. 18:23-35); the parables of the talents and minas that suggest harshness of punishment and imply the use of a *peculium*; and the promise of the reversed master-slave roles (Luke 17:7-9).[107] These may be more easily explained in light of non-Judaistic slave systems.

Nevertheless these observations must be tempered by the remark of A. N. Sherwin-White, who, while objectively evaluating even the most minute of potential links between the gospels and non-Jewish practices,[108] says: "The narratives of the three synoptic gospels is set in a world which reflects hardly a touch of Greek or Roman influence until the arrival of Christ in Jerusalem."[109] Koopmans, for example, denies that any other cultural factors beside those of Judaism were influential on the gospel narratives,[110] and K. C. Russel virtually ignores Greco-Roman practices in his discussion of the slavery references in the New Testament.[111] Keith Hopkins[112] and M. I. Finley,[113] in speaking to the nature of slavery in this period, indicate that there were only two true slave economies in antiquity: Athens in the sixth century, B.C., and Roman Italy in the third century, B.C.[114] Thus, the Palestine of the gospels followed a different economic and social pattern from the slave systems of Rome and Greece. It is not denied that the laws and practices of these cultures might be known; nevertheless they must be seen as less significant. Many scholars caution against the error of assuming that Roman military presence in a region necessarily implies that all its legal practices (e.g., slavery) were rigidly followed.[115] Again Sherwin-White's comments are apt:

> When one lays aside the Graeco-Roman spy-glass, and looks at the narrative in another manner, it coheres beautifully. The pattern of life, both social and economic, civil and relgiious, is precisely what is to be expected in the isolated district of Galilee. . . . The absence of Graeco-Roman colouring is a convincing feature of the Galilean narrative and parable."[116]

In light of this amguity, the Greek and Roman systems must be studied with caution and links established sparingly. A general picture of non-Jewish slavery will be presented, followed by the distinctives of each of the two systems and their possible points of contact with the gospels.

A General Profile of Greek and Roman Slavery

Although the Greek slave system (centered in Athens) was dominant in the sixth century, B.C., while the Roman system (centered in Italy) peaked in the third century, B.C., it is still possible to summarize many features of both systems which are held in common. The Greek system is considered with Rome because, despite its greater antiquity, there is evidence that Greek customs lingered in many provinces that were technically under Roman law[117] and that Hellenism would have at least as great an impact in a Palestine governed by several centuries of Hellenistic Seleucids, Ptolemies, and Herods as would Rome.

The definition of slavery

William L. Westermann suggests four similarities shared by all slave systems: (a) the slave was owned and controlled by another; (b) the slave had no individuality; (c) the slave had no personality apart from his owner; and (d) the slave had no male parent.[118] This can be seen in the Delphic manumission records which imply a slave before manumission cannot represent himself legally, is subject to search and possession by another, cannot earn his living according to his wishes, and lacks the right to travel freely.[119] In the later Roman period, slavery is defined as an institution "in which someone is subject to the dominion of another person 'contrary to nature.'"[120] A major difference between Greek and Roman concepts is that for the Romans slavery was an institution common to all (*ius gentium*), not, as some Greek philosophers believed, a natural situation for certain ones.[121] It was simply a fair exchange between victor and vanquished of one's life for indentured service.[122]

Entrance into slavery

The ultimate cause for slavery, asserts Finley, is economic: the demand for inexpensive labor to support a growing economy.[123] The most universal means for obtaining slaves for this labor supply in both cultures were war, piracy, and kidnapping.[124] By the time of Christ, however, these means had become less significant (due to the *Pax Romana*)[125] and slaves raised in the household probably became a more important source.[126]

Also, a variety of legal reasons for enslavement (*ius civile*) emerged relating to felony, fraud, insolvency, and rescuing of exposed children.[127] But the most common of these was voluntary self-sale into slavery.[128] Likely because of their philosophical ideas about freedom, this practice was less common to the Greeks, but it began to flourish in the Augustinian Age. Bartchy summarizes several of the reasons why such voluntary slavery was attractive: (a) it could provide an easier life, socially and economically, than remaining a poor freeman; (b) it could lead to greater wealth and position in the future; (c) it offered the possibility of full citizenship after manumission; and (d) it could provide funds for the ransom of others.[129]

The status of slaves

The question of the slave's status in society touches upon the larger question of his humanness: is he beast, property, or human being? In answering this question, legal, social, and economic elements are needed to gain a balanced perspective because the slave's status before the law was often more severe than his actual treatment in society. One must remember that the slave's status fluctuated throughout the history of the particular culture: earlier it tended toward the "familial;" later, as the slave economy swung into full operation, it acquired a more exclusively "chattel" aspect; ultimately, when the importance of the slave diminished, he was accorded greater rights and granted manumission more easily.[130] Also bear in mind that the attitude toward slaves varied from place to place even during the same period, so that, for example, Athenian slaves were treated with greater dignity than those of Sparta;[131] and Egypt and the East had a more lax legal approach to the slave than did the West.[132]

Legal considerations

Before the law, the slave was considered to be *res* (literally, "chattel" or "thing").[133] As such they were completely subject to the master's decision regarding purchase and sale, and they had virtually no legal rights. In early Greece, the master possessed the power of life and death, determination of marriage, discipline, sale, purchase, mortgaging and leasing;[134] and in the Roman empire the master had similar sovereignty.[135] Any wrong done against the slave was considered to be a crime against the master who alone had the right of redress. He could sue through *lex Aquila* if only the slave was damaged) or bring an *actio iniuriarum* to court if he could show that he was primarily affected.[136]

By the time of Christ certain legal restrictions had arisen in both systems which limited some of the master's powers. For example, Draco's laws in Greece quite early made the murder of a slave equivalent to the murder of a freeman.[137] Similarly in Rome a non-owner who killed a slave was guilty of homicide according to the *lex Cornelia* of 81 B.C., although it wasn't until after the time of Christ that the master was similarly restricted from killing his own slave.[138] Furthermore, Roman jurisprudence referred to the slave in terms that maintained his chattel status but implied his human nature: the master's authority was called *potestas* (a designation applicable only of human relationships),[139] and a slave's child was called *ancilla* (a human designation) and not *fructas* (a new born animal).[140] Additionally, slaves were allowed in the law to do certain things that only could be applied to humans: (a) act in behalf of the master in making contracts and wills;[141] (b) be designated as the master's heir; (c) be allowed to participate in certain cultic practices[142] (including the Saturnalia festival); and (d) belong to the *collegia*--fraternal societies that crossed socio-economic boundaries and which would at times help a slave member secure a *peculium* to offer his master for manumission.[143]

Social considerations

Though there are evidences of extreme cruelty to slaves,[144] the general treatment of slaves in the Roman empire during the time of Christ was good. Many slaves were better off than free laborers;[145] and slaves in the East were generally better treated than those in the West.[146] Evidence of these conditions exists in the affectionate epitaphs given to deceased slaves by grateful masters and from the fact that many manumitted slaves continued to live with their former masters.[147] The Augustinian laws themselves articulated protective stipulations against the maltreatment of slaves.[148]

Bartchy suggests several reasons for this trend: (a) most slaves were born in the house and thus were personally close; (b) society was influenced by the ethical teachings of the Stoics;[149] (c) slaves were given important tasks to perform that required commensurate status; (d) slaves were valuable investments to be guarded; and (e) slaves, when freed, could provide for the master's needs through *obsequium* obligations.[150] Therefore, despite the severity of slavery before the law, the slave was treated by most as a human being who, if given freedom, could become a citizen with fully invested rights.[151]

Unlike modern slave systems based on racial discrimination, the social distinctions between slave and freedman were often blurred.[152] The Greeks, who developed the most varied vocabulary for slavery, developed a special term (ἀπελεύερος) for the freedman, showing his distinct place in society between slave and free.[153] Yet even so the distinction between slave and free was loose. In Athens a slave could participate in most all activities except political or military ones; and slaves, when freed, were unrestricted yet without citizenship rights.[154] Slaves in Sparta (called helots) were not chattel slaves nor foreigners; they were subjugated Greeks who were tied uniquely to the land and belonged to the state. When freed they acquired a "third status" which was equivalent to any Spartan who, for one of various reasons, had also forfeited his own citizenship.[155]

In Rome, during the classical period, the slave-free distinction was also fluid. Slaves carried on business with a *peculium* (in contrast to the free debt-bondsmen); they acquired citizenship when manumitted; and some slaves achieved a measure of wealth, position, and fame. Most notably were the slaves of Caesar's household who administered much of the empire. Their upward social mobility was seen by their frequent marriages to free women.[156] Yet, Roman freedmen, though citizens, still maintained life-long *obsequiem* obligations to the master.[157]

Finally, one cannot ignore the close analogy that existed in Roman society between the master-slave relationship and the father-son relationship. Alexander Szakats observes,

> Comparing the position of a slave with that of a *filius* under the power of the *paterfamilias* many similarities may be observed. The *patria potestas* gave practically unlimited power to the father both over the child's person and any property he might have possessed. . . . As to property, a *filius* had no capacity to own any; everything he acquired was that of his father. There grew up a practice of *peculium* which initially was similar to that of a slave. . . . Finally, *emancipato* changed the son's status, as manumission changed that of a slave.[158]

While Szakats denies that one can equate the paternal "tenderness" to a slave with that which a son would later receive,[159] the concern of the centurion over his ill slave (Luke 7:1-10; Matt. 8:5-13) suggests such affection was genuine.

Economic considerations

The economic status of slaves revolved around the practice of entrusting to a slave a *peculium*--an accumulation of money or property to which the slave had access and could use with considerable freedom. In Greece (as in Judaism) such monies became the personal property of the slave. Roman practice considered the *peculium* to belong legally to the master.[160] In actual practice, however, the *peculium* for Roman slaves often became a source from which the slave could purchase his freedom.

The tasks and responsibilities of slaves

The tasks and responsibilities of the Greek slave ranged from toil in the mines and on agricultural estates to domestic and professional duties. This vast diversity of occupations was due, says Westermann, to the "accidental nature of slave recruitment" and to the absence of racial distinctions in slavery.[161] In fact, about the only occupation from which slaves were consistently excluded was military and political involvement. Of perhaps the greatest relevance to the imagery of slavery in the gospels is the financial and legal responsibility conferred upon many slaves as their master's representatives. Westermann observes:

> The activities of slaves whose services were leased by their masters and of the slave *emporoi* who travelled overseas in the interests of their owners necessarily entailed some degree of responsibility in the handling of their masters' property as his legal representatives. As a result of these business activities the right of participation in civil actions, in a representative capacity, was necessarily conceded to such slaves.[162]

Thus, the slave performed tasks of great legal and financial value as the master's official representative.

Roman law divided the slave's occupational tasks into *operae illiberales* (tasks related to manual labor) and *operae liberales* (tasks that pertained to skilled occupations). The former category included such occupations as working in the mines, in construction, in galleys, and in various agricultural contexts;[163] and slaves consigned to any of these tasks (particularly in mines) often worked under the worse possible conditions.[164] Slave labor in the West was frequently employed on the *latifundia* (or large estates), and the treatment of these slaves varied considerably.[165] Jeremias suggests that at least for southern Palestine the use of slaves in rural (or agricultural) activities was quite rare.[166] While Jesus does give several parables reminiscent of *latifundian* contexts (e.g., the tares, the wicked tenants, and the prodigal son), in each of these parables the slaves are really peripheral figures who fit the role of domestic or house slaves. In fact, the parable of the wicked tenants probably reflects the common agricultural practice of many landholders to employ free laborers or tenant farmers to handle their estates, a trend that existed among Romans since the second century B.C.[167]

The *operae liberales* classification included a wide variety of domestic and skilled people: craftsmen, teachers,[168] secretaries, doctors, managers of estates,[169] and artisans.[170]

The termination of slavery

Greece

"The best criterion for determining the rigidity and the harshness of any slave system is to be found in the ease and availability of its manumission procedures."[171] In the Greek system, there were basically three methods of manumission;[172] (a) manumission by testament, a practice infrequently used; (b) manumission by friendship, a private procedure usually accompanied by letter; and (c) the increasingly popular and distinctive sacral manumission.[173]

Performed at Delphi's temple of Apollo, sacral manumission was a public entrustment sale in which the slave to be freed handed the required ransom price to the Delphic priest who then paid the master.[174] In this practice, the god himself (represented by the priest) served as the middle man for the slave who, by law, could not represent himself. A debate continues as to this practice's influence on Paul's doctrine of redemption and the atonement,[175] but sacral manumission, by its frequency more than by its uniqueness, affirms the availability of manumission and the increasing integration of slaves into the society of freedmen.

In Greece it was also customary for manumitted slaves to remain bound to their former masters by certain obligations (or *paramone* stipulations) in the manumission contract. At emancipation the legal freedom to serve as one's own representative was transferred to the freedman. However, the *paramone* stipulations of service could limit one or all of the other freedoms accorded the full citizen by reenslaving him if the stipulations were not kept, by requiring payment of fees or performance of services regardless of other obligations, or by demanding respect be shown to former masters.[176] In actuality, *paramone* stipulations were governed by contract, not by the laws of the *polis*; and thus they had considerable variety. Also they were of a set duration, usually expiring after ten years.

Rome

By the turn of the century from B.C. to A.D., the number of manumitted slaves became so great that laws were instituted to restrict the practice. Therefore, it is not surprising that the laws governing the Roman practice of manumission are manifold.[177]

Under Roman law, manumission could be effected either formally or informally. Formal manumission was most effective for the slave because it afforded not only freedom (*liberatas*) but also citizenship (*civitas*).[178] It could occur in three ways: by census (in which the master deliberately allowed his slave to record his name as a freedman on the census list);[179] by testament or will (which upon his death the master conferred freedom to the slave either conditionally with rendering of money or services or unconditionally);[180] and *manumission vindicta* (a legal fiction in which a third party appearing before a magistrate would proclaim the slave free).[181]

Informal means of manumission (also called *manumission inter amicos*, "between friends") conferred only liberty and took any of three forms: an informal announcement by the master to the slave that he was free, usually at the table (*man. per mensam*); a similar announcement to the slave before his friends at a banquet (*man. in convivio*); and advisement of a slave's freedom in a letter from the master (*man. per epistulam*). A benefit of informal manumission to the master was that he retained control of the *peculium* and the children of the liberated slave.[182]

A beneficial result of freedom for the slave was the impartation of Roman citizenship. Rupprecht observes, "slavery had become a well-travelled road to Roman citizenship throughout the empire by the first century A.D.,"[183] showing that the desire for citizenship did serve as a motivation for self-sale on the part of some non-Roman freemen.[184] Citizenship, of course, was only a stepping stone to greater possibilities for advancement among freedmen.[185]

Another result of manumission under the Roman system was a life-long obligation owed by the slave to the master,[186] which consisted of a fourfold responsibility: (a) *obsequium*, the general attitude of loyalty the freedman was to show toward his master even after manumission; (b) *operae*, the slave's obligation to perform certain scheduled service for the master provided it did not involve high risk to the person or to his dignity; (c) *officium*, such general duties as care for the former patron and his children in the event of insolvency; and (d) *bona*, the patron's rights over the slave's inheritance if he left no children.[187] The master also was required to support the freed slave in the event of financial disaster, to grant the freedman an annuity, to allow him to bear the patron's name, and to permit him to be buried in the family tomb.[188] These obligations were lifelong in duration,[189] even though legally the former slave was a freedman and Roman citizen. Bartchy comments: "Although these duties sound harsh to modern ears, the Romans liked to think that a freedman's relation to his patron had something personal and 'filial' about it,"[190] This confirms the earlier observation that the distinction between slave, freedman, and free man was less defined and more fluid than is ordinarily supposed.[191]

Contrasts between Greek and Roman Slavery

Despite the many similarities shared by these two ancient slave systems, several differences of these systems should be noted.

Regarding the slave's responsibilities

Both systems allowed the slave to have control of a *peculium* and to exercise a considerable amount of freedom in relation to it. Greek slave law provided that the slave could own it, add to it, and distribute it freely. It could be presented to the master as a payment for manumission, but only through a middle man because the slave could not legally conduct his own affairs.[192] Of course, the master was under no obligation to accept it. In the Roman system, on the other hand, the slave did not own the *peculium* even though his access to it might be extensive. In the process of manumission, the slave could present the *peculium* directly to the master (without a middle man) because the property was legally the master's.[193]

Regarding the slave's manumission

Both systems put certain stipulations on their slaves at the time of their manumission: in the Greek system it was the *paramone* stipulations; in the Roman system it was the four-fold obligations of *obsequium*, *operae*, *officium*, and *bona*. Both consisted of responsibilities of respect and service and were mutual in their benefits to both freedman and patron. However, under the Greek system these conditions for manumission were usually temporary, established by legal contract at the time of emancipation. By contrast, the Roman obligations between patron and former slave were permanent.

The status of the freed slave in society differed between the two systems. In Roman slavery, the freed slave could be granted full Roman citizenship--a reality which, it has been shown, motivated some free men to voluntarily submit to slavery. Not every form of manumission granted citizenship (*civitas*), and early in the first century A.D. a series of laws were passed which tended to restrict (though not eliminate) this particular feature of the Roman system. The possibility of citizenship was denied in the Greek system, perhaps because the Greeks made a more rigid distinction between citizens and "outsiders," in which group most slaves fell.[194] Yet Bartchy concludes that this denial of citizenship tended to further blur the distinction between slave and freedman.[195]

Regarding philosophic and religious attitudes

Unlike the Romans, the Greeks spent more energy speculating about the philosophic bases and implications of slavery, trying to define the essence of slavery. Their efforts not only give an enlarged understanding of the Greek mentality toward slavery, but also show whether the Greeks ever used slavery in the religious sense of service to God that is found in the Jewish and Christian literature.

A most basic philosophic issue was: Is the slave a slave by nature? Is he naturally inferior? Most early thinkers answered in the affirmative. Homer's *Odyssey* assumed that a slave was somehow half a man;[196] and Plato suggested that the soul of the slave was corrupt.[197] Aristotle gave a classic articulation of the concept of natural slavery: "He who is by nature not his own but another's man, is by nature a slave."[198] Elsewhere, he called the slave a "living possession,"[199] one lacking a deliberation faculty,"[200] and one who could not truly share in human happiness.[201] His most famous statement is:

> The slave is a living tool, and the tool is a lifeless slave. *Qua* slave, then, one cannot be friends with him. But *qua* man one can;

for there seems to be some justice between any man and any other who can share in a system of law.²⁰²

A related ethical question was: Wherein does freedom consist? For example, the early playwrights suggested through their slave characters that a slave may be legally bound but possess inner freedom.²⁰³ Ironically, Aristotle advanced the ethical idea that true freedom consisted in something other than literal bondage, by making a distinction between slavery by law (e.g., through war captivity) and slavery by nature.²⁰⁴ In maintaining that the latter kind of slavery was never true of Hellenes, while the first could be, he reinforced the distinction between inner (spiritual) freedom and external freedom that was later defended by the Stoics.²⁰⁵

It is hard to overestimate the importance of the concept of freedom to the Greek mind. Rengstorf says:

> The distinctive feature of the self-awareness of the Greeks is the thought of freedom. The Greek finds his personal dignity in the fact that he is free. Thus his self-awareness stands out sharply from anything which stands under the concept of δουλεύειν.²⁰⁶

Thus, the Greeks' high regard for service in the πόλις was not expressed in terms that denied self-autonomy or affirmed subjugation to an alien will.

In light of this view of freedom, the inevitable religious question is: Did the Greeks employ the language of slavery to describe their relationship to their gods? Some indicators suggest this is true. First, some of the mystery religions considered an initiate as a slave of the god. The harsh mutilation or branding at initiation, suggests Rengstorf, reflected the practice of marking slaves and thus symbolized the worshipper's entrance into divine slavery.[207] Second, there were examples of people called "slaves of God" in Mycenanean Greece (1450-1100 B.C.), though these may simply be slaves of a lower status.[208] Third, οἰκονομός in the pre-Christian era designated stewards of political offices and private guilds who also performed religious and priestly functions. John Reumann says this common word "has been drawn into religious use, as a cult title, or, at the very least, to describe an office of trust and responsibility in the sphere of the sacred, with the things that belong to the god."[209] He even recognizes a possible application of this in Luke 12:42; 16:1-18.

However, the above indicators appear to be exceptions to the rule. Slavery to God seems alien to Greek thought. Says Westermann: "Among the Greeks the gods, in strict distinction from their temples as organizations did *not* have slaves. Said in other words, the Greeks secularized their institutions of slavery."[210] This is supported by several observations. First, the Greek concept of freedom is too strongly tied to self-sufficiency and self-determination to be compatible with religious service. Second, the Greek gods were not gods of "unconditional majesty and absolute superiority" to man,[211] but were anthropomorphic deities with customary human frailties as well as supernatural strengths.[212] Appropriately, the relationship of the gods to men was portrayed more in familial terms (including marriage and cohabitation) than in servile ones.[213] Third, there was no place for humble kneeling in worship, except as it would put the worshipper in closer proximity to the god.²¹⁴

Contributions of Greek and Roman Slavery to the Gospels' Slavery Motif

It must be reaffirmed that Greek and Roman slavery exerted much less influence on the gospel narratives than did Palestinian Judaism and the Old Testament. Nevertheless, this profile of slavery in the Greco-Roman world confirms a point observed in Judaism: namely that while the slave institutionally was still subject to his master both *de jure* and *de facto*, his position socially was not as harsh as modern slavery. Legal restrictions on masters, freedom to attain wealth and position while a slave (under the Roman system), the very realistic hope of eventual manumission, and the ambiguity of definition between slave and freedman all support the thesis that a slave's position was not abysmal. In fact, some slaves voluntarily entered slavery for the personal benefits they would gain. Therefore, it should not be surprising that Jesus would frequently use slavery imagery to speak of His followers. Neither the experience of Judaism, nor familiarity with Greek or Roman slavery supports the notion that Jesus viewed His disciples as chattel or beasts.

It may be noted that the philosophical attitudes of the Greeks do not fit well with the Old Testament's (and later Judaistic) use of עבד יהוה. To the Greeks, service to God was a mutually exclusive idea; to Israel, it was a high privilege. This difference suggests that Jesus' use of the imagery harmonizes best with Old Testament usage.

Apart from these general observations, slave practices in Greece and Rome may explain some individual references to slavery in the gospels. First, slaves under the Greek and Roman systems functioning as representatives of their lords, often reflected his position and authority. The slavery motif in the gospels includes several examples of slaves acting in this capacity: as ambassadors to invite guests to the great feast (Luke 14:15-24) and the wedding feast (Matt. 21:1-14); as extensions of the vineyard owner in the parable of the wicked tenants (Luke 20:9-18, et al.); and as the master's representatives in the parables of the faithful and the unfaithful slaves (Luke 12:41-48) and the unjust steward (Luke 16:1-13).

Second, the Greek *peculium* may lie behind the parable of the unjust steward (Luke 16:1-14). There the steward not only exercised considerable control of this money but apparently was able to make a profit from it--since the cutting of his own profit "to win friends" is a most plausible explanation for the later praise by his master that he received.

Third, the Roman *peculium* provides a better background for the parables of the talents and minas. The master's distribution of talents and minas in these two parables corresponds with the practice of entrusting slaves with great financial responsibility. And the understanding that the money and profits legally belonged to the master who could claim them at any time also harmonizes with customary practices.

Fourth, the lifelong *obesequium* obligations unique to Roman slavery fit well with Jesus' parables of the talents and the minas.

While faithfulness to the Master produces a changed relationship which moves the master-slave relationship to a different level, obligations continue. In fact, no parable employing the slavery motif implies the cessation of the master-slave relationship.

Fifth, Roman informal manumission practice of *manumission in convivio* is perhaps a backdrop to the Upper Room Discourse, where at a banquet with the disciples, Jesus announces to His disciples that He no longer calls them slaves (a title He had used in reference to them earlier in the evening, John 13:16). Also consistent with *inter amicos* is the principle that such manumission does not guarantee restoration of all legal rights, a reality Jesus maintains in John 15:20-21.

Six, while Jesus' references that the way to greatness is through slavery (e.g., Mark 9:33-37; Mark 10:35-45 and parallels) may strike the modern reader as a shocking reversal, the popularity of voluntary self-sale into slavery makes this more intelligible. Petronius, for example, describes a former prince who voluntarily enslaved himself to gain Roman citizenship.[215] It is possible that Christ's admonition to seek greatness through servitude reflects this practice of Roman culture.

Conclusion

This study of the cultural backgrounds of slavery is an important step in determining the significance of the slavery motif in the gospels. It has shown that of the three cultures influencing Palestine during the life of Christ, Judaism still was dominant. There may be some individual details of the accounts that are better explicated by a Greek or Roman understanding, but on the whole the proposition that Palestine was more directly influenced by its own Jewish customs and regulations (ultimately based on the Old Testament) cannot be set aside.

No more is this true then in discussing the question of the use of slavery imagery to describe one's relationship to God. The Romans were not as concerned with this expression, and such a picture was abhorrent to the Greeks. The Old Testament's (and Judaism's) view of slavery to God as a high privilege then becomes a significant difference that must be preferred in interpreting the gospels.

However, it may be said that nothing in the contemporary culture of Christ exists that would overthrow the thrust observed in the Old Testament that institutional slavery denoted humble, subjected service to the master (without denying the slave's basic human dignity) and that spiritual slavery to God contained the double nuance of humble obedience and exalted privilege.

Notes

¹The literature of Roman slavery is vast. Consult specific listings relating to Roman customs and slave law in the bibliography of the dissertation. Other helpful bibliographies are found in W. L. Westermann, Slave Systems in Greek and Roman Antiquity; S. Scott Bartchy, III, Μᾶλλον Χρῆσαι: First Century Slavery and the Interpretation of I Corinthians 7:21; Thomas Wiedemann, Greek and Roman Slavery; and NIDNTT, s.v. "slave," by Rudolf Tuente, (1978):599. Bibliographical essays by M. I. Finley in Slavery in Classical Antiquity, pp. 229-36; and by Joseph Vogt in Ancient Slavery and the Ideal of Man, pp. 170-87. The most important individual works include: W. W. Buckland, The Roman Law of Slavery: The Conditions of the Slave in Private Law from Augustus to Justinian, and John Crook, Life and Law of Rome.

²Most of the above bibliographies also make references to Greek slavery. Westermann, Bartchy, and Wiedemann are equally helpful here.

³TB: Kid. 69a; Joachim Jeremias, Jerusalem in the Time of Jesus, p. 110; Solomon Zeitlin, "Slavery During the Second Commonwealth and the Tannatic Period," JQR 53 (1962):194.

⁴Josephus Antiquities 20. 9. 2; Zeitlin, p. 198.

⁵TB: Pes. 57a; Tos.: Men. 13. 21. Jeremias, p. 110, questions whether this concerns the period of Jerusalem in the time of Jesus.

⁶M: Ber. 2. 7; M: Pes. 7. 2.

⁷EJ, 1971 ed., s.v. "slave," by Maim H. Cohn, 14:1658.

⁸Zeitlin, p. 194; Jeremias, p. 111.

⁹Ibid., p. 36. This is contrary to Zeitlin, p. 198, who without support denies it.

¹⁰Jeremias, p. 111; cf. Matt. 20:1-6.

¹¹Jeremias, p. 316.

¹²Ibid., p. 312. Jeremias distinguishes Hebrew from Gentile slaves, and all legislation that seems to violate the principle that Jewish slaves are to be treated as kinsmen is applied to the Gentile slave. Since EJ does not so clearly make these distinctions, Jeremias will be followed in this discussion.

¹³TB: Kid. 20a, 22b; Jeremias, p. 316; Bartchy, p. 51.

¹⁴Jeremias, pp. 312-13. Josephus Ant. 4. 8. 27 says if the thief cannot pay the principal and the penalty he can be enslaved for the total restitution. The Talmud stipulates only the principle need be paid. Zeitlin suggests that Josephus was describing the rule in the early part of the Second Commonwealth while the Talmud reflects the practice after Herod, p. 189.

¹⁵Jeremias, p. 313; EJ, 14:1685; M: Git. 4. 9; TB: Kid. 14b.

¹⁶Zeitlin, p. 194. Cf. Philo De Virtutibus 123, who also considers this practice as legitimate.

¹⁷Mek. Exod. 21.7.   ¹⁸Jeremias, p. 314.

¹⁹Ibid., p. 313; EJ, 14:1658.   ²⁰Jeremias, p. 315.

²¹Ibid., p. 314. n. 56. Mek. Exod. 21:2.   ²²Sipre, Deut. 15:18.

²³TB: Kid. 15a; EJ, 14:1659.

²⁴Jeremias, p. 315, points out this must be a Gentile female since an adult Hebrew female would not logically be enslaved.

²⁵M: B.K. 8. 4.

²⁶Sale to a Gentile meant automatic release according to M: Git. 4. 6.

²⁷EJ, 14:1659; M: Shek. 1. 5.; TB: B.B. 51b-52a.

²⁸EJ, 14:1659.   ²⁹M: B.K. 8. 3-4.

³⁰Hillel argued that the slave who is "half a slave" should serve one day for the master and the alternative day be free. The more humanitarian Shimmei, realizing that this would unjustly prevent such a slave from marrying (in disobedience to Isa. 45:18), advised the slave to become completely free--even if it meant going into debt to the partial master, M: Git. 4. 5. See also M: Pes. 8. 1.

[31] Jeremias, p. 314. M: Kid. 1. 2; TB: Kid. 17b. Cf. EJ, 14:1658. Zeitlin believes such boring was a form of punishment, not favor, p. 207.

[32] EJ, 14:1658.   [33] M: Peah 3. 8.   [34] M: Git. 4. 6.

[35] Zeitlin, p. 209.   [36] EJ, 14:1658; M: Kid. 1. 2.

[37] M: Kid. 1. 3.

[38] Jeremias, p. 346, speculates that the slave Malchus was Arabian.

[39] Ibid., pp. 36, 346.

[40] TB: Kid. 22b; EJ, 14:1658.

[41] M: Git. 1. 4.   [42] Jeremias, p. 348.

[43] TB: B.K. 12a and TB: B.B. 68a, 150a show that originally slaves were classed as immovable property. See EJ, 14:1658; M: B.M. 4. 9; M: Sheb. 1. 7. See also Zeitlin, p. 214, who says the law of defrauding does not apply to the slave. Later, however, the slave was considered movable property, says Zeitlin, p. 214. Furthermore, the Gentile slave could not own property; anything he found automatically belonged to the Master. M: B.M. 1. 5; Jeremias, p. 348.

[44] Zeitlin, p. 209.

[45] He could testify that a woman in a Gentile-invaded village was not violated, M: Yeb. 2. 8, but he could not testify in court against priests, M: R.H. 1. 7-8.

[46] Jeremias, p. 351; TB: Kid. 28a.

[47] M: Hor. 3. 8. While the slave would presumably fall just below the freedman, this order is not regularly followed as elsewhere in the Mishna the proselyte is put on par with the freed Gentile, M: Kid. 4. 7. Jeremias, pp. 271-72, ranks some Israelites (e.g., bastard, the fatherless) below the freed slave on the premise that social stigma in Jewish society was indicated by the freedom to marry pure Israelites.

[48] Jeremias, p. 336.

[49] E.g., Gamaliel's affection for his slave, Tobias, M: Ber. 2. 7.

[50] TB: Shab. 135b. Jeremias, p. 349, says they had one year to decide: if they refused they could be sold to a Gentile. Rabbi Akiba said a Jew could not keep an uncircumcised slave. Zeitlin points out, however, this implies a more humanitarian master-slave bond, p. 203.

⁵¹Jeremias, p. 349.   ⁵²M: Ber. 3. 3.   ⁵³M: Suk. 2. 1, 8, 9.

⁵⁴M: Naz. 9. 1.

⁵⁵But cf. Jeremias, on the basis of TB: Git. 43b-44a, who questions this, p. 350, n. 28.

⁵⁶M: Pes. 7. 2.

⁵⁷But cf. Zeitlin, p. 200.

⁵⁸Some rabbis said it had to take place in the presence of witnesses and be shown that the master did it purposefully. TB: B.K. 74; Tos.: B.K. 9. 21; Zeitlin, pp. 206-7.

⁵⁹M: B.K. 4. 5.   ⁶⁰M: B.K. 3. 10.   ⁶¹M: B.K. 8. 3, 4.

⁶²Zeitlin believes that the debate was really over the sale, not the manumission, of Gentile slaves, pp. 204-6.

⁶³R. Ishmael held the former, R. Akiba--the same who said Jews could not keep uncircumcised slaves--held the latter. TB: Git. 38; Zeitlin, p. 204.

⁶⁴TB: Kid. 24b-25a; Zeitlin, p. 207.

⁶⁵M: Kid. 1. 3; Jeremias, p. 335.   ⁶⁶M: Kid. 1. 3.

⁶⁷M: Peah 3. 8; EJ 14:1658.   ⁶⁸Jeremias, p. 335.

⁶⁹TB: Git. 39b-40a.   ⁷⁰TB: Git. 40; Zeitlin, p. 217.

⁷¹TDNT, s.v. "Παῖς θεοῦ," by Walther Zimmerli, 5 (1967):673. Παῖς is used 340 times to translate עבד; δοῦλος is used 327 times. The Hebrew word behind δοῦλος, δουλεία and δουλεύω almost without exception is עבד; עבד is rendered in a variety of ways.

⁷²TDNT, s.v. "δοῦλος," by Karl Rengstorf, 2 (1964):266.

⁷³Παῖς and οἰκέτης are used more often perhaps because Hebrew slaves are in view who were to be treated as "hired men" and as sons of the covenant.

⁷⁴TDNT, 2:266; 5:674.   ⁷⁵Ibid., 2:268.   ⁷⁶Ibid.

⁷⁷Ibid., 5:674.   ⁷⁸Ibid., 2:266.

⁷⁹Cf. TDNT, 5:679, for a complete listing.

80Ibid., 5:677-78.   81Wisdom 9:5.   82TDNT, 5:679, n. 166.

83Ibid., 5:682-83. Its absence in the rabbinic literature is likely explained by the rabbis' aversion to using the designation that Christians were applying to Jesus.

84Ibid., 5:675.   85Ibid.   86Ibid., 5:679.

87Cf. Robert H. Gundry, "The Language Milieu of First Century Palestine," JBL 83 (1964):404-6; Philip Edgcumb Hughes, "The Languages Spoken by Jesus," in New Dimensions in New Testament Study, eds., Richard N. Longenecker and Merrill C. Tenney, pp. 127-43. One evidence of Jesus' use of Greek is the wordplay between πέτρα and Πέτρος (Matt. 16:18) which is insignificant in Aramaic.

88Cicero Pro Archia 23.

89J. A. Thompson, The Bible and Archaeology, pp. 306-7. See also G. A. Barios, in IB, 12 vols., 1:157-58.

90Harold W. Hoehner, Herod Antipas, pp. 184-250.

91Jeremias, p. 74.

92Jack Finegan, Light from the Ancient Past: The Archaeological Background of the Hebrew-Christian Religion, 2nd. ed., 2 vols., 2:305; see Bishop, "Jesus and Capernaum," CBQ 15 (1953):427-37.

93John's reference in 12:21 to Bethsaida of Galilee has led some to conclude that there were two Bethsaidas: one on the west of the Jordan in Galilee and one in the east. Robert L. Alden argues aptly that John's reference to Galilee is likely non-technical; thus, the apostle speaks of the same city that is mentioned in the synoptics. ZPBE, s.v. "Bethsaida," 1:542; Finegan, 2:307. See Josephus Antiquities 18. 2. 1 and 18. 4. 6. Also, Bo Reicke, The New Testament Era: The World of the Bible from 500 B.C. to A.D. 100, p. 126.

94Reicke, p. 116; ZPBE, s.v. "Tiberias," by E. M. Blaiklock, 5:745-46; Josephus Antiquities 18. 2. 3; Finegan, 2:312. Hoehner, p. 91, calls this "the first city in Jewish history founded within the municipal framework of a πόλις."

95Finegan, 2:311; Thompson, p. 364; Reicke, p. 131.

96ZPBE, s.v. "Tyre," by Edward M. Blaiklock, 5:832-35; Jeremias, p. 36.

97The cave of the god Pan was there. Josephus Antiquities 10. 3. 1; Finegan, 2:307.

98Finegan, 2:313; ZPBE, s.v. "Jericho," by Howard Jamieson, 3:455.

99Jeremias, p. 64.

100Naphtali Lewis and Meyer Reinhold, eds., Roman Civilization, 2 vols., vol. 2: The Empire, p. 532.

101Alexandria imposed a five percent manumission tax, Lewis and Reinhold 2:261; Palermo added import, export, and sales taxes for slave transactions, ibid., 2:332.

102Sipra, Lev. 25:42.   103Jeremias, p. 36.   104Ibid., p. 51.

105Josephus Antiquities 16. 1. 1.

106The ambiguity of such references is seen by the following: Westermann, Slave Systems, p. 149, n. 2 believes the centurion is a Gentile; Jochem J. Koopmans, De Servitute Antiqua et Religione Christiana, p. 102, assumes he is Jewish with a non-Jewish slave; A. N. Sherwin-White, Roman Society and Roman Law in the New Testament, p. 124, contends he was a Herodian, not a Roman.

107Koopmans, pp. 109-10, suggests this is reminiscent of the Saturnalia festivals.

108He examines: the ethnic identity of the centurion in Matt. 8:5-13, p. 124; the significance of the Greek and Roman coins, p. 125; the references to tax-gatherers, publicans, and the Roman census, pp. 125-26; the technical distinction between city ($\pi\delta\lambda\iota\varsigma$) and village, pp. 129-133; and the nature of the "king" in the parable of the talents, p. 135.

109Ibid., p. 122.

110Koopmans, pp. 132-133. While he admits some of the more severe customs may be due partly to foreign influences, he also feels they may be deliberate exaggerations.

111Kenneth C. Russell, Slavery as Reality and Metaphor in the Pauline Letters.

112Keith Hopkins, Conqueror and Slaves, pp. 99-100.

113M. I. Finley, Ancient Slavery and Modern Ideology, pp. 9-10.

114Hopkins, pp. 99-100, defines a slave society as one in which slaves play an important part in production and comprises at least 20 percent of the population. Finley, p. 87, adds that three other conditions must exist simultaneously for this to occur: (1) private ownership of land in agrarian societies; (2) sufficient development of community products and markets; and (3) unavailability of an adequate labor supply. Many societies had slaves; only two depended upon them for economic survival as a state.

[115] Lewis and Reinhold, 2:532; Crook, p. 284.

[116] Sherwin-White, pp. 138-39.

[117] Lewis and Reinhold, 2:532, for example, acknowledge that Roman law was altered in the provinces. Crook, p. 284, and Bartchy, pp. 40-41, n. 104, offer a similar observation.

[118] Westermann, p. 20. [119] Ibid., p. 35. Also Bartchy, p. 43.

[120] Justinian Digest 1. 5. 4. 1. See also Bartchy, p. 37; Buckland, p. 2; Alexander Szakats, "Slavery as a Social and Economic Institution in Antiquity with Special Reference to Roman Law," Prud 7 (May 1975):37.

[121] Buckland, p. 1; Westermann, p. 57. [122] Szakats, p. 37.

[123] Finley, Ancient Slavery, p. 86.

[124] Westermann, pp. 2-3, 28-30. See Carol G. Thomas, "On the Origin of the Institution of Slavery," The Ancient World 1 (September 1978):109-10. Buckland, pp. 397-98; Lewis and Reinhold, 2:264; Szakats, pp. 37-38.

[125] John C. Gager, "Religious and Social Classes in the Early Roman Empire," pp. 99-120, in The Catacombs and the Colosseum: The Roman Empire as the Setting of Primitive Christianity eds., Stephen Benko and John J. O'Rourke, p. 109; Westermann, p. 85.

[126] Szakats, p. 38.

[127] Justinian Digest 50. 17. 32; Lewis and Reinhold, 2:264; Szakats, p. 38; Bartchy, pp. 45-49; Buckland, pp. 401-22.

[128] R. H. Barrow, Slavery in the Roman Empire, p. 12.

[129] Bartchy, pp. 47-48. This last reason (1 Clement 55:2) antedates Christ, although its earlier practice is possible.

[130] Finley, "Between Slavery and Freedom," Comparative Studies in Society and History 6 (1963-64):245.

[131] In Athens, slaves did not wear distinctive dress, "mixed"

marriages were allowed, and the slave could participate in the "mysteries," Westermann, pp. 22-24, 122; Bartchy, pp. 41-42.

[132] Westermann, p. 38.

[133] Other legal predicates of the slave in Roman law are *manicipium* and *res mortales*. Justinian Digest 21. 1; 23. 3. See Bartchy, pp. 38-39.

[134] Westermann, pp. 3, 37-38.

[135] Bartchy, p. 39; Szakats, p. 40.   [136] Szakats, p. 40.

[137] Plutarch Lives "Solon" 132; Westermann, p. 4.

[138] Szakats, p. 40.   [139] Ibid.   [140] Ibid., p. 39.

[141] Ibid.; Jérôme Carcopino, Daily Life in Ancient Rome, p. 58.

[142] Lewis and Reinhold, 2:257.

[143] Ibid., 2:272; Carcopino, p. 57.

[144] E.g., Seneca De Ira 3. 40 and Dio Cassius 54. 23.

[145] Bartchy, p. 68.

[146] Westermann, p. 102. He also notes several factors that lessened the severity of slavery in the Hellenistic period: (a) the philosophic tendency (sparked by Stoic egalitarianism) away from the "racial-genetic" approach implied in Aristotle; (b) the proffering of freedom, marriage, etc., as goals for more efficient work; (c) the cosmopolitanism of Hellenism; and (d) the general leveling of class distinctions, pp. 39-40.

[147] Alan Watson, The Law of Persons in the Later Roman Republic, pp. 226-31; Bartchy, p. 70.

[148] Lewis and Reinhold, 2:263-70.

[149] Cf. Seneca Moral Epistles 47; Lewis and Reinhold, 2:266-68.

[150] Bartchy, pp. 68-70.

[151] Finley fully discusses this ambiguity in "On Slavery and Humanity," Ancient Slavery and Modern Ideology, pp. 93-122.

[152] Bartchy, pp. 73-74, 114-15.

¹⁵³Other words included: σῶμα (a popular description not found in legal usage); and οἰκέτης, θεράπων, παῖς, and παιδίον—words used in a variety of rather imprecise ways, Westermann, pp. 5, 42-43; Bartchy, p. 43.

¹⁵⁴Finley, "Between Slavery," pp. 238-39.

¹⁵⁵Ibid., p. 240.

¹⁵⁶P. R. C. Weaver, Familia Caesaris: A Social Study of the Emperor's Freedmen and Slaves, is devoted to proving the reality of upward mobility. See also P. R. C. Weaver, "Social Mobility in the Early Roman Empire: The Evidence of the Imperial Freedman and Slaves," pp. 121-40 in Studies in Ancient Society, ed. M. I. Finley. Cf. Finley "Beyond Slavery," pp. 242-43.

¹⁵⁷See Lewis and Reinhold, 2:256-61. For a clearer picture of the freedman, see Susan Treggiari, Roman Freedmen During the Late Republic.

¹⁵⁸Szakats, pp. 44-45.   ¹⁵⁹Sir Henry Maine, Ancient Law, p. 97.

¹⁶⁰Szakats, p. 41.   ¹⁶¹Westermann, p. 11.

¹⁶²Ibid., pp. 16-17.   ¹⁶³Szakats, pp. 40-41.

¹⁶⁴Lewis and Reinhold, 2:158, 163.   ¹⁶⁵Ibid., 2:166-73.

¹⁶⁶Jeremias, p. 110.   ¹⁶⁷Westermann, p. 91.

¹⁶⁸Slaves called *paedagogi* were in charge of the children at home and escorted them to school, Lewis and Reinhold, 2:288.

¹⁶⁹Szakats, p. 41.

¹⁷⁰Westermann, p. 92. Joseph Vogt places heavy emphasis on the skilled occupations as indicators of the slave's humanitarian treatment in Slavery and the Ideal of Man, pp. 105-121, 127. Cf. Finley, Ancient Slavery and Modern Ideology, pp. 104-10, who feels Vogt's emphasis is overstated.

¹⁷¹Westermann, p. 25.

¹⁷²There are some cases of escape in which Greek law allowed the severely harassed slave to seek asylum at an altar, Bartchy, p. 94; but these instances were, on the whole, exceptional.

¹⁷³Bartchy, pp. 94-95. Westermann, "Athenian Manumission," pp. 92-104, discusses a fourth practice that was found in Athens but not in

Delphi: feigned trials of abandonment in which the court declared a man, in deliberate absence of protest from the master, to be free.

[174] Westermann, p. 92; Bartchy, p. 123, n. 446.

[175] Adolf Deissmann, Light from the Ancient East, p. 323, was among the first to suggest that this practice paralleled the Pauline doctrine of redemption. Bartchy, pp. 121-25, who disagrees with Deissmann, cites the following evidence: (1) there is no precedent legally for asserting the freedmen became the actual slave of Apollo; (2) the linguistic expressions are different (Paul uses ἀγωράζω, which is not found at Delphi; Delphi uses πρίασθαι, which is not found in the New Testament); and (3) slavery to God was a notion repugnant to the Greeks. Note, however, that Tuente, NIDNTT, 3:597, assumes that sacral manumission was the underlying metaphor for the Pauline doctrine; and his bibliography shows he is familiar with Bartchy's work.

[176] Plato Laws 9. 915, prescribes rules which apparently reflect actual practices.

[177] Lewis and Reinhold, 2:53-55.

[178] Bartchy, p. 91; Szakats, p. 42; Lewis and Reinhold, 2:256-57, 261-62; Carcopino, pp. 59-60.

[179] Buckland, p. 440.

[180] Ibid., pp. 442-49, 460; Bartchy, p. 92; Szakats, p. 42.

[181] Buckland, pp. 441-42, 450-60.

[182] Bartchy, pp. 93-94.

[183] ZPBE, s.v. "slave, slavery," by Arthur Rupprecht, 5:458.

[184] The lex Aelia Sentia (c. A.D. 4) prohibited freed slaves of questionable character from becoming full citizens. The Junian law created a new category of "Junian Latins" for freedmen, in which citizenship was not automatic but possible when certain other conditions were met. Szakats, p. 43, dates these laws at A.D. 19, while Lewis and Reinhold, 2:52, put them around 17 B.C.

[185] Westermann, p. 111, reminds us that Felix was the brother of a former freedman.

[186] Crook, p. 191; Lyall, pp. 78-79.

[187] Bartchy, pp. 80-81; Szakats, pp. 43-44; Crook pp. 51-52.

188Crook, p. 54; Bartchy, p. 81.

189Crook p. 191; Lyall, pp. 78-79.

190Bartchy, p. 81.

191Bartchy's discussion on manumission is one of the best contemporary studies of this practice available. For that reason the author has relied heavily on his discussion. Bartchy's thesis is that manumission is something that "happened" to a slave, not something that the slave had the right to initiate, accept, or reject, pp. 96-97, 106-7. While the slave could, through faithful service and accumulation of a *peculium*, make manumission more attractive, he was in the long-run completely at the mercy of the master's decision.

192Bartchy, pp. 98-99.   193Buckland, pp. 187-238.

194Finley, Ancient Slavery, pp. 75-76; Finley, "Beyond Slavery," p. 239.

195Bartchy, p. 118.

196"Servants never do their work when their master's hand is no longer over them, for Jove takes half the goodness out of a man when he makes a slave of him." Homer Odyssey 17. 319-22.

197"But may we not also say that the soul of the slave is corrupt, and that no man of sense ought to trust him" Plato Laws 6. 777-78. See also Phaedrus 238-39.

198Aristotle Politics 1. 4. See also Pol. 1. 2, 5.

199Ibid., 1. 4.   200Ibid., 1. 13.   201Aristotle Nic. Ethics 10. 6.

202Ibid., 8. 11.

203Euripidies wrote: "For in heart, though not in name, I am free," Helen, lines 728-37. Cf. Vogt, Ancient Slavery, pp. 6-25.

204Aristotle Politics 1. 6.

205E.g., Epictetus Discourses 4. 1. His chapter entitled "About Freedom" is particularly relevant.

206TDNT, s.v. "δοῦλος," by Karl H. Rengstorf, 2 (1964):261.

207Ibid., 2:269.

[208] Cf. Edwin Yamauchi, "Slaves of God," JETS 9 (Winter 1966):32-33, with Bartchy, pp. 121-25.

[209] John Reumann, "'Stewards of God'--Pre-Christian Religious Application of οἰκονόμος in Greek," JBL 77 (1958):349.

[210] Westermann, p. 45.

[211] TDNT, s.v. "δοῦλος," by Karl Rengstorf, 2:268.

[212] Ibid., 2:265.   [213] Ibid., 2:264-65.

[214] Ibid. Rengstorf notes several possible exceptions to this conclusion but effectively explains them as arising from compulsion or fear.

[215] Petronius Satyricon 57. 4; cf. Crook, p. 60; Bartchy, p. 47.

CHAPTER IV

THE SLAVERY MOTIF IN THE SYNOPTICS

Introduction

The gospels are not among the earliest written New Testament documents, nor are they mere transcriptions of the *logia* of Jesus. They are integral theological documents reflecting a coherent argument of the individual author which nevertheless do contain the teachings and works of the Lord accurately reported. As such they provide both a firm foundation for considering a motif that is prominent in later New Testament writers and that spans most logically the Old Testament era and the church age.

There is an advantage in dealing with all the occurrences of the slavery motif in the synoptics in one chapter. Because of the considerable similarity in content and expression of the first three gospels, one may avoid undue repetition by treating only one parallel passage where the motif occurs (rather than two or even three) while still placing the event properly in its historical setting, noting the differences and similarities between the accounts, and recognizing the unique perspectives of the evangelists.

Several critical issues relevent to the synoptic material are constantly discussed, including: the synoptic problem (with the questions of literary priority of the gospels[1] and the nature and number of the literary sources lying behind the synoptic records[2]); form criticism, which seeks to distinguish the original words of Christ (the *ipissima verba*) from the later accretions added by the early Christian community;[3] and redaction criticism, which focuses on the theological perspectives of the individual evangelists.[4]

While the writer favors Farmer's Matthean priority because it demands less unfounded assumptions about the existence of proto-gospel sources (e.g., Q), synoptic priority and documentary background do not directly affect this issue. Since the writer's concern here is with the materials in their present canonical shape, such matters need not unduly detain us. It need only be added that the historical integrity of these writings is assumed and that the sayings attributed to Christ, while often selected for an individual author's specific purpose, are authentically the words of Jesus.

The Classification of Slavery Motif Passages

There are four word groups which provide the basis for delineating the slavery motif in this chapter: δοῦλος (including δοῦλος, δουλεύω, and δούλη); οἰκονόμος (οἰκονόμος, οἰκονομέω, and οἰκέτης); διάκονος (διακονέω and διάκονος); and παῖς (παῖς and παιδίον). All of these designate either a person who is a slave or the activity of a slave. The passages in which these words occur are classified below to facilitate the discussion that follows:

I. Literal (or institutional) uses

   A. Of an individual or a group

      1. The healing of the centurion's slave (Luke 7:1-10, δοῦλος, παῖς; Matt. 8:5-13, παῖς, δοῦλος)
      2. Herod's servants (Luke 8:3, ἐπίτροπος; Matt. 14:2, παῖς)
      3. The high priest's slave (Luke 22:50, δοῦλος; Mark 14:47, δοῦλος; Matt. 26:51, δοῦλος)

   B. Of the work of service (exclusively used with διάκονος or διακονέω)

      1. Angels serving Jesus (Mark 1:12-13; Matt. 4:11)
      2. Peter's mother-in-law serving (Luke 4:38-39; Mark 1:29-31; Matt. 8:14-17)
      3. Mary and Martha's service (Luke 10:38-42)
      4. The women serving Jesus (Mark 15:41; Matt. 27:55; Luke 8:3, with ἐπίτροπος)
      5. The ungodly withholding service from God's children (Matt. 25:31-46).

II. Figurative (non-institutional) uses

   A. Personal designations

      1. Mary (Luke 1:38, 48, δούλη)
      2. Israel (Luke 1:54, παῖς)
      3. David (Luke 1:69, παῖς)
      4. Simeon (Luke 2:29, δοῦλος)
      5. Jesus (Matt. 12:51-21, παῖς)
      6. John the Baptist (Matt. 3:11; Mark 1:7; Luke 3:16)

   B. Proverbial uses

      1. "No man can serve two masters" (Matt. 6:24, δοῦλος; Luke 16:1-13)
      2. "A slave is not above his master" (Matt. 10:24-25, δοῦλος)
      3. "If anyone wants to be first he shall be last of all and slave of all" (Mark 9:33-37, διάκονος; cf. also Matt. 18:1-5 and Luke 9:46-48)
      4. "Whoever would be first among you must be slave of all" "Mark 10:35-45, δοῦλος; Matt. 20:20-28, δοῦλος, διάκονος; Luke 22:24-27, διάκονος, διακονέω)
      5. "We are unworthy slaves" (Luke 17;5-10, δοῦλος, διάκονος)
      6. "He who is greatest among you shall be your servant" (Matt. 23:1-12, διάκονος).

C. Parabolic (or analogical uses)

1. Parables in which the slaves are peripheral

   a. Tares (Matt. 13:24-30, δοῦλος)
   b. Prodigal son (Luke 15:11-32, δοῦλος, παῖς, μίσθιος)
   c. Great supper (Luke 14:15-24, δοῦλος)
   d. Wedding feast (Matt. 22:1-14, δοῦλος, διάκονος)
   e. Wicked tenants (Luke 20:9-18; Matt. 21:33-46; Mark 12:1-12, δοῦλος)

2. Parables in which the slaves are central

   a. Alert servants (Luke 12:35-40, δοῦλος, διάκονος)
   b. Faithful vs. unfaithful servants (Luke 12:41-48, δοῦλος, παῖς, οἰκονόμος; also Matt. 24:41-51, δοῦλος)
   c. Unjust steward (Luke 16:1-13, οκονόμος, δοῦλος)
   d. Unmerciful slave (Matt. 18:23-35, δοῦλος, σύνδουλος)
   e. Minas (Luke 19:11-27, δοῦλος) and talents (Matt. 25:14-30, δοῦλος)
   f. Doorkeeper (Mark 13:33-37, δοῦλος)

Examination of the Passages

Institutional Uses

The healing of the centurion's slave

This episode (Luke 7:1-10; Matt. 8:5-13)[5] falls under consideration here for two reasons: (a) the object of the healing is a slave (Luke, δοῦλος; Matt., παῖς); and (b) the centurion's understanding of Jesus' authority is couched in a master-slave metaphor.

Context, theme, and details

The healing occurred after a major discourse by Jesus[6] and was the first miracle Jesus performed when He reentered Capernaum. After the unclean leper (Matt. 8:1-4), Jesus now turns to an "unclean" Gentile.

Although the object of the healing is a slave, the real focal point for the story is the centurion himself. The evangelists are primarily concerned not with Jesus' ability to heal but with the character of a Gentile's faith-response to the Savior.[7] His faith is contrasted with that of the Jew, as demonstrated by the centurion's humble acceptance of Christ's authority even over disease and as reinforced by Christ's prediction about the place of such Gentiles in the Kingdom.

The differing details of the two accounts are not self-contradictory.[8] The most important one is Matthew's use of παῖς (Matt. 8:13, 15) in contrast to Luke's δοῦλος (Luke 7:2, 3, 10). Παῖς is capable of meaning either "boy" or "slave"[9] and often implies affection[10] (as seen by Luke's "δοῦλος . . . ὅς ἦν αὐτῷ ἔντιμος"). In fact, Luke's use of δοῦλος in the context of the centurion's "ὁ παῖς μου" (7:7), shows that δοῦλος and παῖς here are synonymous.[11] Thus, any apparent contradiction disappears.[12]

Slavery motif

Christ healed a male (probably young) who was not a freeman. He made no condemnatory remarks about the institution of slavery to the centurion or His friends; yet the evangelist portrays a close, protective "human" relationship between master and slave. About the greatest implication that can be drawn is that institutional slavery suggested, at its best, mutuality between master and slave with a genuine, sincere attitude behind it.

More important is the centurion's analogy of authority found in Luke 7:8 and Matthew 8:9. There the centurion demonstrates his faith by accurately picturing, and accepting, the authoritative lordship of Christ. He understood his authority to be analogous to, but not equivalent with, Christ's authority as he defined all existence within the framework of authority: he over his slaves, a commander over him, or Christ over all.[13] Thus, the Gentile master pleading for his slave truly sees himself as a slave of the divine Master through a humble recognition of, and submission to, the authority of Christ. Jesus' praise of the centurion makes his an example of legitimate faith; and humility and submission are shown thereby to be corollaries of such faith.

Then, using the centurion's faith as an object lesson, Christ warns the hardened Jewish audience that their own status in the kingdom is in jeopardy without faith. Though calling them "sons of the kingdom" (Matt. 8:12), He predicts their exclusion and proffers the possibility of sonship to faithful Gentiles. In this way Jesus uses the picture of humble submission to authority (as clarified through the master-slave relationship) to depict both soteriological and eschatological truths. True sonship is not based on race but on faith, and is thus open to all, including Gentiles; further, true sonship is defined, ironically, by the elements of humility and submission associated with slavery. The implicit eschatological hope is that present "slave" submission will become realized "sonship" status in the future.

Herod's slaves

Herod's incorrect conjecture that Jesus was really John the Baptist returned from the grave was based partly on a conference with his servants (τοὺς παισίν; Matt. 14:2). While this may suggest a form of mutuality between sovereign and servants, not unlike the Old Testament usage of עבד, the passage only affirms that Herod employed slaves at councillary levels of government, quite in accordance with custom of the day.

The high priest's slave

Context and theme

This use of δοῦλος is represented in all four gospels (Luke 22:50; Luke 14:47; Matt. 26:51; John 18:10). The main point of the story is both proverbial ("for all who take the sword will perish by the sword," Matt. 26:52) and prophetic ("but this has all taken place that the Scriptures of the prophets might be fulfilled," Matt. 14:49; Matt. 26:56). The event shows that Jesus was literally numbered among the transgressors (as predicted in Isaiah 53:12) not only by His arrest but also by his association with men who used swords.

Slavery motif

In none of the synoptics is the name of the slave given. He is identified solely in terms of his servitude to his master, the high priest. When Peter struck the slave, therefore, the action would be seen by the company as an attack against the office and dignity of the high priest himself, whom the slave represented. The evangelists have selected a dramatic incident to introduce the encounter Jesus was to have with the high priest before the Sanhedrin--namely, a garden confrontation with the two representatives of the opposing parties. The synoptists' design to keep both the slave and the disciple anonymous accentuates the representative nature of the conflict. Thus, one purpose of the story may be to focus the conflict first on the representatives and then on the main characters themselves.

Additionally, Peter's aggressive behavior serves as a contrast to the submissive conduct of Jesus. Christ's recent quotation from a crucial Suffering Servant passage (Isa. 53:12; Luke 22:35-38) makes it likely that He is drawing attention to Himself as the Suffering Servant. As the slave of God with the authority to call twelve legions of angels (Matt. 26:53), however, He chose to submit to the will of His Father and thus to fulfill the prophecies of Scripture. The contrast is clear: while Peter functioned as the slave of Christ in opposing his counterpart, the disciple lacked the real slave-like quality of submission to the will of God that was manifestly evident in the Master he represented.

Institutional Uses of the Work of Service

Angels serving Jesus

The temptation of Jesus is retold in all three synoptics, but only in Mark and Matthew are there allusions to the angels serving Jesus following His ordeal (Mark 1:12-13; Matt. 4:11). Service in this context meant, first, providing food that Jesus had previously denied Himself (much like Elijah was fed by the angel in 1 Kings 19:5-8).[14] There was also a form of spiritual service rendered to the Lord--a ministry suitable for refreshing Christ in victory.[15]

The angels' service to Christ may underscore the loyalty and joy of proper service, although the brief account adds little to the notion of slave service.

Peter's mother-in-law's service

The details

This brief healing episode is mentioned in all three synoptics (Luke 4:38-39; Mark 1:29-31; Matt. 8:14-17), but Mark and Luke place the incident before the great sermons and directly following an exorcism. Matthew, on the other hand, describes the incident as the third link in a trilogy of healings of "untouchables": the unclean leper, the Gentile centurion's slave, and the woman (Matt. 8:1-15).[16] Peter's mother-in-law begins to serve both Jesus and the disciples after her healing, and the point of the story seems to be twofold: she was healed quickly (for she immediately responded); and she was healed completely (with no confining aftermath of sickness).[17]

The slavery motif

Several implications surface. (a) There is mutuality of service between the woman and Christ; her response to Christ was in response to His positive action. (b) Her service is expressed concretely in a display of hospitality both to Jesus, because of who He was, and to the disciples. (c) Matthew relates the Suffering Servant motif to the Savior by applying Isaiah 53:4 to Christ (Matt. 8:17).[18] Mutuality of service is thus underscored in this picture of a healed woman diligently serving the Master who is tirelessly serving a corrupt world.

Mary and Martha's service

Context and theme

This episode (Luke 10:38-42) follows the parable of the good Samaritan, where Jesus stressed the reality of a practical, active expression of love through unstinted service. It may be Luke's intention to use this account to more clearly define one's love for God just as the parable defines one's love for neighbors.

The main point of the story depends on whether one takes the focus to be on Mary or Martha. Those who prefer the former emphasis take Martha's action as distracting "religious busyness,"[19] see the Lord's rebuke as harsh,[20] tend to argue for the contemplative life,[21] and view Jesus as actively dissuading anyone from serving Him.[22] If Martha is seen as the center, which is more likely, then Jesus' response is tender[23] and His purpose is not to deprecate her service but to defend Mary's seeming lack of it.[24] Martha's problem was not in serving but in her attitude of frustration (μεριμνᾷς and θορυβάζῃ), her subsequent self-pity, and her dissatisfaction with her sister.[25]

The slavery motif

Several lessons for one who would serve Christ are suggested. (a) Service is a balanced response of activity guided by instruction. Martha's response to both Jesus and her sister shows her unbalance in the area of activity; without further action, Mary could opt for an unproductive life of listening. (b) Service is not defined as mere busyness but as fulfilling activity. (c) Service involves an attitude of total devotion to the Master as evidenced by Mary.[26]

The women serving Jesus

Two passages cameo the women who stood by the cross as the Savior died (Mark 15:41; Mark 27:55). Ironically, they serve as witnesses to the central event of Jesus' life while the Twelve are nowhere to be seen. Their credentials are simply their faithful service to Jesus while He was still alive. Their service is exemplary in two ways. First, it was continual, being based on a series of acts of service, not a single act. In addition to hospitality (Luke 4:38-40; 10:38-42), this would also have included specific financial support (Luke 8:3).[27] Second, it had the earmarks of total loyalty to the end, in marked contrast to the disciples who fled.

The ungodly withholding service from God's children

In the Olivet Discourse, Jesus presents the idea of service as the standard of judgment (Matt. 25:31-46). M'Neile believes the thrust of this pericope is Christological--exalting the coming of the Son of Man.[28] But certainly the standard of kindness toward the "least of these brothers of Mine" has ethical implications.[29]

Service in this context is suggestive of two things. First, service to God is defined by service to others (cf. Matt. 23:1-2, etc.). Second, Christ defines this devotion to Him in tangible terms: feeding the hungry, giving water to the thirsty, welcoming the stranger, clothing the naked, and visiting the sick and imprisoned. Just as the literal slave's tasks are tangible and defined, so spiritual service is measured by meeting concrete needs.[30]

Figurative Personal Designations

All of the examples considered below are either drawn from Old Testament quotations or are evocative of an Old Testament usage. As such, they may be seen as important transitionary links between the Old and New Testament slavery motifs.

Mary

Twice Mary refers to herself as a bondslave of the Lord (δούλη); and submission and obedience are the keynotes. In Luke 1:38, Mary responds to the problematic announcement that she, a virgin, would bear the Messiah. Her acceptance of the blessing as well as the possible shame provides an unparalleled model of slavery. Luke's rare use of δούλη (occurring only in 1:38, 48 and in the Acts 2:18 quote from Joel 2) seems deliberately intended to relate this idea with the Old Testament understanding of slavery to God as both humble service and exalted privilege. In the Magnificat (1:46-55), Mary's reference to herself as "bondslave" (δούλη) reiterates this dual theme in a context reminiscent of Hannah's prayer in 1 Samuel 1:11.[31]

Israel

Also in the Magnificant, Mary calls Isarel "His servant" (παῖς, not δούλος in Luke 1:54). This alludes not simply to Israel's responsibility to obey God but to her covenantal relationship with God who intervenes for His people. Slavery is not simply a synonym for sonship[32] because it suggests a mutual obligation between God and Israel that better fits the master-slave motif.

David

In Zechariah's "Benedictus," παῖς is used to designate King David (Luke 1:69). By no stretch of the imagination can this describe a person of lowly position, means, or ability in society. This is a title of honor suggesting proven loyalty and obedience.

Simeon

In Luke 2:29, Simeon uses not παῖς but δοῦλος to stress his absolute servitude to God. Further, he addresses God not as κύριος but as δεσπότης--a title used only rarely of God in the New Testament (e.g., Acts 4:24).[33] Simeon could be using that title to stress God's lordship over Gentiles and Jews (since salvation to the Gentiles is in the context in verse 32);[34] but this term, rather than the more personal κύριος, emphasizes the sovereign character of God. Simeon thus sees himself as one totally submissive to the control of a sovereignly authoritative, omnipotent Lord.

Jesus

Context, theme, and details

In Matthew 12:15-21 (quoting from Isa. 42:1-4), the Suffering Servant theme is applied to Christ using παῖς in accordance with familiar LXX style.[35] Matthew does this to explain both Jesus' refusal to confront the Pharisees openly and His urgency for silence: namely, as the Servant of Yahweh, His mission is to proclaim justice to the Gentiles (not constantly engage the rejecting Jews) and, by remaining quiet and non-recalcitrant in manner, to accomplish a great work of justice from which even the Gentiles will benefit.

The main problems of this section are textual and hermeneutical. Textually, Matthew does not follow either the Septuagint or the Massoretic text very closely,[36] although each varient can be shown to be consistent with the context of Isaiah 42:1-4. Some suggest Matthew's text is a translation of an unattested recension;[37] others assert it is a targumizing of the Hebrew text characteristic of a Matthean school of interpretation;[38] this writer believes it is Matthew's own interpretative rendering of the Hebrew with a comparative knowledge of the Septuagint. Hermeneutically, the Servant of Isaiah 42 could be taken either as corporate Israel or as the individual Messiah. In view of Matthew's pesher method of interpretation,[39] and in accordance with this study's acceptance of the messianic interpretation of the Servant, Albright's assessment that "Messiah is the embodiment of Israel's vocation as servant of the Lord" probably is the best resolution.[40]

The slavery motif

First, in His work as the Suffering Servant, Jesus shows that obedience and responsibility are attributes of such service: specifically the responsibility to carry out God's will for which the Spirit of God is given and whose purpose is the bringing of justice. Second, Jesus as the Suffering Servant enjoys a privileged relationship to God, described by the terms "chosen," "beloved," and "well-pleased." The Servant thus expresses devoted loyalty and enjoys mutual identification with the Father. Third, the manner of the Servant, as predicted in Isaiah and personified in Christ, is one of quiet and humble submission (12:19-20).

John the Baptist

John the Baptist describes his relation to the Savior by an unworthiness to unloose His sandal (Matt. 3:11; Mark 1:7; Luke 3:16). Although there is no use of any of the four terms for slave or service discussed above, the removing of shoes is in accord with a specific act of slave service. In Leviticus 25:39, Moses protected the Hebrew slave from performing a "slave's service," ruling that he should be treated as a hired hand. Roland de Vaux says the acts of feet washing (1 Sam. 25:41) and sandal-removing are included under this prohibition. The implication of this for John the Baptist is that he considered himself, in comparison to Jesus, to be "less than a slave."[41]

As a slave of God, John's behavior gives an excellent model of obedience to God as he proclaimed repentance, baptized, and prepared the way for Christ; of humble submission both to God and to Christ, as evidenced not only by this figure but also by his willingness to point others to Christ; of representing his Master by fulfilling the predicted role of a preparatory ambassador to the Messiah; and of loyalty to the task even when it meant death for him.

Figurative Proverbial Uses

"No man can serve two masters"

Context, theme, and details

The Matthean setting for this familiar proverb about "singleness of service" (Matt. 6:24) is the Sermon on the Mount and is the third in a trio of contrasts pertaining to riches: corrupt (earthly) versus incorrupt (heavenly) wealth; a clear eye versus a bad eye; service to God versus service to Mammon.[42] Luke's use of the proverb in a different context (Luke 16:1-13) suggests Jesus used this pithy saying frequently.[43]

Culturally, it was not unknown for a slave to be owned by more than one person.[44] In terms of the literal obligations of slavery, this probably meant serving only one master at a time.[45] But Jesus is not protesting a social phenomenon. Rather He is pointing to the spiritual attitude of single-minded devotion that must characterize every disciple. Matthew underscores this by using the broader οὐδείς instead of Luke's more restrictive οὐδείς οἰκέτης.[46]

In the proverb itself, bonded servitude is emphasized not only by the contrast between master and slave but by the twofold repetition of δουλεύειν. This inability to serve two masters is then explained by a double contrast: loving versus hating and clinging versus despising. In this parallel fashion, both the attitude and the consequent behavior of true service is delineated.[47] "Mammon" itself (μαμωνᾶς) could come either from the Hebrew מטמון ("something hidden or stored up") or מאמון ("something entrusted") although μαμωνᾶς is not found in the Septuagint.[48]

Its validity as a proper name for a god or idol is unattested; rather the context suggests Jesus personifies wealth.

The slavery motif

A most obvious submotif to the theme of slavery is loyalty. Also present is the concept of exclusiveness of service. Loyalty must be undivided loyalty. The double repetition of the phase "you cannot serve" makes this point emphatic. Finally, the context of financial stewardship into which the proverb is placed shows service to God is proven concretely by the way the slave of God relates to money.

"A slave is not above his master"

Context and theme

When Jesus granted to His disciples authority to preach and perform miracles and exorcisms, He warned them that association with Him might mean persecution. As the followers of one who was being harassed, they had no right to expect a more favorable reception. Such is the context and thrust of this proverb in Matthew 10:24-25.[49]

The triple analogy upon which the proverb hangs includes disciple and teacher, slave and master, and household and master of the house (10:24-25). The first two are closely associated and describe both voluntary and compulsory relationships.[50] The two figures also present a two-sided perspective to relationships between unequals: (a) realistically, the inferior is never superior to the master or teacher (v. 24); but (b) ideally, it can be hoped that unequals will evidence similar behavior.⁵¹

The third part of the analogy--οἰκεδεσπότην versus τοὺς οἰκιακούς (v. 25b)--is a play on words with Beelzebul, a word that means "lord of the dwelling."⁵² Jesus appears to be using a pun on the title for Satan in order to stress His lordship over His own representatives.⁵³ Further, this reference to "household" augments the slavery imagery by making it more familial or personal.

The slavery motif

Therefore, to be related to the Master as His slave means to be identified with Him and His cause, to become a recipient both of the honor and the suffering that comes to Him, for the world, through its hatred of Christ, will persecute His true disciples. They find comfort in this task, however, by the knowledge that their Master also has endured persecution. As Schweitzer says,"solidarity with Jesus in suffering and absence is a central token of discipleship. Jesus always remains the Master, the head of the family; the disciple remains His slave, a member of His household."⁵⁴ But slavery also implies the slave will represent the Master to the world, as demonstrated by the disciples sent with Christ's authority to preach His message and duplicate His miracles.

"If anyone wants to be first, he shall
be last of all and servant of all"

Context, theme, and details

Dennis E. Nineham correctly describes the "collating factor" of

Mark 9:33-50 to be the prediction of the passion.[55] It is at this point that the disciples, in ignorance of the meaning of Jesus' words, choose to discuss personal greatness. In response, Jesus takes a child to illustrate His answer about the real meaning of greatness.

While Matthew 18:1-15 and Luke 9:46-48 record this dialogue, only Mark includes Jesus' proverb about greatness and servitude. Some modern critics suggest that Mark has conflated two stories--one on precedence and one on the child.[56] Vincent Taylor goes as far as to believe that Matthew's interpretation (Matt. 18:3) is more appropriate to Mark because Mark 9:37 is too incoherent in its present form.[57] On the other hand, Matthew Black postulates that Jesus used the Aramaic word *talya*--an expression that could represent either διάκονος (9:35b) and παιδίον (9:36)--and formed a subtle word-play on the meanings of servant and child. To him, the idea of servanthood and the exhibition of the child are related by this Aramaic word.[58]

Closer observation, however, reveals that the child has a different purpose in Matthew than he does in Mark and Luke. In Matthew 18:3-4, the child is the subject of the action, manifesting the qualities of humility and lowliness which the disciples should possess. But in Mark the child is the object of the action, being received into the arms of Jesus (9:37). Here the disciples are not to be like the child, but are to be like Jesus in showing hospitality and acceptance toward the "little ones" in the faith (Mark 9:42). The disciples' concern over their own greatness is refocused on their present responsibility: namely, to serve those who are weak.

The slavery motif

Mark's account of the child is much more conducive to the slavery motif since greatness through slave services comes by showing hospitality, as the concept of "receiving" a child "in My name" suggests (Matt. 25:31-46). There is also the implication that serving others precludes arrogance. Slavery means being engaged in immediate service, not debating over future status.

"Whosoever would be first among you must be slave of all"
Mark 10:35-45 and Matthew 20:20-28

Context, theme, and details. The contexts of Matthew and Mark are identical. Following a prediction of Christ's death, James and John request places of honor in Christ's glory. Though Jesus makes no promise, the Ten become indignant and Jesus responds by outlining the true path toward greatness.

The two accounts are in disagreement on two harmonizable points: (a) in Matthew the mother of James and John makes the request for her sons while Mark omits this; and (b) Matthew refers only to the "cup" while Mark includes both "cup" and "baptism." But both include the request, Jesus' response that such a privilege is bestowed only by the Father, the indignation of the Ten, Jesus' own explanation of greatness, and His concluding reference to His impending sacrifice.

The main issue of the pericope is simply that one becomes great

by willingly performing lowly slave-like service. Robertson correctly
points out that Jesus is not condemning the disciples' desire for greatness, but rather He is rebuking their measurement of greatness as
human honor, rank, and authority.[59] Jesus makes His point by a double
illustration. Negatively, greatness is not to be defined by the
Gentile's behavior, an ironic twist in light of a Jew's natural antipathy to the Gentile and Christ's earlier prediction that Gentiles
would crucify him (Mark 10:33; Matt. 20:19). The Gentiles' wish to
"lord it over" (κατακυριεύω) and to "exercise authority over"
(κατεξουσιάζω) implies a desire for power and status antithetical to
Jesus' ideal. The principle itself (Matthew 20:26-27; Mark 10:43-44)
is repeated in Semitic style and given intensity by the use of increasingly severe vocabulary. To be great (μέγας), one must serve (διάκονος):
to be first (πρῶτος), one must be a slave (δοῦλος).[60]

Positively, greatness is exemplified by Jesus Himself as one who
came to meet people's physical needs and to provide salvation (Matt.
20:28). Again, there is a touch of irony in Jesus' reference to Himself
as one who does the service of a slave (διακονεύω), yet ultimately who
has come to free other slaves (as suggested by λύτρον, a word used
frequently of the manumission of slaves).[61] The death of which Christ
just spoke to uncomprehending disciples is the ultimate act of service
to enslaved mankind and the highest example of true greatness.

The slavery motif. The slavery motif is evidenced by the way
the words διάκονος and δοῦλος are intertwined with the concept of ransom.

Some commentators justifiably believe that Jesus' allusion to His salvific purpose evoke the Suffering Servant theme of Isaiah.[62] Specific aspects include: (a) submission, which is explicit in Christ's description of His own relation to the Father (Matt. 20:33; Mark 10:40); (b) the importance of serving (διάκονος) with humility (δοῦλος) in comparision to the behavior evidenced by the Gentiles; (c) suffering, seen in Christ's prediction that the disciples pursuing greatness would suffer ("drink of the cup"); and (d) implicitly, reward, in the veiled hint that service now does mean true greatness later, though the age is unmentioned.

Luke 22:24-27

<u>Context, theme, and details</u>. Like the above passages, Luke relates a dispute the disciples had over who was the greatest. Jesus' rebuke entails a reference to Gentile overlords, a proverbial statement about true greatness, and an allusion to Himself as one who proves His greatness by service. However by contrast, Luke 22:24-27 describes a discussion in the upper room before the crucifixion which likely stemmed from a dispute over positions at the table (Luke 22:27),[63] while Matthew and Mark describe an event before the triumphal entry involving the request of the Zebedee sons.

There seems here to be the presupposition that some indeed are elders and leaders. The issue is how those who are great should act. They were to avoid the Gentile tendency to exercise lordship and not to seek honorific titles (εὐεργέται καλοῦνται). Such titles as εὐεργέτης, Deismann points out, were in actual use by Egyptian and Syrian kings,[64] and the middle form, καλοῦνται, connotes a wish that others would bestow the honor--the very thing the disciples also desired.[65] Jesus then gives three comparisons: the greatest should become as the younger; the leader should become as one who serves (διακονεύω); and the one who sits at the table should become as the one who serves. Service and lowliness are the keynotes of Jesus' response, and when He includes Himself as the final example of such service, it is possible that this final saying was punctuated by the washing of the disciples' feet.

The slavery motif. That Luke presents his story from the perspective of how leaders should display greatness is clear. In 22:28-30 Christ gives a decidedly eschatological promise to the disciples concerning kingdom fellowship and authority, thus supplying some basis of reward for leaders who faithfully and humbly serve. The other suggestions of humility, submission, and service described above also occur in this account.

"We are unworthy slaves"

Context, theme, and details

Luke 17:5-10 teaches that the slave must perform exacting, continual, and unrequited service to the Master. He should not expect thanks or preferential treatment from his master, Jesus says; neither should he indulge in self-praise.

Christ's words follow immediately upon a discussion of faith
(17:5-6). In response to the disciples' desire to have their faith
increased, Jesus explains that even the smallest amount of faith would
be sufficient to move the most entrenched tree into the sea. However,
such power could lead to pride and a misuse of faith. What is really
needed is faith exercised by slaves (δοῦλοι) who recognize that "service
of God is not a subject for God's congratulation and gratitude."[66] God
wants men of faith who are also obedient slaves.

The phrase "we are unworthy (ἀχρεῖος) slaves," though somewhat
shocking (Matt. 25:30 uses ἀχρεῖος of the unfaithful slave), is defined
by the parallel phrase, "we have only done what was our duty" (17:10).
Ἀχρεῖος, therefore, must mean "unmeritorious" in the sense that a slave
does not earn favor by obedience but gains disfavor by failing to do his
tasks.[67]

This episode reveals Jesus' starkest expression of what slavery
means and the closest parallel to contemporary chattel slavery. Unlike
other passages where future reward is implied (e.g., Luke 22:24-30;
12:37, 41-48; Mark 13:33-37; Matt. 24:45-51), there is no hint here of
any reversal in position.

The slavery motif

The implications for the slavery motif should be obvious. (a)
Humility of the slave is an evident predicate as shown by the word
ἀχρεῖος. (b) The story stresses the necessity of performing exacting,
obedient service--service that is constant (it does not cease even after

a day's plowing is done), unrequited (no thanks should be expected), perfect (punishment is to be expected for failure), and preferential (the master, not the slave, is always served first).

"He who is greatest among you shall be your servant"

Context, theme, and details

In Matthew 23:1-2 Jesus introduces the ideas of humility and slavery to God shortly before His passion. In context, this is a warning about hypocrisy (Matt. 23:1-4) and ostentation (Matt. 25:5-7),[68] following an extended debate with the Jewish leaders. Unlike Mark and Luke, however, Matthew includes five verses that deal specifically with the problem of honorific titles. It is here that the slavery motif is again introduced. (Cf. Luke 22:24-27 discussed above.)

Verses 1-6 anticipate the slavery motif by describing the pharisaical method of handling Torah as a chain that binds the people (23:4, δεσμεύουσιν). Jesus is politely saying, "if one follows the Pharisees, one is essentially a fettered slave." A logical question then is implied: as a follower of this new rabbi, what is my status?

In answering the question, Jesus discusses three titles that were circulated among prominent religious leaders: (a) "Rabbi," a transliteration from the Hebrew meaning "my master" and a common designation for scribes; (b) "Father" (πατήρ), a title applied primarily to patriarchs and famous rabbis who had died;[69] and (c) "Master" (καθηγητής),[70] a word which means "interpreter" (or perhaps "professor") and another designation for one who taught.[71] Jesus' general antipathy to these titles stems from one's tendency to use them for self-exaltation since the passive command, "don't be called" (μὴ κληθῆτε) Rabbi or teacher censures the person who wishes to be addressed. The proscription against calling anyone "Father" is an active command. Based upon the unique Fatherhood of God, it is an absolute prohibition against the use of this as a title of religious honor. In all cases, such titles place the disciple in positions uniquely reserved for Christ and the Father.

By contrast, Jesus suggests His followers must serve (διάκονος). While implying there are distinctions within His ranks (some being greater), He affirms the greater ones should act as a servant (23:11). Jesus concludes with a final ironic prediction: the one who exalts himself (i.e., through following the pharisaical practice of acquiring titles) will be humbled; but the one who humbles himself (by implication, in this age), will be exalted in the age to come.

The slavery motif

Jesus teaches several things about spiritual slavery: (a) the slave of God is to be humble and does not seek the plaudits of men; (b) the slave of God shows his greatness by service, in contrast to the Pharisee who use their authority to bind heavy burdens to the oppressed people they are supposed to serve; (c) slavery to God involves reward in the form of future exaltation (23:11).

Figurative Parabolic Uses

Some of Jesus' most profound, though often perplexing, teaching is to be found in the parables; and no less than eleven parables or similes contain the slavery motif to varying degrees.

The parable itself is a distinctive feature of Jesus' ministry. Jeremias states: "We find nothing to be compared with the parables of Jesus, whether in the entire intertestamental literature of Judaism, the Essene writings, in Paul, or in Rabbinic literature."[72] Jesus used them frequently (about forty-one parables are in the synoptics) to emphasize one main point from a true-to-life situation. Although form and redaction critics frequently question the authenticity of the parables, this dissertation will accept the observation of Jeremias: "It is generally recognized today—despite the need for a critical analysis of every single parable and the history of its tradition—that the parables belong to the bedrock of the tradition about him."[73] Thus, rather than differentiating Christ's "authentic" words from the community's developed" ones, it will be sufficient to place the parable in its historical context, to interact with modern criticism as needed, and to derive the implications for the slavery motif.

This will not be the first attempt to consider a group of the parables in terms of a motif of slavery. Alfons Weiser[74] discusses a group of the servant parables, using the dual criteria of (a) expressions of the master-slave relationship and (b) explicit servant terminology to isolate the parables for study. In a later article,

John Crossan uses his own criteria of master-slave relationships and critical confrontation between the parties, while rejecting lexical considerations.[75] Though Weiser's criteria seem more appropriate for the purposes here, Crossan has made some interesting observations about the different structure of the parables he discusses.[76] Yet, neither men include all the parables that contain elements of the motif.

Parables in which slaves are peripheral

The tares

   Context, theme, and details. In the parable of the tares (Matt. 13:24-30) Jesus describes the nature of the kingdom of heaven, explaining that the kingdom will be composed of evil elements which will only be purged when the Son of Man returns. Dodd groups it with other "parables of growth" (e.g., sower and mustard seed);[77] and Jeremias links it thematically to the drag-net parable (vv. 47-50).[78] Some have questioned its authenticity because of its uniqueness to Matthew and its closeness to Mark's secret seed parable.[79] Many scholars take it as genuinely Jesus';[80] some even argue it may have been an actual historical event,[81] yet then reject the authenticity of Matthew's interpretation (13:36-43).[82] On the other hand, the authenticity of the interpretation is accepted by many scholars[83] who cogently refute form-critical denials.[84] Both parable and interpretation are taken as fully genuine in this study.

   The seed (the sons of the kingdom), the darnel (the sons of the

evil one), the sower (the Son of Man), the reapers (the angels), and
the enemy (the devil) are primary characters whose identification is
given. The slaves (δοῦλοι) are secondary elements which are not
identified but who cannot be the angels (13:30), the divine Sower, or
the sons of the kingdom. Perhaps they are simply parabolic features
which round out the story, although the suggestion that they are the
disciples is a common, and not unwarranted, conjecture.[85] Their
status is consistent with trusted members of a large rural household;
and their behavior still is exemplary, even if their identification is
uncertain.

The slavery motif. The actions of the slaves suggest several
things: (a) they possess a willingness to serve--in this case to pull
up the weeds from the field; (b) they are entirely obedient to their
Lord, accepting His decision about the harvest even though they show
evidence of not fully understanding; (c) they are patient in waiting
until the Lord's timing for the harvest; and (d) they enjoy a certain
freedom of interaction with the Master which is confirmed by the confidence He expresses in them.

The prodigal son

Context and theme. This famous Lucan parable (Luke 15:11-32)
is one of three parables Jesus used in responding to the Pharisees'
criticism of His association with sinners. Like the finding of a lost
sheep by a shepherd, a lost coin by a woman, and a lost son by a

father, so the repentance of sinners before God produces celebration. Jesus associates with outcasts to encourage repentance and to celebrate when it occurs.

The basic elements of the story are familiar: the younger son asks for his inheritance, squanders it far away, is caught in disgusting poverty, and returns humbly home to his father who welcomes and restores him with wild celebration. The ironic factor of the parable is the elder brother's bitterness to the father's acceptance of the lost son. Most would agree that the lost son is the publican or sinner that turns penitently to God; most would also concur that in the account of the elder brother, Jesus is gently needling the Pharisees for failing to properly understand their relationship to God the Father and to be as concerned with the repentance of sinners as He is.[86]

Sonship versus slavery. An underlying element of this parable is the interaction between the concepts of sonship and slavery. The father's view of sonship is quite clear: both are fully his sons despite their differences. The sons, on the other hand, view sonship in terms of slavery: the younger son, after coming to his senses, seeks to return to the father as a hired servant (μίσθιος), disbelieving that his sonship would endure unscathed. The elder son views his relationship to the father as one who slaves (δουλεύω) for him. It is only the younger son who gives evidence of having his misshapen viewpoint set straight. Both illustrate the danger of underestimating the exalted position that true sons (whether literal or spiritual) should enjoy.

The slavery motif in this parable is supported by other details as well. For example, Luke uses three different terms for slaves in this short account: "hired hand" (μίσθιος, 15:17, 19), "slave" (δοῦλος, 15:22), and "slave" or "boy" (παῖς, 15:26). Μίσθιος is used by the poverty-stricken son as an example of one who was well paid for his labor. Δοῦλοι denotes the father's bonded slaves, suggesting the father's total authority over them (the son never seeks to become one of them). Παῖς is used of one who is closely associated with the household and probably enjoying the feast--a stark contrast to the elder son who deliberately ostracized himself from the household. Thus, while none of the main characters were slaves, the two sons are often described in comparison to those household slaves.

The response of the father in welcoming the younger son heightens this contrast between sonship and slavery. The father kisses the son (likely on the cheek as a sign of equality; slaves kissed their masters on the feet).[87] The son was given the best robe (a sign of high honor), a ring (likely a signet ring symbolizing authority), and sandals (a sign that a man was a freeman).[88] Thus, though the younger son had envisioned himself as a slave, the father clearly affirms his sonship.

The slavery motif. While the slaves of the parable do not receive the primary attention, the details do serve as a foil for Jesus in presenting more starkly the honor of sonship with the Father. Several implications about the meaning of slavery can be drawn: (a) slavery involves mutuality with the master, illustrated here by their willingness to obey the master and also by his willingness to include them in the celebration; (b) it involves security, as seen by the younger son's desire to become his father's μίσθιος; and (c) it is nevertheless subordinate to sonship. Despite the advantages of being a slave in the master's household, it is superior to be his son.

The great feast

Context, theme, and details. As Jesus dines at the house of a Pharisee, He responds to the glib and possibly self-assured statement by one guest who anticipates the happiness of the feasting at the messianic banquet by telling this parable (Luke 14:15-24).[89] In it, a man gives a feast for invited guests; a group of guests give valueless excuses to the man's slave-messenger as to why they will not be coming;[90] the man invites the poor, maimed, blind, and lame (see Luke 14:13) to fill the banquet hall; and the man gives a second invitation to the unfortunate classes, "compelling" them to come in.

The parable has some similarities with Matthew 22:1-14, but numerous specific details argue that Jesus gave it a different time.[91] And, because of the complexity of detail in the parable, there is some debate over its actual purpose.[92] But, despite numerous good suggestions, it seems clear that the primary purpose of the parable is found in Luke 14:24: "None of those men who were invited shall taste my banquet." Thus, the criterion for participation in the messianic banquet is not simply to be invited (i.e., be a part of the religious elite of Judaism) but to properly respond to God's invitation. So both a soteriological and an eschatological theme is prominent in the parable.

The slavery motif. The slave is a secondary character of the story whom many commentators attempt to identify. Plummer concludes he is God's messenger, typical of either John the Baptist or Christ,[93] although Christ's use of the plural ὑμῖν in verse 24 indicates He is the host and the slave is a representative of the disciples.[94] Whatever the slave's particular identification, the following observations can be made about a slave of God: (a) he was a representative of the man, and the excuses given to the slave were insults to the master; (b) he was obedient and submissive to the master in carrying out the unusual tasks; and (c) he was diligent and conscientious in "compelling" the poor in the outer reaches of the city to attend the banquet. Morris observes that the fact only one servant was sent indicates that he could not use force but rather had to be earnestly persuasive.[95]

The wedding feast

Context, theme, and details. The parable of the rejected invitations to the wedding feast of the King's son (Matt. 22:1-14) is polemical. Given after the parable of the wicked tenants, it manifests greater tension; and Matthew, emphasizing the Jewish rejection of Christ, includes a parable of Jesus consistent with that thrust. It is more eschatological than the Lucan parable of the great feast, due to its connection with the wicked tenants parable and to the specific details of the king, the wedding feast, and imposition of judgment included in the story.[96]

Its similarity of theme (i.e., the importance of a proper response to God's invitation) with the parable in Luke seems apparent, although two crucial differences must be considered. First, Matthew records an additional pericope about the man without a wedding garment (22:11-14) which slightly alters the thrust of the parable and contributes to its harshness.[97] The episode infers a plea to "make certain you are prepared for accepting the invitation."[98] Or, as Hill puts it, "entrance into the kingdom is gratuitous but it is not characterized by libertinism."[99]

Second, there is a tendency for this parable (unlike the great feast) to include a richness of details susceptible to allegorizing. These include: (a) the double invitation of the original guests (variously interpreted as either the ministry of the former and latter Old Testament prophets,[100] or the ministries of the Old Testament prophets and the New Testament apostles and evangelists);[101] (b) the murder of the servants by the invitees (perhaps the persecution by the Jews of either the Old Testament prophets[102] or the apostles[103]); and (c) the judgment of the king on the killers (thought to be a reference to the sack of Jerusalem).[104] Though the lack of consensus as to the meaning of details is a caution against pressing the allegory too far, their cumulative effect is to suggest that the parable may intend to chart a predictive overview of *Heilsgeschichte*--particularly as the message has been rejected by the nation.[105]

The slaves, while not the focus of the action of the story, are significant interpretative details. Though a specific group of people with whom the δοῦλοι can be positively identified may be impossible, it is sufficient to say they represent any of God's messengers. The διάκονοι of 22:11-14 perhaps are different individuals (Alford suggests they are angels[106]), although there is precedence in Matthew for believing the terms may be synonymous (Matt. 20:20-28). Jesus could have used different terms to suggest the difference between the past and future aspects of God's redemptive plan; as such they should not be specifically identified but merely recognized as essential components of God's household. However they are to be identified, their relationship with God and their responsibilities to Him are fully consistent with the disciple of Christ.

The slavery motif. Implications from this parable for the slavery motif are: (a) obedience in delivering the invitations and calling the guests; (b) loyalty in continuing to obey even after the setbacks of persecution; (c) suffering at the hands of the invited guests; (d) an identification of the slaves with the king as his representatives in taking the invitations and in receiving the abuse. As representatives of the king himself, the slaves killed in service are avenged by the king. This matter of identification and representation is heightened even further by the parable's sequential link to the parable of the wicked tenants.

The wicked tenants

   Context, theme, and details. The parable of the wicked tenants is found in three parallel passages (Luke 20:8-18; Mark 12:1-12; Matt. 21:33-46) which occur at the beginning of Jesus' passion week debate. Matthew puts the parable between the parables of the unequal sons and the marriage feast which Mark and Luke do not include. Though there are some differences of detail, the parable contains the following features: a householder (ἄνϑρωπος ἦν οἰκοδεσπότης in Matt.; ἄνϑρωπος in Mark and Luke) builds a vineyard with hedge, pit for winepress, and tower. He sends a slave (δοῦλος in all accounts, but plural only in Matthew) to gather the produce from the tenants who is beaten. Other slaves are sent and mistreated.[107] Finally, the longsuffering householder sends his "beloved" son[108] (Mark 12:6; Luke 20:13) to the tenants who cast him out and kill him.[109] The parable concludes with Jesus' rhetorical question about the fate of the wicked tenants.[110]

   The slavery motif. Like the δοῦλοι of the previous parable, these slaves have received various interpretations. Taylor refers to the many Old Testament servants of the Lord (from Moses, Joshua, and David to the prophets) and their rejection by Israel.[111] Most simply say these represent the prophets as emphasized by Matthew's reference to stoning (Matt. 21:35).[112] As messengers of God, and likely his prophets, they suggest several traits about what it means to be God's slave: (a) suffering on behalf of the master while doing his bidding; (b) service for the master in the gathering of what was due him, regardless of the personal jeopardy it involved; (c) identifying both with the Son (because He suffered the same treatment as they did) and with the Lord (because their treatment represented a lack of respect for the householder Himself); (d) being a representative of the Lord to the wicked tenants; and (e) acting responsibly and conscientiously for the Lord in His absence--a distinctly eschatological idea.

Parables in which slaves are central

The alert slaves

Context and theme. The historical context of this parable in Luke 12:35-40 is the final days of Jesus' Galilean ministry. A parallel exists with Mark 13:33-37 (the doorkeeper); and Dodd even suggests that Matthew 24:42 is a summary of the same parable.[113] But since in Luke Jesus gives the parable earlier in Galilee and in Mark the similar parable is given by Jesus during passion week, it is concluded here that the parables are distinct.[114]

Thematically, the parable deals with discipline; but there is an unmistakable eschatological mood as represented by the metaphor of the wedding feast (12:36), the unexpected coming of the Son of Man (12:40), and the blessing to be granted by the returning Lord for faithful service (12:37).[115]

The point of the parable is alertness and preparedness.[116] Speaking to the disciples (12:22, 32), Jesus expresses the necessity for preparedness in a double figure: the Son will return inevitably like a master to his slaves (12:35-38); and the Son will return unexpectedly like a thief (12:39-40).[117] Verses 35 and 36 both stress the hortatory aspect of this parable in that the ὑμεῖς is in the emphatic position (Ἔστωσαν ὑμῶν αἱ ὀσφύες . . . καὶ ὑμεῖς). Thus, Jesus is urging prepared alertness for His disciples because the hour of return is always unexpected.

The slavery motif. Several elements make this parable especially significant for the slavery motif. First, there are details which, consistent with slavery, stress obedient service and alertness: the girded loins (i.e., robes tucked in the belt for active service) and burning lamps. Slaves are to keep at their posts even during the long hours of the night. Second, there is a rather unexpected promise to the disciples (who are subtlely identified as δοῦλοι, vv. 36-37, 40ff.) that faithfulness will be rewarded in the future when the master girds himself (περιζώσεται, also v. 35) and serves (διακονέω) the slaves--a sharp contrast to Jesus' description of the slave in Luke 17:5-10, yet reflective of His own role while on earth (Luke 22:27; John 13:4-5).[118] This strongly eschatological thrust allows the parables to be classed with others that suggest future reward or judgment for a slave's present faithfulness. Third, the change to the thief metaphor still includes the slavery motif. The implication is that the absent householder need not fear for his house because his alert, responsible slaves will be prepared even for a clandestine invasion by a thief.

Therefore, several implications for the slavery motif may be inferred: (a) the slave of God must be alert even during long periods of the Lord's absence in order to be of immediate service when the Lord returns and demands it; (b) the slave of God must be prepared for any eventuality (i.e., loins girded, waiting to open the door, even able to thwart a thief); (c) the slave of God can expect reward for faithful service, a reward that will even take the form of being served; (d) the faithful slave of God experiences, therefore, a certain mutuality with the Master who requires complete preparedness on the part of His slave, but who, in blessing the faithful servant, will show to him the same respect and service.

The faithful and unfaithful slaves

<u>Context and theme</u>. Immediately following the parable of the alert slaves, Jesus includes a similar parable (Luke 12:41-48).[119] It too is highly eschatological,[120] and even more clearly describes discipleship in slavery imagery. As Lenski observes, Luke 12:35-40 is a positive admonition to alertness, while these verses form a negative warning against irresponsibility during the Master's absence.[121]

Although the parable stresses the importance of being trustworthy during the Lord's absence,[122] Luke's conclusion adds the thought that the greater one's responsibility, the greater one's potential reward or loss. This is confirmed by Peter's question (v. 41): "Lord, are you telling this parable for us or for all?" Peter could be making a distinction between Jews and Christians,[123] but more likely, the contrast is between the mass of followers of Jesus (Luke 12:1) and the

Twelve who were to be apostolic leaders.[124] Jesus does not answer Peter's question directly, but the idea of graded punishment as expressed in Luke 12:47-48 certainly suggests that Jesus is referring to those in leadership positions.

The slavery motif. This parable contains two concepts of slavery. The slave is described both as owned property subject to the complete disposal of the master (δοῦλος, Matt. 24:45 and Luke 12:43, 45, etc.) and as a personal representative of the master in society, responsible for the keeping of his goods and household (οἰκονόμος, Luke 12:42).[125] Furthermore, the responsibility of the slave or steward is stressed (e.g., to feed the household), not only as a onetime discharge of duty but also as an ongoing activity to continue until the master returns.

Finally, the idea of recompense pervades this parable. Rewards exist for the wise and faithful slave in the form of promotion over all the master's possessions (Luke 12:44; Matt. 24:47); but the slave who beats fellow slaves (Matt. 24:49, σύνδουλοι) and selfishly eats and drinks will be severely punished by being "cut in pieces (διχοτομέω) and sequestered with the hypocrites (Matt. 24:51) or unfaithful (Luke 12:46).[126] Nevertheless, those who are ignorant of their responsibility will receive a lighter beating than those who deliberately abuse their position.

Therefore, the implications for the slavery motif can be summarized as follows: (a) the slave of God is given responsibility over the Master's possessions and "fellow slaves." (b) As such he is accountable for the manner in which he discharges his responsibility. (c) He will receive rewards in accordance with his faithfulness and his responsibility. (d) Obedience is as much a part of this responsibility as is alertness. (e) The slave who is wise and faithful can expect further association with the Master by being given more responsibility over His possessions.

The unjust steward

Content, theme, and details. This uniquely Lucan parable (Luke 16:1-13) is perplexing because an unjust οἰκονόμος is an example for behavior. It follows the parable of the prodigal son with which there is slight affinity (i.e., both main characters are guilty of wasting, [διασκορπίζω], another's goods), but unlike that parable (which is directed primarily to the Pharisees regarding repentance) this one is directed toward the disciples and deals with financial stewardship. It unfolds in three scenes: (a) the master terminates the steward (16:1-2); (b) the steward alone seizes on his plan (vv. 3-4); and (c) the steward rewrites the debts to procure friends after his release.[127]

This short parable raises several complex interpretative difficulties.[128] One is the question of the identity of the speaker in verse 8a. Jeremias argues rather forcefully that it is Jesus, not the Master (ὁ κύριος refers to Jesus in Luke 17:6; 18:6), who commends the steward for such behavior.[129] Others,[130] however, take the more plausible position (in light of the literary flow of 12:9-13 where

Jesus speaks in the first person) that the master does commend the slave.¹³¹ A simple explanation of this curious commendation may be seen in the Hellenistic practice of a slave's *peculium*. The steward then, in rewriting the debts, may have cancelled his own exorbitant profit and not the master's.¹³²

Another question is the meaning of the parable. Initially it shows how an unrighteous steward's cleverness in a crisis should be an example of how righteous stewards of God should behave. Jesus does not stop there, however, but continues in 12:9-13 to render several other principles tied together by the concept of financial stewardship and by the catchword "mammon."¹³³ First, the prudent use of "unrigheous mammon" will have eternal consequences (i.e., the making of friends for eternal habitations). Second, the proper use of mammon will indicate a person's faithfulness (12:10-11): (a) faithfulness in little indicates faithfulness in much; (b) faithfulness in material things indicates faithfulness in eternal (or true, ἀληθινός) riches;¹³⁴ and (c) faithfulness with another's possessions indicates a potential for handling one's own.¹³⁵ Third, loyalty to both God and money is impossible.¹³⁶ Thus, the unjust steward functions now (vv. 12-13) not as an example to follow but as a warning of dishonesty and unreliability to be avoided.¹³⁷ Jesus' point: God's steward must temper shrewdness with faithfulness.

The slavery motif. The qualities of a proper steward¹³⁸ include: (a) responsibility for a large sum of money with a great deal of independence; (b) accountability to the master for his behavior; and (c) the importance of shrewdness in a crisis, of faithfulness to the master (in small things, in material things, and in things belonging to others), and of loyalty.

The unmerciful slave

Context and theme. The parable of Matthew 18:23-25 deals with the issues of forgiveness and mercy in response to Peter's question about the extent of forgiveness (12:21).[139] The parable itself unfolds, according to Crossan, in three scenes.[140] Scene one involves the slave who owes a tremendous debt[141] and the king who out of mercy entirely cancels it (12:23-27). Scene two depicts the merciless confrontation of that slave with a fellow-slave who is indebted to him for a mere pittance (12:28-30). It deliberately expresses this confrontation in language and details that parallel scene one.[142] In scene three the fellow-slaves report the unmerciful behavior of the first slave, and the lord harshly condemns and punishes him (12:31-34). Jesus' own conclusion about forgiveness sums up the parable.[143]

The slavery motif. The slave himself was perhaps a satrap[144] who collected taxes or handled other great revenue for the king.[145] Also, some details of the story reflect slave conditions of the day: slaves had the ability to take other slaves to court (8:28-30); lords could sell men and families for debt; one could be imprisoned and tortured for failing to pay a debt.[146] But since Judaism condoned neither the selling of one's family (cf. Neh. 5:1-13; Amos 2:61; 8:6)[147] nor the imprisonment and torture for the repayment of debt, the background to this parable probably lies in Hellenistic slave practices. Such allusions by Jesus would have unusually stressed the harshness of the deserved judgment to a Jewish audience.

The interrelationship between the slaves is worth noting. Although σύνδουλος implies equal status among the slaves, the first slave must have had authority over at least the one he imprisoned, if not over others. Thus, the slaves are equal, not in their relative position to each other, but as equally owned by and responsible to their lord. Consequently, as Green says, "the unmerciful servant was at fault not only in refusing to forgive his debtor, but in forgetting that the two of them stood in the same relation to the king, and in exacting strict justice where the king had waived it."[148]

There are several implications for the slavery motif: (a) the slave has a responsible position, inferred by his apparent freedom to use the lord's money in order to accumulate such a debt; (b) the slave is accountable as shown by the lord's demand to settle his accounts; (c) the slave is to be punished for unfaithful service--punishment that is rightly deserved and within the proper scope of the lord's authority; (d) the slave has responsibility to behave properly to fellow-slaves of the same master; and (e) the slave's relationship to the lord is personal, not just legal, as seen by the lord's merciful decision to cancel the heavy debt against the slave. Such mutuality of interest and concern, this parable cautions, is not to be presumed upon. Failure to show mercy to another can evoke justice by the lord.

The minas and the talents

Context and contrasts. Perhaps Christ's most familiar teachings on the theme of a slave's faithfulness and accountability are found in the parables of the minas (Luke 19:11-27) and talents (Matt. 25:14-30). Because there is value in juxtaposing the emphasis of these similar parables, they will be treated together. However, the difference in context and detail argue forcefully that Jesus gave the parable twice in His ministry.[149] For example, in Luke the parable of the minas is delivered to a crowd near Jerusalem (19:11) after Jesus passed through Jericho (19:1). The expectation of the people that Jesus would very soon come into His kingdom in Jerusalem forms an important eschatological backdrop for the details that the Lord chose to include, although the emphasis on financial stewardship must not be overlooked either (cf. the preceding encounter with Zaccheus, 19:1-10). In Matthew, Jesus gives the parable of the talents in Jerusalem to the disciples during the Olivet Discourse; and its details also evoke eschatological implications (e.g., Matt. 25:30), although with a slightly altered emphasis.

Several other differences should be noted. First, Luke emphasizes the delay between the nobleman's departure and return (Luke 19:12, "a far country"), likely to instruct the people that their expectations of an immediate literal kingdom may be premature.[150] Second, Matthew's parable deals specifically with three slaves, while

Luke records the selection of ten slaves out of an untold number of which only three examples are later explained. Third, the denominations of money distributed is the rather small mina in Luke while in Matthew it is in valuable talents. Fourth, the distribution in Luke is equal--all are given ten minas; in Matthew it is proportional according to ability--one has five talents, one two, another one. Fifth, Luke alone adds the event of the rebellious citizens (Luke 19:14) and their punishment (19:27), a double-pronged thrust by Jesus on the judgment that the returning Lord will execute.[151] Sixth, the faithful slaves of Matthew had proportionately similar increases, and thus were given the same commendation; the faithful slaves in Luke had disproportionate returns on their money and were rewarded accordingly. Seventh, the wicked (πονηρός) slave of Luke hid his mina in a napkin, an indictment of insincerity since according to the rabbis secreting goods in a napkin did not preclude liability.[152] In Matthew the slave buried his talent in the ground. Finally, Matthew concludes with the wicked slave's talent being taken away and his consignment to outer darkness; Luke also mentions the deprivation of the minas but concludes with the lord's judgment on the rebellious citizens.

Themes and purposes.[153] Most commentators will agree that accountability and faithfulness are keynotes, as seen by Jesus' concluding principle: "I tell you, that to every one who has more will be given; but from him who has not, even what he has will be taken away" (Luke 19:26; Matt. 25:29).[154] Morris comments on the respective purposes of the two parables:

> In Matthew He [Jesus] is concerned with men of different abilities to whom are assigned tasks according to their capacities. The sums are large and represent the discharge of serious and important tasks. Here [Luke] the sums are small and the same amount is given to all. The servants are being tested to see whether they are fit for larger tasks. The Matthean parable reminds us that we all have different gifts, the Lucan that we all have one basic task, that of living out our faith.[155]

<u>The slavery motif</u>. From these two parables applications can be made for the slavery motif. (a) Most obviously, the slave of God is to be obedient in the exercise of his tasks for his Master, whether the thing entrusted is large (ten talents) or small (a mina). (b) In this capacity, the slave is God's representative during the interadvent period (as suggested most prominently by Luke 9:12). This is seen not only by the slave's activity with the Master's money during His absence as His delegate but also by the nature of the reward: namely, authority over cities (Luke 19:17, 19). (c) He is accountable to the Master and rewards and punishments become inevitable. (d) The Master rewards His slaves appropriately (and proportionately) for faithful service rendered. Rewards take the form of commendation (Matt. 25:21, 23; Luke 19:17), fellowship with the Lord (Matt. 25:21, 23), and further responsibility involving greater authority (Matt. 25:21, 23; Luke 19:17, 19). (e) With responsibility and accountability comes punishment to the wicked and unfaithful servant in the deprivation of the things committed to him (Luke 19:26), in the loss of fellowship with the Master (Matt. 25:30), and in eschatological punishment (Matt. 25:30).

(f) The slave is to display an attitude of loyalty to the Lord. The wicked slave showed a disloyal attitude by his rationalization that the lord was a severe man who reaped where he did not sow. (While this comment was not denied directly by the lord, it was refuted by the lord's graciousness to the other slaves.) He also manifested disloyal actions by refusing to put the money in the bank (Luke 19:23; Matt. 25:27) and rather hiding it in the ground (Matt. 25:25) or in a napkin (Luke 19:20). This perhaps revealed a secret desire to secure the money for himself in the event the lord never returned. (g) Finally, an increased freedom and fellowship grows between faithful slaves and Master because of their obedience.

The doorkeeper

Context and theme. The parable of the doorkeeper, which has its closest affinities to Luke 12:35-48, is found only in Mark 13:33-37. It closes Mark's account of the Olivet Discourse and builds a fitting climax toward Jesus' final exhortation of 13:37: "And what I say to you I say to all, 'Be on the alert.'"

This passage falls into four parts: Jesus' exhortation to be alert because the time of the second advent is unknown (cf. 13:14-32); His parable of the departing man who puts his slaves in charge of things and especially cautions the doorkeeper to be on guard (13:34); His second warning to be alert to the master's unexpected return (13:35-36); and His third "Be alert" warning (13:37).[156]

The message of the parable is extremely clear: be actively

alert in light of the master's undetermined arrival. Or, as Cranfield has put it, ". . . ignorance of the date of the Parousia is not an excuse for being unprepared but a reason (γάρ) for unceasing vigilance."[157]

The slavery motif. The implications for the slavery motif are also evident. (a) The slaves are to be given responsibility (δοὺς τοῖς δούλοις αὐτοῦ τὴν ἐξουσίαν, 13:34) over the house while the Master is gone with every slave given their individual responsibilities. (b) As a result, the slaves are to function as the Master's representatives or ambassadors (seen by the eschatological context which denotes the absence of the Lord during the interadvent period). (c) The slaves are to be alert (a thrice repeated admonition--13:33, 35, and 37) since the Master could return at the most inconvenient and unexpected time of the day. (d) The slave is to be as vigilant as a doorkeeper.[158] (e) Finally, the slave is to be accountable. This is implicit from Christ's veiled warning "lest he come suddenly and find you asleep." Though rewards and punishments are not mentioned, being found asleep by the Master could produce harsh reprisals.

Conclusion

In the synoptics the slavery motif is pervasive. Thirty-one separate passages (apart from parallels) contain the motif in any of its institutional or non-institutional uses. One finds examples of individuals who display the qualities of the true slave of God; and the prominence Jesus Himself gives the motif in His own teachings and parables is impressive.

The Continuity of the Synoptic Slavery Motif with the Old Testament

The slavery motif in the synoptics forms a thematic bridge between the Old Testament and the epistles, building upon and expanding the concepts of spiritual service laid by the Old Testament writers.

The continuity of the motif in the synoptics with the Old Testament is seen in two specific ways. First, the synoptics (especially Luke) apply the term "slave" to individuals in ways that parallel the Old Testament usage. Israel and David, for example, are designated as God's slaves in Luke, and the use of slave for Mary and Simeon evoke the characteristic Old Testament predicates of humble submission combined with a privileged relationship with Yahweh. Furthermore, Jesus is called servant ($\Pi\alpha\tilde{\iota}\varsigma$) in Matthew's direct application of a Suffering Servant passage to Him.

Second, the synoptic use of the slavery motif sustains the two complimentary ideas of humble submission and exalted status that was observed in the Old Testament occurrences. The allusions to slavery contain, on the one hand, the notions of service, stewardship, accountability, faithfulness, acceptance of hostility from others, and alertness. These stress the slave's unquestioned responsibility to, and absolute ownership by, the Master. On the other hand, the synoptics picture the slave as a full member of the household, give him responsibilities requiring trust, promise rewards for his faithfulness, and even depict him as being served by the returning Master. These suggest the slave of God also occupies a position of exalted privilege.

The Expansion of the Synoptic Slavery
Motif beyond the Old Testament

Not content to simply repeat the form of the motif in the Old Testament, the synoptics expand the way the slavery imagery is utilized. This is evident in three areas.

First, Jesus' application of the imagery is much broader. The Old Testament tends to restrict the motif to certain religious individuals (unless the nation's covenant relationship is in view); Jesus, while applying it primarily to the Twelve, often introduces it in such a way as to make slavery to God a possible status for any who wish to faithfully follow Him.[159] The following outline displays the ways the imagery is used in the synoptics of individuals and groups:

I. Of specific individuals
   A. Literal slaves (e.g., centurion's slave; Herod's slaves; slave of the high priest)
   B. Those performing godly service (e.g., angels, women, Peter's mother-in-law; Martha; the righteous)
   C. Those fulfilling special divine tasks (e.g., Mary, David, Israel, Simeon, John the Baptist, Jesus)

II. Of those without specific identity
   A. Parable of the tares
   B. Parable of the lost son

III. Of Old Testament prophets
   A. Parable of the wicked tenants
   B. Parable of the wedding feast (at least the first group sent out)
   C. Parable of the great feast (may also be apostles)

IV. Of New Testament disciples[160]
   A. Of disciples in a broad sense
      1. Proverb: no man can serve two masters
      2. Parable of the faithful and unfaithful slaves

3. Parable of the alert slaves
   4. Parable of the doorkeeper (also may be more restrictive)
   5. Parable of the minas
 B. Of the Twelve, primarily
   1. Proverb: a slave is not greater than his lord
   2. Proverb: to be first, be a slave
   3. Proverb: we are unworthy slaves
   4. Parable of the unjust steward
   5. Parable of the unmerciful slave
   6. Parable of the talents
 C. Of leaders within the Twelve
   1. Proverb: he who is greatest shall be slave
   2. Parable of the doorkeeper

This summary highlights the synoptic emphasis. The majority of references is addressed to and describe the individual who is, or aspires to be, a follower of the divine Master. The axiomatic nature of Jesus' proverbs and parables lend themselves to a broader application of "slave" to anyone who follows Him; and the identification of all members of Christ's body with the foundational apostles (e.g., Eph. 2:20) makes Jesus' specific teaching to the Twelve about slavery to God relevant to all believers. Therefore, in contrast to the Old Testament use of the motif, entrance into this special relationship with the Master is no longer restricted to a few members of the nation of Israel but is broadened to include all disciples whom Jesus calls, regardless of ethnic orientation. But, while opportunity is greatly expanded, the obligation of faithful service still is tightly retained.

Second, the motif of slavery in the synoptics (and particularly in the parables) has an eschatological emphasis. Disciples are to serve as slaves in light of the Master's absence, in the face of the world's hostility, alertly and faithfully in view of eternity, and with the prospect of future reward. In fact, eschatological realities and rewards become frequent motivators for the disciple's faithful service during the difficult interadvent period. This is a startling departure from the Old Testament's עבד theme which has a primarily present and earthly focus.

Third, the obligations of a slave of God are much more specific. Probably this is true because slavery to God is now presented as an opportunity which anyone can choose to pursue rather than a divine pronouncement of what certain ones have done for God. This also follows from the eschatological thrust: if one is to serve God now in anticipation of His future return, then the details of what comprises that service must also be delineated. The synoptics present an amazingly rich pattern of ethical behavior which the Master expects. Those details will be summarized in chapter six.

Notes

[1] Donald Guthrie, New Testament Introduction, p. 132, calls the popular view of Marcan priority an almost "undisputed canon of criticism." Guthrie, pp. 133-35; Joachim Jeremias, New Testament Theology, pp. 37-41; Werner Georg Kümmel, ed., Introduction to the New Testament, pp. 42-80, mention Mark's primitive Greek style, the tradition of Mark's Petrine influence, the 90 percent proportion of Mark reproduced in Matthew and Luke, and the propensity of Matthew and Luke to diverge from each other when they do not share Marcan material as support. In contrast, B. C. Butler, The Originality of Saint Matthew, argues for a Matthew, Mark, Luke order while William R. Farmer, "A Skeleton in the Close of Gospel Research," BR 6 (1961):18-42; and The Synoptic Problem, pp. 199-233, argues for a Matthew, Luke, Mark sequence.

[2] See Kümmel, pp. 63-80 and Guthrie, pp. 143-57 for an evaluation of the "Q" document hypothesis. Burnett Hillman Streeter, The Four Gospels, pp. 223-70 posits two additional sources. Interestingly, Jeremias, pp. 38-39, accepts Marcan priority but rejects Q.

[3] Guthrie suggests six assumptions of Formgeschichte which themselves assure "that eyewitness testimony had no influence upon the development of community products," p. 208. See p. 211 for his critique of these assumptions. Those who embrace this approach include Rudolf Bultmann, History of the Synoptic Tradition, p. 205; Norman Perrin, What is Redaction Criticism?, p. 71. Jeremias, pp. 1-33, focuses on the criterion of "dissimilarity" as a form-content tool. See Richard Longenecker, Biblical Exegesis in the Apostolic Period, pp. 52-57, for a cogent refutation of these criteria.

[4] Guthrie, pp. 214-19, critques redaction criticism. See also William L. Lane, Commentary on the Gospel of Mark, NIC, p. 6.

[5] Leon Morris, The Gospel of John, NIC, p. 228, gives strong evidence for rejecting John 4:46-53 as a parallel account.

[6] Though the Sermon on the Mount (Matt. 5-7) differs from the Sermon on the Plain (Luke 6:14-49) in content and in proximity, they likely were given about the same time in Jesus' early Galilean ministry.

[7] Sherman E. Johnson, in IntB, 12 vols., 7:339.

⁸See H. Benedict Green, The Gospel According to St. Matthew, p. 99; Alan Hugh M'Neile, The Gospel According to Saint Matthew, p. 103.

⁹BAG, 4th rev. ed., s.v. "παῖς," pp. 609-10.

¹⁰Adolf Schlatter, Der Evangelist Matthaus, p. 274.

¹¹Alfred Plummer, The Gospel According to St. Luke, ICC, p. 196.

¹²There are other variations: in Luke, the centurion communicates through two sets of delegates; in Matthew, Jesus speaks directly to the soldier. Also, Luke's mention of the philanthropic reputation of the centurion is absent in Matthew's account. John Calvin, A Harmony of the Gospels Matthew, Mark and Luke, CC, p. 247, resolves the first discrepancy by saying "Matthew attributes to the centurion what was done at his request," thus correctly assumes that "what a man does through agents he may be said to do himself." Leon Morris, The Gospel According to Saint Luke, Tyndale, p. 137, concurs. The second variation merely reveals that Matthew stresses faith and the issue of nationality; Luke, the man's faith plus his overwhelming humility.

¹³In verse 8 the centurion makes his contrast with Christ not as ἄνθρωπος but as ὑπὸ ἐξοθσίαν, M'Neile, p. 104. This precludes on the one hand that he viewed Christ simply as another man and assumes on the other that Christ had authority over a vast sphere.

¹⁴David Hill, The Gospel of Matthew, The New Century Bible, p. 102.

¹⁵M'Neile, p. 42. Cf. Dennis E. Nineham, The Gospel of St. Mark, p. 64, who suggests the association of angels, wilderness, beast, and temptation implies a "reverse" Edenic temptation with the Second Adam victorious.

¹⁶Hill, p. 160. Other distinguishing details include: (a) Matthew's portrayal of Jesus as alone, Mark's and Luke's more complete scene (Mark 1:29, 30; Luke 4:38); (b) Matthew's placing Jesus as the object of service, Mark's and Luke's broadened scope that includes the disciples; (c) Matthew's and Mark's depiction of the illness as a fever (πυρέσσουσαν), Luke's more medical terminology (πθρετῷμεγάλο); (d) Matthew's and Mark's description of Christ touching the sick one, Luke's reference to Christ as "rebuking" (ἐπετίμησεν) the fever.

¹⁷Nineham, p. 81.

¹⁸Tasker, p. 90; William F. Albright and C. S. Mann, The Gospel According to Matthew, AncB, p. 94.

[19] E. Earle Ellis, The Gospel of Luke, p. 60.

[20] G. H. P. Thompson, The Gospel According to Luke, The New Century Bible, p. 168.

[21] C. B. Caird, The Gospel of St. Luke, p. 149.

[22] Ellis, p. 160.

[23] Morris, Luke, p. 191. He suggests this tenderness is shown by the repetition of Martha's name in Jesus' address.

[24] Caird, pp. 149-50.

[25] Geldenhuys, Commentary on the Gospel of Luke, NIC, p. 316.

[26] Mary's response to Jesus while in His presence may not be normative behavior in His absence. See, for example, the illustration of the bridegroom in Matthew 9:15.

[27] Chuza was Herod's "steward" ($\dot{\epsilon}\pi\acute{\iota}\tau\rho\sigma\pi\sigma\varsigma$) which could have denoted that he held a political office or simply that he was in charge of Herod's estate. Morris, p. 150.

[28] M'Neile, p. 370.

[29] In context, the "brethren" likely apply to the nation of Israel since this occurs at the Second Coming and is a judgment involving the nations (Matt. 25:32).

[30] Eduard Schweizer, The Good News According to Matthew, p. 478. $\Delta\iota\alpha\kappa\sigma\nu\acute{\epsilon}\omega$ is only used in v. 44 by the ungodly. Schweizer's explanation that the unsaved are using more religious language to express their piety is overdrawn; $\delta\iota\alpha\kappa\sigma\nu\acute{\epsilon}\omega$ merely summarizes all the desired responses to people in need.

[31] So thinks Ellis, p. 72; Plummer, p. 32; Thompson, p. 57; and A. R. C. Leaney, A Commentary on the Gospel According to Luke, p. 22. Luke 1:15 is seen as a possible link to Hannah's prayer since the LXX uses $\delta\sigma\tilde{\upsilon}\lambda\eta$ to translate אמה in 1 Sam. 1:11.

[32] R. C. H. Lenski, The Interpretation of St. Luke's Gospel, pp. 92-93.

[33] Cf. also Rev. 6:10; 2 Pet. 2:1; and Jude 4 (which likely refers to Christ). Plummer, p. 68, avers that the Greeks often reserved this title only for their gods when they spoke in reference to one another.

See Euripides <u>Hippolytus</u> 88: ". . . we needs must call upon the gods, our lords. . . ."

³⁴Lenski, p. 149.

³⁵This conclusion comes despite M. D. Hooker's thesis in <u>Jesus and the Servant</u> that neither the evangelists nor Jesus saw Himself as the embodiment of the Suffering Servant in Isaiah. Modern scholarship has for the most part rejected her analysis. See for example Jeremias' review in <u>JTS</u> 11 (1960):140-44. What is more surprising is that the evangelists do not make this application more frequently, perhaps because it was so commonly assumed to be true.

³⁶For example: Matthew, following the MT reads, "Behold, My servant, (Ἰδοὺ ὁ παῖς μου), while the LXX reads, "Jacob is my servant" (Ἰακὼβ ὁ παῖς μου).

³⁷Albright, p. 153.

³⁸Krister Stendahl, <u>The School of St. Matthew</u>, pp. 107-10.

³⁹Longenecker, p. 149.   ⁴⁰Albright, p. 153.

⁴¹Roland de Vaux, <u>Ancient Israel</u>, 2 vols., vol. 1: <u>Social Institutions</u>, p. 86. See also Edwin Yamauchi, "Slaves of God," <u>BETS</u> 9 (Winter 1966):46-47.

⁴²Lenski, <u>The Interpretation of St. Matthew's Gospel</u>, p. 278.

⁴³Calvin, p. 219, believed it was a common proverb of the day. The Gospel of Thomas, 47, ascribes the following to Jesus: ". . . and it is impossible for a servant to serve two masters, otherwise he will honor the one and offend the other." Edgar Hennecke and Wilhelm Schneemelcher, eds., <u>New Testament Apocrypha</u>, 2 vols., vol. 1: <u>Gospels and Related Writings</u>, p. 291.

⁴⁴Theodore H. Robinson, <u>The Gospel of Matthew</u>, p. 56.

⁴⁵Calvin, p. 219.   ⁴⁶Schweizer, p. 163.

⁴⁷M'Neile, p. 85. That love and hate are comparatives and not harsh absolutes can be seen from other New Testament uses of this literary device (e.g., Matt. 5:43; Luke 14:26; John 12:25; cf. also Gen. 29:33; Deut. 21:15; Mal. 1:23).

⁴⁸The Hebrew equivalent to μαμῶν is found in Sirach 31:8 which the LXX renders χρυσίον ("gold"). Compare this with Psalm 36:3 (LXX 37:3) where מתחנאה is rendered πλοῦτος ("riches"). M'Neile, p. 86;

Hill, p. 143.

⁴⁹A similar rabbinic proverb in TB: Ber. 58b suggests such sayings were common property and frequently adapted, Hill, p. 191. Luke 6:40 makes a similar point, but lacks the master-slave figure.

⁵⁰Lenski, pp. 406-7.

⁵¹Matthew 10:24 reads: τῷ μαθητῇ ἵνα γένηται ὡς ὁ διδάσκαλος αὐτοῦ, καὶ ὁ δοῦλος ὡς ὁ κύριος αὐτοῦ. The unparallel form of τῷ μαθητῇ and ὁ δοῦλος is explained by the attraction of ὁ δοῦλος to γένηται. A. B. Bruce, in EGT, 5 vols., 1:165.

⁵²Hill, p. 191; M'Neile, p. 143. It does not mean "lord of flies," 2 Kings 1:2, or "lord of dung" as the poorly attested Beelzebub would indicate.

⁵³Schweizer, p. 244. ⁵⁴Ibid., p. 245. ⁵⁵Nineham, p. 251.

⁵⁶Joseph Schmid, The Gospel According to St. Mark, p. 178.

⁵⁷Vincent Taylor, The Gospel According to Saint Mark, p. 404.

⁵⁸Matthew Black, An Aramaic Approach to the Gospels and Acts, pp. 218-22. While this interpretation has its attractions, it must be asked why Mark did not use παῖς (still a more suitable equivalent to talya than παιδίον), whether it is beyond doubt that Jesus only spoke Aramaic, whether it is valid to speculate on a hypothetical wording when the Greek text is quite clear, and whether that is another better alternative.

⁵⁹Arichbald Thomas Robertson, WPNT, 6 vols., vol. 1: Matthew and Mark, p. 162.

⁶⁰M'Neile, p. 290.

⁶¹MMVNT, s.v. "λύτρον," pp. 382-83; Adolf Deissmann, Light from the Ancient East, pp. 331-35.

⁶²See Albright, pp. 242-44; Hill, pp. 258-59.

⁶³Plummer, p. 500. Lenski's view, Luke, pp. 1056-57, that strife would occur after the foot-washing incident seems unlikely.

⁶⁴Deissmann, pp. 253-54. ⁶⁵Morris, p. 307. ⁶⁶Thompson, p. 218.

⁶⁷Joachim Jeremias, The Parables of Jesus, p. 193, suggests ἀχρεῖος means "miserable" and thus is an expression of modesty.

⁶⁸Greene, p. 189.

⁶⁹Cf. Jeremias, New Testament Theology, pp. 61-67, for his discussion of Jesus' use of "Αββα."

⁷⁰Though the UBS text reads διδάσκαλος here and gives no indication there is any textual disagreement, καθηγητής has stronger geneological and geographical support. See Kurt Aland, ed., Synopsis of the Fourth Gospels, p. 251.

⁷¹R. S. Barbour suggests that καθηγητής was a technical term for the Qumran community's Teacher of Righteousness; Jesus used it in reacting against the false claims to authority and prominence that were circulating. "Uncomfortable Words (VIII): Status and Titles," ET 82 (February 1971):141. See also Hill, p. 371 and C. Spicq, "Une Allusion au Docteur de Justice dans Matthew 23:10," RB 66 (1959):387-96. This suggestion is not essential in understanding Jesus' point.

⁷²Jeremias, Theology, p. 29.   ⁷³Ibid., p. 30.

⁷⁴Alfons Weiser, Die Knechtsgleichnisse der Synoptischen Evangelien, pp. 42-48. Cf. also John Crossan, "The Servant Parables of Jesus," Semeia 1 (1974):17-19.

⁷⁵Crossan, p. 19.

⁷⁶For example, he sees two groups of parables structurally: (1) Group A (doorkeeper, overseer, talents, and throne claimant) which stresses action that leads to reckoning, the master's departure and return, rewards that are appropriate; (2) Group B (unmerciful servant, unjust steward, wicked husbandmen and vineyard workers) which illustrates a movement from reckoning to action, the servant departing and returning, and rewards and punishments not in accord with audience expectation (pp. 17-18). This ingenious structure does not accommodate the wicked husbandmen parable, and his conclusion tenuously distinguishes between an apocalyptic eschatology of Jesus' audience ("the ending of this world"), and a prophetic eschatology of Jesus ("the ending of world"), p. 44.

⁷⁷C. H. Dodd, The Parables of the Kingdom, p. 175.

⁷⁸Jeremias, Parables, p. 224.

⁷⁹Benjamin W. Bacon, Studies in Matthew, pp. 216-17.

⁸⁰Dodd, p. 183; Jeremias, pp. 224-25; M'Neile, pp. 202-3; Albright, p. 169.

⁸¹Jeremias, Parables, pp. 224-25.

⁸²Jeremias, pp. 81-84, claims it is too allegorical, the interpretation misses the point of the parable, it contains words Jesus would not use, and it exhibits thirty-six peculiarities linguistically unique to Matthew. M'Neile alleges the explanation is too "stilted" and "mechanical" and feels it reflects stereotyped apocalyptic formulas that do not characterize the early teaching of Christ, pp. 202-3.

⁸³Hill, p. 235. See also Michel de Goedt, "L'Explication de la Parable de l'Ivraie," RB 66 (1959):32-54.

⁸⁴The argument that allegory or "developed" eschatology could not be a part of Christ's teaching is circular and the emphasis on the linguistic peculiarities of Matthew is somewhat overdrawn. Two of Jeremias' examples—διάβολος and κόσμος—not only occur in Matthew on the lips of Jesus (Matt. 25:41; 16:26) but also in the other synoptics (Luke 8:12, διάβολος, and Luke 9:25; Mark 8:36, κόσμος).

⁸⁵Johnson, p. 415; Hill, p. 231.

⁸⁶Eta Linnemann disagrees that Jesus' audience would think of the Pharisees as the elder brother because the brother's protest differs from the Pharisees' in 15:2 and because slavery is inappropriate to the Pharisees' view of their task, Parables of Jesus: Introduction and Exposition, pp. 79-80.

⁸⁷Ibid., p. 77.   ⁸⁸Plummer, p. 376; Linnemann, p. 77.

⁸⁹Geldenhuys, p. 395, suggests that the contrastive δέ introducing Jesus' response is a rebuke to this self-assurance.

⁹⁰To Linnemann, such excuses were believable, p. 89; see Morris' evaluation of their transparent worthlessness, p. 234.

⁹¹These differences are as follows: (1) Luke's parable takes place at the latter part of the Galilean ministry; Matthew's takes place during Passion Week in Jerusalem. (2) Luke speaks of a man who gave a feast; Matthew mentions a king who gave a wedding feast for his son. (3) Luke's account mentions only one effort by a single slave to ask the guests to come; Matthew records a double invitation of the original guests, each taken by a group of slaves (Matt. 22:3-4). (4) The response in Luke to the invitations is the giving of various refusals; the responses in Matthew include a refusal to come and then a reaction of either making light of the invitation or of mistreating and killing the slave-messengers. (5) Luke is specific about the three excuses; Matthew only vaguely hints at what might have been given. (6) Luke depicts the man's response to invite new guests; in Matthew the king first destroys

the murderous invitees and then invites the others. (7) Luke includes a double invitation of the lower class; Matthew, having included a double invitation of the original guests, records only one invitation. (8) Luke says nothing about the guest without the wedding garment while Matthew's account includes it. (9) Finally, the parable in Luke concludes with the point, "none of those men who were invited shall taste my banquet" while Jesus' point in Matthew is "for many are called but few are chosen." Scholars who consider the two accounts to be parallel are: Jeremias, p. 63; Hill, p. 301; M'Neile, p. 314; and Leaney, p. 214. See Henry Alford, GT. 4 vols., vol. 1: The Four Gospels, p. 218; Albright, p. 270; Plummer, p. 359; Geldenhuys, p. 395; Morris, p. 233; and possibly Dodd, p. 121 (who sees only the differences as coming from different sources) for scholars who deny Matthew and Luke are parallels.

[92] Linnemann, pp. 91, 93-95. Linnemann, for example, sees Jesus' own intention to stress the urgency of being prepared now for the banquet, in contrast to the Pharisees' concern about the hereafter (v. 15); while the early church's interest is in the parable first as a dominical teaching on the contrast between earthly interests and a heavenly calling and second as Jesus' answer to the question of why the Jews rejected, and the Gentiles accepted, Him. Cf. Dodd, p. 119, who says this is one of the parables where the *Sitz im Leben* is not the early church but Christ's era. Morris suggests the purpose is to show "that men are saved, not by their own effort, but by responding to the invitation; if they are lost, however, it is by their own fault," p. 233. Thompson recognizes the variety of purposes is due to emphasizing different elements. His own emphasis is on the difficulty in finding guests, which teaches that discipleship is costly, p. 202.

[93] Plummer, p. 360. Lenski concurs it is Christ, p. 778.

[94] Geldenhuys, p. 396. [95] Morris, p. 235. [96] Schweizer, p. 416.

[97] Linnemann, p. 96; Jeremias, Parables, p. 64; and Albright, p. 269, view this episode as a separate parable not spoken by Christ but invented by the evangelists because of the lack of historical precedents for the giving of wedding garments to guests (Linnemann) and because of the change in terminology from δοῦλος (22:1-10) to διάκονος (22:11-14). Jeremias, pp. 64-65. However, "wedding garment" may mean "newly washed" or "unsoiled" garment, Jeremias, p. 187, so historical precedence ceases to be an issue, and the change in terminology may be intentional by Christ.

[98] Linnemann, p. 97. [99] Hill, p. 301. [100] Jeremias, p. 68.

[101] Alford, p. 218; Schweizer, p. 417.

[102]Willoughby, C. Allen, *A Critical and Exegetical Commentary on the Gospel According to St. Matthew*, ICC, p. 235.

[103]M'Neile, p. 315.   [104]Ibid.; Jeremias, p. 68.

[105]Jeremias, p. 69, says this was the evangelist's purpose, not Jesus'.

[106]Alford, p. 227.

[107]Plummer, p. 459; Jeremias, p. 71.

[108]The close connection of this term with the Lord's baptism and transfiguration is seen by Schmid to be a later addition; Leaney, p. 251, relates the son to Jesus and Jeremias admits that Jesus Himself could have had this connection in mind, pp. 72-73.

[109]So reads Matthew and Luke; Mark reads "killed him and cast him out" (12:8). Morris, following Derrett, suggests Matthew has the right order and reads this way so the tenants would not defile the ground with a corpse; Mark is reconcilable in that the death-blow was probably given in the vineyard (i.e., the tower) and the son was carried outside to die, p. 285. See J. Duncan M. Derrett, *Law in the New Testament*, pp. 307-10, for more detail.

[110]Much discussion centers around the authenticity of the parable. Some reject its historic plausibility and see the details simply as the later accretions of the early church to provide an interpretation of "salvific history," e.g., Bultmann, p. 9; Schmid, p. 219; Nineham, p. 309; Johnson, p. 511. Jeremias, p. 70, and Dodd, p. 125, allege the parable contains some allegorical features and some authentic elements. Actually it is historically probable in light of practices in the upper Jordan Valley and many Galilean uplands for foreign overlords to own land and hire tenants to run it, Jeremias, pp. 74-75, note 97. Cf. TB: B.B. 35b, 40b, for other confirmation. The Newells take the historical plausibility too far in their suggestion that the Zealot background of the story would have put the audience's sympathy with the tenants rather than with the Lord. Jane and Raymond Newell, "The Parable of the Wicked Tenants," *NT* 14 (July 1972):226-37.

[111]Taylor, pp. 474-75.

[112]Geldenhuys, p. 498; Hill, p. 478; Albright, p. 264; Schweizer, p. 413.

[113]Ibid., p. 164.

[114] Even Aland, p. 184, is tentative about making this parable parallel with either Mark 13 or Matthew 24:42.

[115] Morris rightly rejects as too limited the view that only the crucifixion crisis is in view here, p. 216.

[116] E.g., Dodd, p. 165; Leaney, p. 201; Thompson, pp. 188-89; etc.

[117] This sudden change of metaphors, says Plummer, is not strange in Oriental language, p. 331.

[118] Plummer wisely rejects the view that this has reference to the Saturnalia rituals, p. 330.

[119] Luke's account has many close literary parallels to the parable found in Matthew 24:45-51, although the contexts of these two, and some details, are quite dissimilar.

[120] Jeremias, p. 58, like others, sees the delay as the inter-advent period.

[121] Lenski, *Luke*, pp. 704-5. [122] E.g., Jeremias, p. 56.

[123] Thompson, p. 189. If so, then Dodd's proposed theme logically follows: "to pillory the religious leaders of the Jews as God's unfaithful servants, exactly as in another parable they are pilloried as wicked husbandmen," p. 160.

[124] Leaney, p. 202; Geldenhuys, p. 363. Cf. Jeremias, p. 58; Ellis, p. 180.

[125] *TDNT*, s.v. "δοῦλος," by Karl Heinrich Rengstorf, 2 (1964):261.

[126] While many see διχοτομήσει as referring to a cruel execution (so A. W. Argyle, *The Gospel According to Matthew*, p. 187), others suggest it may refer to the dividing of his goods or to his own segregation from the faithful slaves. See Hill, p. 325; Dodd, p. 159.

[127] Crossan, p. 32.

[128] See I. Howard Marshall, *The Gospel of Luke: A Commentary on the Greek Text*, pp. 614-17, for a lucid explication.

[129] Jeremias, p. 46. Also Ellis, p. 201.

[130] Dodd, p. 30; Geldenhuys, p. 415; Morris, p. 248; Thompson, p. 211; Marshall, p. 620.

[131]Morris, p. 246; Derrett, pp. 72-73. Morris, following Derrett, suggests the master was party to usurious practices against the debtors. When the slave rewrote the bills and eliminated the heavy usury, the master, having no evidence to regain his profit, had to commend the steward to avoid revealing his own guilt.

[132]Thompson, p. 383.

[133]Leaney and others deny that these verses are authentic sayings of Jesus in this context but are rather "an assorted collection of sayings brought here to explain points in the parable, a task for which they are not well fitted," p. 223.

[134]M'Neile, p. 86.   [135]Thompson, p. 212.

[136]See the discussion on Matt. 6:24, pp. 144-45 above.

[137]Jeremias, p. 47.

[138]It should be of little concern whether the steward in this parable is actually a slave or a freeman. Plummer concedes he could be either, p. 381; Lenski argues with some cogency that because the master would discharge him he was likely free, p. 824.

[139]Linnemann believes the Lord's response is a reversal of Nimrod's ideas on blood-feud revenge in Genesis 4:24, p. 106.

[140]Crossan, p. 28.

[141]While the debt could have been simply an exaggerated figure, Jeremias, p. 210, Josephus does affirm that large amounts of money (e.g., 460 talents) were paid for ransoms, The Antiquities of the Jews 12. 2. 3.

[142]Schweizer, p. 378.

[143]Jeremias believes that the themes are forgiveness and the last judgment, p. 213; Schweizer, p. 379. Linnemann observes the issue that mercy should not be the exception and personal rights the norm, but adds "mercy has the character of an ordinance," pp. 111-12.

[144]Jeremias, p. 213.   [145]Allen, p. 200; Tasker, p. 178.

[146]M'Neile, p. 269; Deissmann, p. 267.   [147]Schweizer, p. 377.

[148]Green, p. 165.

[149]While Dodd, p. 146, believes these are the retelling from different sources of the same parable, Plummer, p. 437, Tasker, p. 236. and

Morris, p. 273, agree the parables are different.

[150]Josephus, Ant. 14. 14. 1-5, on Herod the Great, and Ant. 17. 9. 4-7, on Archelaus and Antipas, shows this may have historical parallels to the Herodian kings who traveled to Rome to acquire sanction and authority.

[151]Though some see this Lucan protion as a conflation (Jeremias, p. 59), Thompson, p. 231, concurs that it fits the judgment-motif of the parable. It also fits better historically with Jesus' impending entry into hostile Jerusalem. Crossan observes, pp. 23-25, that Matthew is more symmetrical and more in keeping with a threefold Semetic construction without the episode. Plummer, p. 438, suggests Luke's parable may evoke the rebellion against Archelaus in 4 B.C.

[152] TB: B. M. 42a. See Lane McGaughy, "The Fear of Yahweh and the Mission of Judaism: A Post-exilic Maxim and its Early Christian Expansion in the Parable of the Talents," JBL 94 (June 1975):235-45.

[153]Dodd sees these as multi-layered edifices of tradition, distinguishing Jesus' initial purpose (e.g., to avoid the Jewish leaders' desire for security through a cautious use of the law) from that of the early church (to urge faithfulness) and from later theologians (to stress the variety of gifts, eschatological delay, and accountability), pp. 151-53. See also Jeremias, p. 62. McGaughy suggests the saying about the master as a "hard man" reflects a post-exilic Jewish maxim of the bitterness toward Yahweh, pp. 243-45. However, the details make sense as they stand, and it is gratuitous to assume the eschatology could not be Jesus' own.

[154]Although Dodd sees this as a misapplied addition by the evangelists, p. 49, Plummer sees it as explaining the principle of opportunity, p. 443.

[155]Morris, pp. 273-74.

[156]While Vincent Taylor describes this as "a homiletical echo of several parables" including the parables of the talents and the minas, p. 524, there is no reason to deny Jesus spoke it here. Form critical assumption about the inappropriateness of the eschatology expressed here influences others to agree: Jeremias, pp. 53-55; Aland, p. 263; C. E. B. Cranfield, The Gospel According to St. Mark, CGTC, pp. 411-12.

[157]Cranfield, p. 411.

[158]Cole points to this as the door motif, citing Matt. 16:19; 25:11; John 10:7; 1 Cor. 16:9; Col. 4:3 and Rev. 3:20 as supporting

references, p. 307. To suggest some Christians have the specially commissioned task to be watchers (in contrast to other tasks) is disproved by the universal command in v. 37.

[159]The question as to whether the slave status is to be applied to all Christians or only certain ones of special rank is a matter of debate in the epistles. Gerhard Sass, "Zur Bedeutung von δοῦλος bei Paulus," ZNW 40 (1941 Juni):29-31, for example, argues from the Old Testament and from Paul that it should be restricted to a few; Kenneth C. Russell, Slavery as Reality and Metaphor in the Pauline Letters, pp. 50, 88-90, asserts Paul intends the imagery to suggest the ideal behavior of all Christians. The synoptic pattern seems to anticipate more clearly Russell's conclusions.

[160]This category is not rigid. The broadest grouping refers to slaves where the multitudes are either present, directly addressed, or specifically included by Jesus (e.g., Matt. 13:37). The "Twelve" grouping includes references where Jesus exclusively addresses the twelve disciples. The greatness proverb and the doorkeeper parable may distinguish common disciples from leaders; they may simply be distinguishing true disciples from the curious multitudes.

CHAPTER V

THE SLAVERY MOTIF IN THE FOURTH GOSPEL

Introduction

The evident distinctiveness of John's purpose, focus, style, literary structure, and theology underscores the importance of investigating its slavery motif separately from the synoptics. Of interest in this chapter will be not only the meaning of slavery to God and Christ found in the Fourth Gospel, but also how these meanings reflect the distinctive character of John.

Many of the introductory issues concerning the Fourth Gospel (e.g., the identity of the author, the date of composition, the purpose, the possible religious and philosophical background, the destination, and the theological thrust) need not be discussed here. The position accepted in this dissertation is that the evidence supports Johannine authorship, the gospel was written later than the others but within the first century, and that it accurately reflects Jesus' teachings spoken from a Judaistic milieu.[1]

Critics frequently question the gospel's unity--and hence its reliability--because of stylistic differences, sequential inconsistencies, and unnecessary repetition.[2] The suggested explanations of these features as "accidental displacement,"[3] multiple sources,[4] and multiple editors[5] are rejected by this writer as being too subjective, too unaccepting of the cohesiveness of John's own structure, and too dependent upon unnecessary and unfounded assumptions.[6] Rather the gospel's unity and reliability are affirmed in this discussion, confirmed by the progression and continuity observed in studies done by Raymond Brown and C. H. Dodd.[7]

John does contain references to slavery in accounts that parallel the synoptics (e.g., the testimony of John the Baptist, the anointing by Mary, and the Passion narrative);[8] yet, it also differs from them. Donald Guthrie points out four kinds of Johannine dissimilarities:[9] (a) synoptic material excluded by John (e.g., the parables containing the master-slave motif); (b) material unique to John (e.g., the washing of the disciples' feet); (c) differences in literary and theological presentation (e.g., the interplay between discourse and sign material);[10] and (d) dissimilarities in factual detail. Since it is accepted that the gospel is reliable, it is appropriate to ask what its relationship is to the other gospels. Guthrie summarizes the four basic options:[11] (a) John is independent from the synoptics (a position which cannot explain why certain crucial details are omitted and which must assume the readers were unaware of the other accounts); (b) John is an interpretation of the synoptics (a view often beclouded with unfounded assumptions of gnostic, Hellenistic, or Mandean religious influences); (c) John is a substitute for the synoptics (in which case John failed in his purpose); or (d)

197

John is intended to be supplemental to the synoptics. Guthrie's own position that John supplements the other gospels is accepted here as the best understanding of the gospel's relationship to the other three.[12] The existing differences in this "supplemental" gospel likely find their origin, explains Dodd, in an independent, primitive, and largely oral tradition.[13]

Investigation of the Motif
Classification of the Passages

The Johannine passages in which the slavery motif emerges are determined both lexically and contextually. Lexically, the word groups pertaining to the slavery motif are: δοῦλος (δοῦλος is used eight times, δουλεύω, once); παῖς (while παῖς, παιδάριον, and παιδίον do occur in John, their usage is always of "child" and not "slave;" παιδίσκε, however, is used once of servant); διάκονος (διάκονος is used three times; διακονεύω, twice); ὑπηρέτης (nine times); and λατρεία (once). The basic meaning and relative significance of these words has been discussed in the introduction and in chapter four; the focus in this chapter will be on the frequently used word groups of δοῦλος, διάκονος, and ὑπηρέτης. Three passages are included that do not contain any of these words yet which contain elements describing the service of a slave. These are the testimony of John the Baptist, the anointing by Mary of Bethany, and the footwashing by Jesus. All the discussed usages are outlined below:

I. Literal (or institutional) uses

   A. Of ones who serve

      1. The servants at the wedding feast (John 2:1-11, διάκονος)
      2. The service of Martha (John 12:1-8, διακονεύω)

   B. Of household slaves

      1. The slaves of the nobleman (John 4:46-54, δοῦλοι)

   C. Of officers and representatives

      1. Officers sent to seize Jesus (John 7:32; 45-49, ὑπηρέτης)
      2. Servants associated with the passion (John 18:1—19:6 ὑπηρέτης, δοῦλος, παιδίσκε)

         a. Officers at Jesus' arrest and trials
         b. Peter and Malchus
         c. Slaves prompting Peter's denials

II. Figurative (or non-institutional) uses

   A. Descriptive uses

      1. The testimony of John the Baptist (John 1:19-28)
      2. The anointing by Mary of Bethany (John 12:1-8)
      3. The footwashing by Jesus (John 13:1-20, δοῦλος)

   B. Proverbial uses

      1. "A slave does not remain in the house forever." (John 8:31-36, δοῦλος, δουλεύω)
      2. "If any would serve me, let him follow me." (John 12:20-26, διάκονος, διακονεύς)
      3. "A slave is not greater than his master." (John 13:12-20, δοῦλος)
      4. "A slave does not know what his master is doing." (John 15:12-16, δοῦλος)
      5. "A slave is not greater than his master." (John 15:17-27, δοῦλος)

Explication of the passages

Literal (or institutional) uses

The literal uses of slave or service are included to understand the reality of service and slavery so that the figure of slavery can be grasped with more accuracy. However, since the language of the Fourth Gospel is capable of multi-levels of meaning, it is worth studying the literal uses of slavery and service with the view toward discovering whether John selects these details to communicate not just background detail but deeper theological truths.

Individuals who serve: the servants
at the wedding feast (John 2:1-11)

The account of Jesus' first sign is replete with detail and theological significance, but the references to servants (διάκονοι) are slight. At first glance at least, they seem to function as background details to the story.[14]

General observations about the story. The structure of this short pericope is simple enough:[15] (a) the circumstances of the wedding are described (2:1-2); (b) the dilemma of the wine shortage is introduced (2:3a); (c) the dialogue between Jesus and Mary ensues (2:3b-4); (d) the directives are given to the servants, first by Mary and then by Jesus Himself (2:5-8); (e) the results of Jesus' actions are both immediate (the guests enjoy the wine) and ultimate (the disciples believe on Him, 2:9-10).

The account conveys more than simply that Jesus was a miracle worker. Brown interprets the story primarily in light of the glorification of the Son and the belief of the disciples.[16] And the association of a wedding feast with the glorification of the Messiah is consistent with Jesus' parables of the wedding feast (Matt. 22:1-14), the waiting servants (Luke 12:35-36), and the ten virgins (Matt. 25:1-13).[17] Dodd suggests the theme of the passage is "that with the coming of Christ a new order was inaugurated,"[18] and Leon Morris believes:

> this particular miracle signifies that there is a transforming power associated with Jesus. He changes the water of Judaism into the wine of Christianity, the water of Christlessness into the wine of richness and the fulness of eternal life in Christ, the water of the law into the wine of the gospel.[19]

Jesus' proverb about new wine in old wineskins (Luke 5:37-39 and par.) is commonly acnowledged. Dodd, who admits the parallel exists, maintains that the focus is somewhat different: in the synoptics, Jesus criticizes those who have acquired a taste for the old wine; in John, Jesus praises the new wine and those who taste it.[20]

The servants in the story. Servants at a wedding feast would likely aid the guests in the ceremonial washing of hands[21] and be available to serve the groom in a variety of ways. However, these servants are διάκονοι, not δοῦλοι. The word itself stresses the functional service of the individual (in contrast to the servile status of the bondslave);[22] Lenski concludes from this that these men were voluntary assistants who rendered service out of love for the groom.[23]

The primary characteristic of these servants was their quick and accurate obedience to a variety of strange directives, both from Mary[24] and Jesus. But though John keeps the servants well in the background in this story, another item about the servants comes to light: the phrase "but the servants who had drawn the water knew." In contrast to the headwaiter who discovers the newly created wine without knowing its origin, the servants possess special knowledge of the event.

Most commentators attach little significance to this remark. Lenski believes they simply were too stunned to reply;[25] and Bernard asserts that the servants only knew that it was originally water, but did not know that it had changed.[26] However it is difficult to imagine that the servants would be unaware of the miracle of the water changing to wine. Thus, John's comment about their knowledge of the event may be given to explain more clearly why the disciples now believed in Jesus: namely, there were eyewitnesses to the miraculous change who could confirm the sign to anyone who inquired. This probable explanation for the inclusion of this comment gives insight into the importance of such otherwise insignificant people in the ministry of Jesus. He left as His witnesses not the nobles (e.g., the ἀρχιτρίκλινος) but the servants.

Implications about servanthood. One may draw several implications about the meaning of servant from this literal use: (a) servants obey promptly, completely, and accurately. There is no questioning of either the command of Mary or the directives of Jesus. The account highlights Jesus' authority since He, an outsider, commands them. (b) The servants here are defined by their service, not by their ownership by any master. This is consistent with John's use of διάκονος (not δοῦλος). (c) The servants are not pictured as mindless animals; they are intelligently aware of what happens around them. This positive treatment of the servants by John may serve to prepare the reader for Jesus' later identification of His disciples as both διάκονοι (John 12:26) and δοῦλοι (John 13:16; 15:20).

Individuals who serve: Martha
of Bethany (John 12:1-8)

The story of the anointing of Jesus' feet by Mary of Bethany will be considered in depth below. However, the brief allusion to the service of Martha (John 12:2) deserves some comment here.

<u>General comments about the incident</u>. Jesus and the disciples gather with the family of Lazarus, Mary, and Martha in Bethany just before Jesus' triumphal entry.[27] The story portrays three kinds of service: the table service (διακονεύω) of Martha, the devoted service of Mary, and the false service of Judas.

The reference to Martha may be, as Lenski suggests, included out of a sense of fairness, since Mary's act of devoted anointing is the focus of the pericope.[28] However, it is difficult to separate this allusion to Martha from two other occasions: (a) Martha's fretful service in Luke 10:40; and (b) Martha's belief in the Lord of resurrection in John 11:20-28. Jesus in Luke 10:40 taught Martha that devoted service must not be merely an end in itself, nor be characterized by a self-pitying spirit of criticism. In John 12:2 Martha seems to have learned the Lord's lesson of serving without frustration or rancor. Perhaps Martha's transformation is evident just prior to the resurrection of Lazarus where, in contrast to Mary who weeps at home, Martha meets Jesus expressing her absolute confidence in His person and power, even though she does not understand all that Jesus says or intends to do (John 11:20-28).

Implications about servanthood. Martha's service in this context is voluntary, performed for the Master's benefit. In a context where her sister performs an incredible act of humble service, Martha's patient waiting at table (in contrast to her earlier frustrated busyness) is illustrative of the patient, quiet, consistent service that is as essential as the more heroic efforts of self-giving.

Individuals as household slaves;
the slaves of the nobleman
(John 4:46-54)

The story of the healing of the nobleman's son manifests the slavery motif in its references to literal slaves (δοῦλοι) who were a part of the nobleman's household.

General observations about the story. This incident immediately follows Jesus' contact with the Samaritan woman, who forms a striking contrast with the nobleman: she is a sinner who seeks for no miracle from Jesus; the Capernaum nobleman is a wealthy and reputable Jew who wants Jesus to heal his son. In both stories many believed as a result of Jesus' ministry--thus furthering the Johannine theme of faith.[29]

The miracle of healing a person at a distance through Jesus' spoken word finds some antecedents in the healing of the centurion's slave (Matt. 8:5-13; Luke 7:1-10) and the exorcism of the Syrophonecian woman's daughter, Mark 7:24-30. Dodd observes that the story in John 4 is, in a formal way, closest to the account of the Syrophonecian woman.[30]

However, the content and theme of the two stories differ: Jesus' response to the Gentile woman concerns the exclusiveness of His ministry to Israel while His response to the nobleman focuses on faith.[31]

Thus, the healing of the nobleman's son is more parallel to the healing of the centurion's servant. Brown believes the stories have more in common than their differences suggest.[32] However, a closer analysis of the different details[33] leads one to concur with Morris[34] and Dodd[35] that these are likely separate incidents.

Elements of the slavery motif. The term nobleman (βασιλικός) could denote either a man of royal blood or a servant of a king, and most concur that the latter is John's meaning[36] and that the king served is Herod.[37] That the nobleman might be a servant of Herod (in the official sense in which servant was used in the Old Testament of royal ministers) subtly evokes the master-slave theme, particularly when he addresses Jesus as "lord" (κύριος).[38] This may be a Johannine way of stressing Jesus' authority, much as the obedience of the διάκονοι in John 2:1-11 also suggested Jesus' divine authority.

Certain details explicate the status and position of slaves. First, they enjoy a close association with the family or the household. For example, the reporting slaves refer to the nobleman's son as παῖς (John 4:51), and not as παιδίον (the endearing term the father himself used, 4:49, which would be too familiar) nor as υἱός (the term used by Jesus, 4:50, which would be too formal). Their use of παῖς shows their consciousness of both their inferior status in the house and their closeness to the master, which was typical of the οἶκος of that time.[39]

Second, because the slaves were apparently left with the son while the father sought Jesus, and are informed of the child's physical status, it follows they were given important responsibilities in that household. Mere messengers would not anticipate the master's desire to know the exact moment of recovery.

Third, this association with the family is carried into the spiritual decisions of the master. The conversion of the nobleman's entire household would logically include the slaves as well. Household conversions are not unique; Cornelius (Acts 10:2, 44-48), the Philippian Jailor (Acts 16:34), and Crispus (Acts 18:8) are among the best examples.[40]

While the slaves are only a peripheral element to the story's greater focus on the miracle of healing and the theme of faith, John's reference to slaves is not unimportant. The salvation of the entire household (including, presumably, the δοῦλοι) enlarges the theme of the universal offering of the gift of salvation begun with the Samaritan woman and the climaxing with the coming of the Greeks in John 12:20-26. Furthermore, this anticipates a major discourse (John 8:31-36) in which Jesus contrasts slaves who are temporary occupants of the house with sons who are permanent residents. John subtly depicts the relationship of son and slave in the present story as one in which there is close affinity yet firmly defined barriers.

<u>Implications of slavery</u>. The major implications about the nature of slavery are as follows: (a) there is a close affinity between

the slaves and the rest of the household; yet (b) there is a distinction
constantly maintained between slaves and sons; (c) slaves are given
considerable responsibility by the master, even to the extent of caring
for the ill son in the master's absence. All in all, the picture of the
slave is positive, a feature which prepares the reader for Jesus' later
application of the figure to the disciples.

**Individuals as officers and
representatives (1): officers
sent to seize Jesus
(John 7:32, 45-49)**

The Johannine use of ὑπηρέτης. This passage marks John's first
use of ὑπηρέτης. He uses this word nine times in the gospel, and
Morris recognizes this use is unusual.[41] The word itself is almost
synonymous to διάκονος except that it often expresses a closer relationship with the master and frequently connotes serving in an official
capacity.[42] In the Fourth Gospel, ὑπηρέτης, in its literal sense, does
not refer to Jesus' disciples but only to officials of those opposed to
Christ.[43] As such, it heightens the contrast between Jesus and His
disciples, on the one hand, and the ruling Jews and their officers, on
the other. It also intensifies the atmosphere of hostility that
exists between Jesus and His enemies.

Contextual observations. During the feast of tabernacles the
Jews sent ὑπηρέται to arrest Jesus, apparently with instructions to seize
Him when the opportunity was right (7:32).[44] These ὑπηρέται were no
ordinary slaves but operated in an official capacity. Though sent out

by the chief priests, they reported both to the priests and the Pharisees, a detail which strongly indicates they were officers of the Sanhedrin (in contrast to the slaves of the high priest in John 18:10, 18, 26).[45]

The officers return impressed by Jesus; and their statement—οὐδέποτε ἐλάλησεν οὕτως ἄνθρωπος—underscores their conclusion that Jesus is no ordinary human. They were more influenced by Jesus' words (either His manner[46] or His content[47]) than by his miracles. This would make them somewhat distinct from the sign-seeking multitudes and more typical of men used to heeding verbal commands. Their willingness to admit these observations to the Sanhedrin rather than excuse themselves by suggesting the opportunity was not suitable is striking.[48] For servants accustomed to obey, not question, their superiors, these men are extraordinarily independent. John possibly includes this detail to emphasize the effect Jesus was having on a cross-section of people.

<u>Implications for the slavery motif</u>. The officers of the Sanhedrin in this context do not provide a clue as to how a slave of God should behave, but they do prompt some observations which may prove fruitful later. (a) The officers serve as their superiors' representatives, reminding the reader of the values and motives of the ones who command them. (b) Nevertheless, the ὑπηρέται are somewhat independent in this context, forming their own judgments in contrast to the rather close-minded opinions of their superiors. (c) These dual (and seemingly contradictory) characteristics further the impression that Jesus possesses the real authority. It is Jesus, not the Sanhedrin, who will

determine the time of His seizure; and it is Jesus' authoritative manner and message that makes such an impression.

Individuals as officers and representatives (2): servants associated with the passion (John 18:1--19:6)

The passion narrative contains some interesting allusion to slaves and servants. While most of the references are intended literally, the tenor of the passage suggests some theological themes which build upon the ideas of authority and slavery. The section can be broken into these basic divisions: Jesus' arrest (18:1-14); Peter's first denial (18:15-18); Jesus' trial before Annas (18:19-24); Peter's final denials (18:25-27); Jesus' trial before Pilate (first phase, 18:28-37; and second phase, 19:1-16). However, it is more profitable to discuss the slavery motif under the following three headings: (a) the arrest and trials of Jesus; (b) Peter's attack on Malchus; and (c) Peter's denials.[49]

<u>The arrest and trials of Jesus (John 18:1-14, 19-24, 28-19:16)</u>. Except for Malchus, each functionary in these passages is denoted by ὑπηρέτες. In John 18:3, the officers of the Sanhedrin are sent with a Roman cohort (likely under the command of another high-ranking officer, στρατηγός)[50] to aid in the capture of Jesus. In John 18:12 the officers conduct Jesus to Annas' residence. Here the ὑπηρέται are not as impressed with Jesus' authority (though He exerted it in 18:6) as they were in John 7. It is obvious that Jesus' hour had come (John 13:1).

The progressive hostility toward Jesus is not simply reflected by

Judas and the Jews but also hinted in the change of attitude among the officers. During Jesus' inquisition by Annas (18:19-24)[51] an officer struck Jesus for His remark to the high priest. Jesus was simply asking for the fair evaluation of His openly expressed beliefs which justice demanded. Whether the officer was acting out of genuine concern for the high priest's honor, or to "curry favor" with his master[52] (who certainly does not rebuke the man), Bernard's statement is apt: "conduct of this kind on the part of an underling would not have been permitted at a formal meeting of the Sanhedrin."[53] The officer, depicted in a violent role for the first time by John, is more and more representative of the master he serves.[54]

John 18:36 is the gospel's one non-literal use of ὑπηρέτες. In a discussion of kingship, Jesus explains to Pilate that His servants (ὑπηρέται) are not fighting to defend Him as servants of an earthly king would do.[55] Lenski believes Jesus is only referring to hypothetical subjects, and a positive identification of these subjects with the disciples is impossible because they failed to stay with Jesus.[56] Bernard thinks the reference is to angels, since Jesus could call twelve legions of angels (Matt. 26:53)[57]; and Brown adds it could be any who listen to Jesus' voice.[58] The author is convinced that Jesus had the disciples in mind.[59] Jesus' concern for the disciples is prominent from His upper room discourse and throughout the arrest and trial.[60] Also, John's arrangement of the material keeps the disciples (especially Peter) constantly before the reader. Thus any other explanation of the ὑπηρέται in 18:36 is foreign. Consequently, Jesus contrasts two kinds of ὑπηρέται: the temple police on the one hand and His disciples on the other. Thus, Brown's remark, "perhaps there is a deliberate contrast with those who arrested Jesus," is almost an understatement.[61] Jesus' use of ὑπηρέτης becomes an interpretative key to understand the dichotomy between servants of the Sanhedrin and servants of the Savior that unfolds throughout the entire passion narrative.

In 19:6, when the officers and the chief priests cry for Jesus' crucifixion, John's expression highlights the separateness of the two groups (οἱ ἀρχιερεῖς καὶ οἱ ὑπηρέται).[62] He may intend to show that such official servants do not merely mindlessly obey their superiors but partake of their values. This is an especially poignant message in the context of Jesus' suggestion that His followers are ὑπηρέται, too.

A theme which intensifies and illuminates the slavery motif is the authority of Jesus. In the garden He is in command with powerful words; His submission to arrest is voluntary; and He rebukes and protects His disciples.[63] Another theme is kingship seen in Jesus' confrontation with Pilate, in Pilate's presentation of Jesus as king, in the inscription above the cross, and in the soldiers' mock enthronement ritual.[64] Thus, this narrative conveys a tension between the true authority of Christ and the false authority of His Jewish and Roman enemies whose definition of power is totally different. Similarly the same conflict emerges in the interplay of the characters (ὑπηρέται and δοῦλοι) who are the officers and slaves of the antagonists.

What does this passage contribute to an understanding of being a slave of God? (a) The slave is a representative of the master, personifying his values and directives. While this quality of a servant has been observed before, the unique contribution of this study is in comparing such service to Christ with the service of forces hostile to Christ. (b) As the slave obeys the master, he also increasingly embraces his values, often operating without direct orders but in accordance with his master's intentions. The loyalty of the Jewish ὑπηρέται manifested itself increasingly in hatred for those hated by the master. (c) The slave is the defender of the master as seen by the common role that kingly subjects usually take in an earthly kingdom (18:36).

Peter's attack on Malchus (John 18:10-11). John 18 alternates its focus from Jesus to Peter. Peter's cutting of the high priest's ear begins the interchange which is continued by the recurring glimpses of Peter's denials. This account is found in every gospel, although only John identifies Peter and Malchus.[65] Like Luke, he places the incident before the arrest, thus picturing Peter's act as one of prevention.[66] John also omits the healing of the slave, which Barrett credibly suggests may be included to stress the great gulf between Jesus and His enemies.[67]

Peter's victim was a slave (δοῦλος) of the high priest and plainly distinguished from the Sanhedrin officials (ὑπηρέται).[68] Although Bernard dismisses Malchus as a man whose servile position would not cause much excitement if his ear was cut off,[69] it is more probable that Malchus was a prominent person, "especially delegated by the high priest to accompany the expedition."[70] Perhaps it was his conspicuousness that attracted Peter's sword.[71]

Like before, the primary implication for the slavery motif is the slave's function as his representative. Malchus was the high priest's agent. But the confrontation between Peter and Malchus seems to typify the more serious confrontation between Jesus and the Jews. In that sense, both Peter and Malchus, though participating in a real event, emerge in John's narrative as the representatives of their respective masters who are also in conflict.[72]

The denials of Peter (John 18:15-18; 25-27). The interweaving of the denials of Peter with Jesus' trials provides some interesting ironies: the Peter who at first used a sword to prevent Jesus' arrest now fails to defend him with his lips;[73] Jesus will always defend His disciples, but His disciples will deny Him.

Allusions to slavery abound in these few verses as three different terms for slaves are used. In John 18:17 a slave girl (παιδίσκη) asks whether Peter is a disciple. Her question is perhaps asked innocently because she expects a negative answer. Morris concludes that Peter, braced for stiff opposition, was caught off guard by the girl's simple question and uttered a denial that became increasingly harder to retract later.[74]

The second reference to slaves (John 18:18) proves there is a distinction between the slaves (δοῦλοι) who apparently were residents of the palace and the officers (ὑπηρέται) who were outsiders that, after bringing Jesus to Annas, remained beside the fire until the interrogation was finished. Trench postulates that John might intend to distinguish the officer who struck Jesus from the one who was struck by Peter;[75] but more likely, John's purpose is simply to identify the ones who inquired of Peter's association with Jesus.

The third use of slave occurs when a relative of Malchus asks whether Peter was in the garden with Jesus (18:26-27). Unlike the first two questions, this question expects a positive reply, perhaps because this close relative (possibly also a slave) recognized the one who assailed his kin. This may explain Peter's fear. As Bernard says, it was not as serious to be known as Jesus' disciple as it would be to be unveiled as the one who assaulted the high priest's slave![76] Since admission to being in the garden could very well have led to arrest of the sword-wielding Peter, he utters the third denial.

The implications for the slavery motif are similar to those observed above. The interchange between Peter and a variety of other servants, slaves, and officers (ὑπηρέται, δοῦλοι, and a παιδίσκη) can easily be seen as an interchange between the representatives of the major antagonists. The confrontation is perhaps illustrative of Jesus' prediction that the slave would suffer a fate similar to the master.

Figurative (or non-institutional) uses

The three descriptive uses of the slavery motif are identifiable not by slave terms but by details which describe the type of lowly and humble service a slave performs. They are figurative because the persons performing these acts are not literal slaves but depict slave-like attitudes. Interestingly, these three incidents relate to each other in that all depict the lowly task of attending a person's feet.

Descriptive uses (1): the testimony
of John the Baptist (John 1:19-28)

In John 1:27, John the Baptist declares: "It is He who comes after me, the thong of whose sandal I am not worthy to untie." The task of unfastening the thong of a sandal was considered the job of a slave (along with removing the shoes, bathing the feet, and cleansing the sandals).[77] Furthermore, it was such a lowly and degrading task that Hebrew slaves were not required to perform it.[78] And although the disciples of a rabbi, while not legally slaves, would often perform services for them, later rabbinic law (which undoubtedly also reflects the customs of these days) expressly excluded removal of the rabbi's sandals from such service.[79]

Therefore, for John to depict himself as unworthy to loosen the thong of the coming One is an extraordinary declaration of his humble and servile position. In comparision to Christ, he considered himself as less than a slave. Two specific implications may be drawn: (a) John, as an example of a slave, recognized his inferior status before His Master, expressing it in terms that denote the lowest forms of humility. (b) John also expresses his willingness to obediently execute any form of service for his Master, even the degrading tasks that other slaves would refuse.

Descriptive uses (2): the anointing
by Mary of Bethany (John 12:1-8)

An account of a woman anointing Jesus' feet is found in all four gospels (cf. Mark 14:3-9; Matt. 26:6-13; and Luke 7:36-50). There is little question that John's story is parallel to the Marcan and Matthean incidents with only slight differences.[80] However, while Bernard equates this incident with the Luke 7 story, identifying Mary Magdalene with Mary of Bethany,[81] Brown is inclined to distinguish the two incidents. The many different details argue for separate events.[82] As to the purpose of the story Barrett says John is interested "in the anointing as a means of expressing the royal dignity of Jesus in preparation for His triumphal entry in Jerusalem."[83] But while that may be a secondary emphasis, it does not conform to Jesus' own explanation that Mary's act is anticipatory of His burial.

Mary's anointing of Jesus' feet with ointment and wiping them with her hair is an enacted example of functioning as the Master's slave. The lowliness of Mary's service is seen by her attention to Jesus' feet, a detail that John repeatedly emphasizes in verse 3.[84] Furthermore, she subjects herself to possible ridicule by expending a vast quantity of expensive ointment and by loosing her hair to wipe it.[85] Her act of devotion thus contrasts both with Martha's serving at the table (by its extreme lowliness and costliness) and with Judas' comment about the poor (by its sincerity). Of the latter Westcott writes, "Mary in her devotion unconsciously provides for the honor of the dead. Judas in his selfishness unconsciously brings about the death itself."[86]

Mary's example of service suggests several implications. (a) True service is costly. For her it not only was financially expensive but possibly socially damaging. (b) True slave service is an act of humility. Mary's attention to Jesus' feet and her use of her own hair suggests a deeply personal involvement to a lowly task. (c) True service always has the master as the first priority. Unlike Judas, Mary correctly elevated Jesus above all others.

Descriptive uses (3): the footwashing by Jesus (John 13:1-20)

Introductory remarks. Perhaps the most poignant example of slave service is Christ washing the disciples' feet. This incident, unique to John, occurs at the beginning of the upper room discourse and forms, as Dodd puts it, the "'frontispiece' to the whole passion narrative."[87] It is the first of two significant acts that Jesus performs privately with His disciples before His death: the footwashing, symbolic of what He will undergo, and the giving of the sop to Judas, initiating that event.[88]

Its importance is seen by its correspondence to several other scriptural references. First, Mary's anointing of Jesus' feet, a "preenactment" of Jesus' burial, complements the footwashing which preenacts Christ's work on the cross.[89] Both similarly involve the work of a slave.[90] Second, Jesus' interpretation of the act suggests Luke 22:27, where, after the disciples dispute who is greatest, Jesus tells them that He is among them to serve. Third, Jesus' action partially fulfills the prediction in Luke 12:37, where the faithful slave will be served by the master upon his return. Finally, the act anticipates the Pauline kenosis (Phil. 2:6-11) as Christ's servanthood is expressed with a basin and a towel.

Brown analyzes the passage as follows: (a) the introduction to the gospel's second "book" (13:1); (b) the event with its first interpretation (13:2-11); and (c) the second interpretation (13:12-20).[91] The event and the two interpretations will be investigated in turn.

The footwashing and the first explanation (13:2-11). A primary theme identified with the footwashing in verses 2-11 is the death of Christ. Several details keep the cross clearly in focus: the allusion to Judas' betrayal during the footwashing (13:11); Jesus' awareness of His divine origin and destiny, an item best explained as Christ's submission to the cross (13:3); and Jesus' promise that Peter will understand later (probably after the crucifixion) what is happening (13:7). That Jesus makes participation in the footwashing a prerequisite to having a part (μέρος) with Him,[92] and that the act takes place at the passover feast (which symbolizes atonement) also contributes to this soteriological emphasis.[93]

Furthermore, footwashing illustrates the cleansing aspect of Christ's death, as seen by Jesus' threefold reference to washing (13:8, 10, 11). But cleansing cannot be separated from Christ's humiliation. As Brown puts it: "The simplest explanation of the footwashing, thus, remains that Jesus performed this servile task to prophesy symbolically that He was about to be humiliated in death."⁹⁴

Thus, Jesus' act bears directly upon the slavery motif for His work with the towel (and later with a cross) is a clear example of humble service.⁹⁵ Westcott calls this "a parable in action" and correctly concludes that "when Christ serves, He serves perfectly."⁹⁶

In verses 4-5, each part of Jesus' procedure is delineated. His preparation for washing the feet—putting off His garments, taking up a towel, and girding Himself—stresses slave service. The word for towel (λέντιον) is used in classical literature for the towel a slave used;⁹⁷ and the process of girding is mentioned of servants in Luke 12:37 and 17:8. Not coincidentally, the word for laid down (τίθησιν) is used elsewhere of Christ laying down His life (John 10:11, 15, 17, 18), and the word for taking up (λαβών) is used of His retaking it (John 10:7, 18; 13:12).⁹⁸

The actual act of washing itself, in which the details are almost ponderously repeated (13:5), also highlights Christ's example of slave service. He performed the task during the supper, probably in an ironic reaction to the disciples' dispute over who was greatest (cf. Luke 22:24).⁹⁹ Further irony is added to this scene of humiliating service when Peter addresses Jesus as κύριος (not rabbi) in objecting to being washed.¹⁰⁰

Of course, not every instance of footwashing is done out of obligation; some are performed voluntarily, out of loving devotion.¹⁰¹ Christ's action, consequently, must always be defined by His awareness

of His divine authority, origin, and destiny (13:3); and that gives an
added force to the directive to follow Christ's example. Bernard is
certainly right in saying that Christ's act is "a lesson both in humility
and dignity of service,"[102] but he does not go far enough. When the
slave shows the same humility, it is because he also has received divine
authority from the Father. Barrett concludes: "The church is the
responsible envoy of Christ, sharing his dignity and obliged to copy his
humility and service."[103]

Thus, Christ's footwashing example shows that true slavery
involves: (a) service that is lowly and humble; (b) service that may
demand the ultimate sacrifice, since Christ's act of washing the
disciples' feet anticipated the cross; and (c) service that has dignity,
because the Master set the example and because the disciple-slave shares
with his Lord the Father's authority.

The second explanation (13:12-20). Christ's second and more
explicit interpretation of the footwashing is that the disciples should
follow His example in washing one another's feet. He gives the basis
of the explanation in 13:13, the logical deduction in 13:14-15, and the
explanatory proverb about the slave and his lord in 13:16: "a slave
($δοῦλος$) is not greater than his master."

The basis of the explanation (v. 13) is Christ's affirmation
that He is indeed the Teacher and the Lord. While these descriptions
are not unique to Jesus, their articular form (in contrast, for example,
to the anarthrous use of $κύριος$ in 12:21 by the Greeks[104]), suggests

Lenski, are not vocatives but nominatives describing Christ's character.[105] Christ is not simply to be respected (as "Sir") but served (as the "Lord").

An *a fortiori* deduction from Christ's lordship is that the disciples should so serve one another (v. 14). Here, Christ reemphasizes His own position of master (or κύριος, which Brown here takes to mean as "owner")[106] by reversing the two nominatives to "the Lord and the Teacher." While this may simply be a stylistic change, some see it as Christ's deliberate affirmation of His status as the divine Master.[107] His example is neither a sacrament[108] nor an ordinance.[109] Rather, it is a nondiscriminatory act of service (both Peter and Judas were washed) that all disciples might follow (13:15).

The explanatory proverb, "a slave is not greater than his master," was used by Jesus on several occasions (Matt. 10:24-25; John 15:20). It constitutes a call to reevaluate both one's view of himself[110] and one's view of the Lord. Lenski cautions that if one thinks himself too great to stoop, then he implicitly believes himself to be greater than the Lord Himself.[111] Furthermore, it implies how others should be viewed: don't expect others to serve you, rather be willing to serve them.[112] The rationale for willing service is expanded with the second line of the proverb, "neither is one who is sent greater than the one who sent him." Jesus, by using the word ἀπόστολος (its only use in John) and not μαθητής (cf. Matt. 10:24-32) which one would expect in comparison to ὁ διδάσκαλος, underscores the slave's commission as coming from God. This element of divine authority implies the slave of

Christ is not only a humble servant to other disciples but the highest representative of the Master to the world.[113]

In conclusion, slavery to Christ implies several things: (a) a correct understanding of the exalted position of the Master as "the Lord;" (b) a consequential obedience to His command to follow His slave-like example in serving others--not only because He commands it, but because refusal implies the disciple consider himself superior to the Master; (c) an awareness that the mandate to serve is based upon a commission to represent both Christ and the Father; and (d) a willingness to humbly serve other similarly commissioned disciples.

Proverbial uses (1): "a slave does
not remain in the house forever"
(John 8:31-36)

Introductory remarks. Jesus' discourse on the light of the world contains a most complex interweaving of themes relating to the slavery motif. In John 8:30-31 Jesus introduces the theme that freedom comes from knowing the truth and abiding in His word (8:31-32). To the Jewish objection that they are already free, Jesus introduces the second theme: that the barrier to freedom is universal slavery to sin (8:34). While the slave may have temporary residence in the house, his tenure is only provisional (8:35). This leads to Jesus' third theme of the contrast between sonship and slavery. The son has privilege in the house (8:35b) while the slave must depend upon the Son for emancipation (8:36). Thus, sonship in Jesus' sense is different from mere physical Abrahamic descent (8:37-39).[114]

In addition to the complexity of themes, the figurative use of slavery is unique: it is the only instance in the gospels in which Jesus uses slavery to depict spiritual bondage to sin and it is one of the few times in which Christ applies the imagery to His enemies. Therefore it is not surprising that this passage is called a "*locus classicus* of Johannine theology," one containing a richness of theological expression that represents other New Testament theology.[115] This can be seen, for example, in the Pauline expression of the three themes of freedom, slavery, and sonship. In Pauline thought, one is enslaved not only to sin but also to the law and consequently to death. Freedom through Christ and the gospel liberates man from all three so he can become a son of God (Rom. 6:18-23; 7:3; 8:2, 21; Gal. 2:4; 4:21-31; 5:1, 13).[116] Such use of slavery is also reflected in Peter's phrase, "slave of corruption" (2 Pet. 2:19).

The theme of freedom: the result of abiding. Freedom could have a Judaistic or a Greek connotation. In Judaism, freedom was obtained through the study of the Law.[117] By contrast, the Greeks viewed freedom as the opposite of enslavement.[118] Both nuances are present here. The Jews, by responding that they are not enslaved (δουλεύω, 8:33), juxtapose bondage with freedom; and Jesus contrasts the one who is free with the one who is enslaved to sin (8:34). However, more in keeping with the Jewish notion, the bondage from which one is released is sin (not, for example, restrictive desires or the "pressures of existence"),[119] the truth which frees is the Word or revelation of

Christ (not a philosophic freedom from ignorance),[120] the agent of emancipation is Christ (8:36),[121] and freedom itself becomes equivalent to salvation.[122]

The Jews reveal their misunderstanding of freedom. If they thought in political terms, they were poor students of history.[123] If, as is more likely, they thought in spiritual terms (because of the link with Abraham and, implicitly, the divine covenant),[124] then they were ignorant of the enslaving nature of sin and their own unrighteousness.

<u>The theme of slavery: the barrier to freedom</u>. Christ explains that the one who sins becomes its slave,[125] and He includes all who do not abide in the truth in this category. While the notion that sin enslaves is closer to a Greek conception than to a Hebrew one,[126] the point is that those who considered themselves free because of their lineage are really enslaved because of their behavior. This then is a soteriological use of the slavery motif which helps to establish not so much what a slave of God does but who he is.

<u>The theme of sonship: the manumission from slavery</u>. In verse 35, Jesus changes the figure from one who is bound to one who serves in a household. Dodd believes this verse is essentially a shortened parable.[127] As such, it contrasts two stock characters: the slave and the son. The slave is one whose position is temporary, without security, and without rights. He has no "tenure,"[128] and the picture fits either the Gentile slave who could be sold at any time or the Jewish slave

whose term of service would last no more than six years. The son, on the other hand, has security and privilege.

The short proverb raises some obvious questions: Who is the son? Who is the slave? What is the house? The Jews saw themselves as sons in the household of God through the Abrahamic covenant. But since Christ already identified the slave as anyone who lives a life of sin, the "son" of the proverb can only refer to the perfect Son. Furthermore, verse 36 affirms that only the Son, because of His honored position, can liberate; and Jesus' use of "Son" as self-designation (8:28) and His word as the avenue of freedom (8:31) lead to the conclusion that Christ is the liberator. Jesus, therefore, in referring to Himself offers both a hope and a warning. The hope is that the slave can become emancipated by allowing the Son to intervene. But the warning is that the house in which the Son dwells (and which, implicitly, the Father owns) will not tolerate the permanent indwelling of persons enslaved to sin. They must either be manumitted by the Son or dispossessed. Delusions by the slave that he is really a son can only lead to ultimate disenfranchisement.

Implications for the slavery motif. The imagery of slavery from which the following implications are drawn describes not the disciple of Jesus but the sinner. But, the varigated use of the slavery imagery in the discourse does contribute to the understanding of what it means to be a slave of God--if not by its affirmations, at least by its exclusions. (a) Being a slave of God excludes being a slave to sin (i.e., remaining in habitual sin).[129] (b) Being a slave of God demands liberation from sin's bondage through emancipation by the perfect Son. (c) Being a slave of God implies no longer having a temporary, uncertain resident in God's οἶκος, but enjoying the security of the house.

Proverbial uses (2): "if any would
serve Me, let him follow Me"
(John 12:20-26)

This proverb occurs at the close of Jesus' public ministry when a group of Greeks express their desire to see Jesus. There is some question as to whom Jesus addresses His remarks. Morris feels that they are given primarily to Philip and Andrew,[130] while Brown believes it is a comment on the whole scene with neither the Greeks nor the disciples specifically intended.[131] Since the Greeks are never again mentioned, and since Jesus' remarks seem reflective of ideas that transcend a single incident, Brown's comment is acceptable. But regardless of the audience, the coming of the Greeks functions in John's gospel to show that Jesus died for the entire world (John 3:16) and to contrast the response of the Jews to that of the Gentiles.[132]

The main thrust of Jesus' response is the allusion to His glorification (12:23). All the other verses in the paragraph explain the implications of that: the parabolic illustration from nature (the analogy of the grain of wheat, 8:24); the explanatory aphorism about loving and losing life (8:25); and the series of statements about the one who would serve Christ (i.e., the command to follow, the promise of association, and the comfort of honor, 8:26).[133] Service intertwines with the theme of Christ's glorification to highlight the slave of God motif.

These verses have several parallels in the synoptics. Christ's use of the grain of wheat corresponds to other uses of this figure in Matthew 13:24-30 and Mark 4:3-9, and it perhaps is anticipatory of Paul's use of grain in 1 Corinthians 15:36-38 which he uses to illustrate the resurrection of believers. The aphorism about loving and hating life has its parallels in Mark 8:35 (which is similar in vocabulary with Luke 9:24); Matthew 10:39 (similar to Matt. 26:25); and Luke 17:33.[134] Finally, the command to follow Christ as a slave has a close ideological parallel to Mark 8:35. In Mark, Jesus predicts His death (8:31), stresses the necessity of discipleship (through self-denial, cross-bearing, and following, 8:34), and utters the proverb about losing and saving one's life. In John, Jesus also predicts His death (as seen in the phrase "to be glorified," 9:23, and in the analogy of the dying wheat, 8:24), utters the proverb about life (8:25), and stresses discipleship (8:26).[135]

The analogy of wheat: the ultimate service. The main point of this analogy of the grain of wheat is that "the way of fruitfulness lies through death."[136] This illustration, which would be more appropriate to a Greek audience than Jesus' earlier illustration of the uplifted serpent (John 3:14), directly refers to Christ Himself.[137] Those who wish to see Him must recognize His glorification only comes through the cross. Thus Christ, the supreme Servant, here describes the ultimate service He will perform.

The aphorism of loving and hating life: the attitude for service.
Jesus' proverb expands His previous illustration from His own death to the expected attitude of others. The saying compares the loving of life),[138] which results in life's destruction (ἀπολλύει), with the hating of life, which results in eternal life. The meaning, says Morris, is that loving one's life is a self-dstructive process. One's attitude should be, rather, to set "no store by this life in itself."[139] The implication however seems to be even stronger than that. As Brown observes, Jesus' followers must realize that they might not escape death (just as their Lord did not); they must be prepared to face that option.[140]

Statements about ones who serve: implications of service. The three statements in this verse are addressed to those who serve. The words for serve and servant (διακονεύω and διάκονος) are rarely used in John, and here only in a metaphorical reference to Christ's followers.[141] The synoptic parallels to this context (Mark 8:35; Matt. 16:24) seem to interchange διάκονος with "take up the cross." Therefore, the kind of service implied is severe, extensive, sacrificial and total. The basic command given to such a servant is to follow Christ, a word used frequently in John to mean "follow as disciples" (1:44; 8:12; 10:4, 27; 21:19, 20, 22).[142] It suggests the possibility of following

Christ to the death.

With such a serious command, Christ gives two promises. The first is that one will have intimate association with the Master ("where I am, there shall My servant also be."). This close, personal relationship with Jesus is confirmed grammatically by the personal pronouns for Christ which are consistently placed in the emphatic position;[143] and it constitutes an eschatological assurance.

The second promise is that the Father will honor the servant. Exactly how the Father will show honor is uncertain (e.g., He honored Christ by speaking in 12:28), although both future reward[144] as well as present suffering may be involved. Both aspects are explicit in Mark 10:30: Christ affirms that in the present the disciple will receive a hundredfold in brothers and family yet may undergo persecutions; in the future he will receive eternal life (a more than coincidental connection with John 12:25).

Implications for the slavery motif. (a) Being a servant of Christ involves assocation with the Master: being with Him, enjoying His companionship, and having the hope of future relationship. (b) Being a servant associated with Christ, however, also implies partaking of His sufferings. This may include martyrdom since Christ's service, like the buried grain of wheat, meant going to the cross. (c) Being a servant of Christ carries with it eschatological implications of companionship with the Master and reward from the Father. (d) Service to Christ is, therefore, a service that has dignity, not degradation.

This is true not because of who the servants are but because of who the Master is.[145]

Proverbial uses (3): "a slave is not greater than his master" (John 13:12-20)

This passage has been discussed above. It is listed here for the sake of completeness.

Proverbial uses (4): "a slave does not know what his master is doing" (John 15:12-16)

This proverb makes a different kind of contribution to the slavery motif in John because it describes what is not true of a disciple-slave. The disciples, says Jesus, are no longer to be considered slaves but friends. It is therefore pertinent to discover what Jesus means by "friends" (φίλοι) and by "slaves" (δοῦλοι) in order to determine how this discourse harmonizes with the slavery motif.

Three different figures are used in John 15: vine and the branches (15:1-11); friends versus slaves (15:12-16); and slaves (15:17-27). John 15:12-16 is probably best seen as part of a major subdivision of the upper room discourse that focuses on the theme of the uniting power of love (15:1-17).[146] Verse 15 contains the allusion of slavery. It follows the command to love (15:12); the standard of love (i.e., dying for friends, 15:13); the identification of the friends as obedient disciples (15:14); and the positive and negative explanation of what friendship means (15:15).

Details of the slavery motif. The slavery motif in this passage revolves around the contrast between "slaves" (the old designation) and "friends" (the new one). Since the old designation of slave is not used as frequently by Jesus in John as it is in the synoptics, He is likely referring to John 13:16 where the proverb, "a slave is not greater than his master," is uttered in connection with the footwashing. Jesus' definition of what a slave is, however, now limited to one trait: namely, the slave is uninformed of the master's purpose. He lacks knowledge because he lacks the intimacy with the master that a friend possesses. That, and only that, is the condition that has changed between Jesus and His disciples. As Barrett observes, "the difference between a δοῦλος and a φίλος lies not in doing or not doing the will of God, but in understanding or not understanding it."[147]

The new designation of friend thus carries with it the idea of intimacy. The title of friend could evoke several assocations in that day: a small group of influential intimates (as in the "friends of the emperor");[148] the Jews as a group (whom the rabbis sometimes designated as God's friends);[149] or the patriarch Abraham, who as the friend of God (2 Chron. 20:7; Isa. 41:8; James 2:23) enjoyed special intimacy with God. That Abraham is perhaps the best example of what such friendship means can be seen from Genesis 18:17-19 where God's relationship to the patriarch is characterized by both the revelation of His intimate plans to Abraham and His choice of Abraham. Both knowledge (15:15) and election (15:16) are traits of the disciples whom Jesus calls friends.[150]

The scope of friendship includes not only a special relationship with Christ but also a bond with Christ's other friends.

Although Christ contrasts the slave and the friend, there is nevertheless a continuity between these two designations. For one thing, the disciples are still called slaves just five verses later (15:20). Also, friendship is defined in this passage by two traits that are also true of the slave: obedience (a condition for friendship, 15:14) and election (15:16). Further, throughout the New Testament, the title δοῦλος is used as self-designations by many of the apostles (e.g., Rom. 1:1). Nevertheless, there are references in which believers are expressly called sons and not slaves (e.g., Gal. 4:7). How is this to be resolved? Bernard suggests that being a slave is the first stage of discipleship; the later stage of being a friend comes as more divine knowledge is shared.[151] Since this view does not adequately explain why the designation of slavery continued throughout the epistles, perhaps Brown's resolution is better. He sees the difference between slave and friend being one of perspective: "Thus, in New Testament thought the Christian remains a δοῦλος from the viewpoint of service that he should render, but from the viewpoint of intimacy with God, he is more than a δοῦλος."[152]

Implications for the slavery motif. From this passage three characteristics of slavery can be deduced: (a) the slave is to be obedient; (b) the slave is chosen by the master, not the reverse; (c) and the slave is uninformed of the master's doings. The first two of these are true of the slave of God who is also called, "friend." The difference between the literal slave and a slave of God lies in the intimacy and knowledge that the slave of God enjoys with his Lord.

Proverbial uses (5): "a slave is
not greater than his master"
(John 15:17-27)

This final proverb that compares the master and slave reflects a slight change in emphasis in this portion of the upper room discourse. While John 15:1-16 is unified by the theme of love to be expressed to Christ and to other disciples, John 15:17--16:4a is united by the theme of the world's hatred.[153] The immediate context in which the proverb occurs can be outlined as follows. (a) The world's attitude toward the disciples is hatred (15:18-19). The certainty, permanency, and basis of this hatred is expressed in 15:18, and the unique position of the disciple is stated in 15:19.[154] (b) The world's action toward the disciple is persecution which stems from the hatred (15:20-21). The principle by which the disciples are persecuted is stated in the proverb (15:20), and the cause of this persecution is ignorance of God (15:21).

Brown observes a striking parallel between this passage and Matthew 10:17-18. In John 15 the themes of hatred and persecution are separated by the proverb that the slave is not greater than the master. In Matthew 10, the same themes of hatred (10:22) and persecution (10:23) are followed by the proverb (10:24).[155] Thus these ideas are not new to the slavery motif in the gospels, and they would not need special explanation for the disciples.

    <u>Details of the slavery motif</u>. The fundamental detail that relates this passage to slavery is the proverb itself.[156] The point is that the treatment the master receives will be no better for the slave. In other words, the disciples can expect persecution since Christ received it.[157]

    The proverb, however, must be seen in light of two other factors. One factor is that although this is the second time in the same discourse that Jesus uses the proverb (the first is John 13:16), the application of the proverb in these two contexts differ. In John 13 the application concerns the relationship of believers with each other; in John 15 it concerns the believer's treatment by the world. The former instance is an encouragement to imitate the master's humility; the latter is a warning to undergo the master's fate.[158]

    Another factor is that this follows shortly after Christ calls his disciples friends, not slaves (15:15). That He freely uses this proverb of the disciples reinforces the conclusion made above that in the sense of possessing intimate knowledge the disciples are friends but in the sense of receiving hostility accorded the Master they will be treated as His slaves.

    In addition to the proverb, the idea of slavery to Christ is expanded by other details. One is the idea of election which, by stressing the uniqueness of the disciples, also suggests their ownership by Christ. Another is the notion that the disciples act as representatives. This is seen by the promise that if the world accepts Christ's word (an assumption made for the sake of argument) it will also accept theirs (15:20b). Thus, the disciple is the slave who represents the Master both in receiving the world's abuse and exercising the Master's authority.

Implications of the slavery motif. This proverb affirms that there are senses in which the disciple still can be considered a slave of Christ. (a) He is owned by his Master (in election); and (b) he is the representative of the Master.

Religious use: improper spiritual service to God (John 16:1-4)

The theme of the world's hatred is continued in John 16:1-4 with a specific example (16:2): namely, the world will persecute believers with the conviction that they are offering service (λατρεία) to God. This word for religious service (used in John only here) is capable of meaning either worship or service to God (Rom. 9:4; 12:1; Heb. 9:1, 6).[159] Because of the redundancy of the expression,[160] and because of the activity associated with persecution, perhaps service is in view here. However, its use is ironic and pejorative, for the kind of service being offered God is the destruction of God's very servants. Consequently, the one use of the word for religious service has no applicability to the slavery motif.

Summary and Conclusion

Several observations may be made about the slavery motif in the

Fourth Gospel. Generally speaking, the motif emerges rather frequently in a variety of contexts (from Cana to the upper room) and in a variety of uses (from the literal διάκονοι and ὑπηρέται, to Jesus' proverbial allusions to slavery). Many of the ideas of association, service, humility, obedience, and representation are reinforced.

There are, however, some distinctive qualities of the motif in John. First, John includes a discourse by Jesus in which slavery describes the bondage to sin that the non-believer endures (John 8). In doing so he charts a different path from the synoptics and anticipates Pauline and Petrine uses of the figure to speak of the same thing.

Second, John employs three descriptive uses that are somewhat singular. The testimony of John, the anointing by Mary, and the foot-washing by Jesus all depict the status of a slave in humble service. All are also associated with the most humble servile task of attending the feet. While John's testimony and an anointing story are found in every gospel, the footwashing of the disciples is unique to John. The inclusion of all accounts in one gospel employes a repetitive emphasis that attracts attention.

Third, there are no parabolic uses of the motif. The motif does emerge in contexts where there is imagery reminiscent of parabolic structure (e.g., the son and the slave in John 8), but such instances are rare.

Fourth, generally speaking, the motif in John has more of a soteriological emphasis. For example, slavery is used to depict bondage

to sin (John 8) or association with the Master through the cleansing of
the cross (John 13). On the other hand, the synoptics tend to reflect
more of an eschatological thrust. There is an eschatological under-
current in John 12:20-26 where the comfort of the Master's companionship
and the promise of honor by the Father come close to a doctrine of
reward, but it is not prominent.

Fifth, there is a solid emphasis by John on the slave as a
representative of the Master. This is done directly in John 15 where
the slave, functioning as the representative of the divine Master, both
receives the hatred intended for Him and wields the authoritative Word
He bestows. It is also conveyed indirectly. In the passion narrative
(18:1--19:6), the interchange between the officers of the Sanhedrin
and the subjects of Jesus and the contrast between Peter and Malchus
seem to underscore the representative function of the respective
slaves for the principle antagonists. John, in his remarkable subtle
way, carries the basic narrative with its strong emphasis on Christ's
authority on one plane, and supports it with the interaction of the
slaves and disciples on another. Such multilayered composition is a
characteristic of John in many places where the motif occurs.

Notes

¹See Donald Guthrie, <u>New Testament Introduction</u>, pp. 237-335; Leon Morris, <u>Studies in the Fourth Gospel</u>, pp. 139-279; Leon Morris, <u>The Gospel According to John</u>, NIC, pp. 8-64, for conservative views with which the author is in agreement. Raymond E. Brown, <u>The Gospel According to John</u>, AncB, 2 vols., pp. xxi-cxxix, with bibliography, is an extremely valuable source, though not all the conclusions are adopted.

²See Brown, pp. xxiv-xxv, for specific examples of these irregularities.

³Ibid., p. xxvi-xxvii; J. H. Bernard, <u>A Critical and Exegetical Commentary on the Gospel According to St. John</u>, ICC, 2 vol., ed. A. H. M'Neile, pp. xvi-xxx.

⁴C. K. Barrett, <u>The Gospel According to St. John</u>, pp. 34-36; Rudolf Bultmann, <u>The Gospel of John: A Commentary</u>, pp. 6-7.

⁵Bultmann, pp. 10-11; Brown, p. xxii.

⁶Morris, <u>John</u>, pp. 50-51; Brown, pp. xxvi-xxvii, xxx-xxxiv.

⁷See especially C. H. Dodd, <u>The Interpretation of the Fourth Gospel</u>, pp. 289-453.

⁸Guthrie, p. 288.   ⁹Ibid., pp. 293-97.

¹⁰Guthrie acknowledges the often raised position that the differences between Jesus' synoptic discourses and His Johannine ones are so great as to be contradictory. He reconciles them by appealing to the differing audiences of Jesus (in the synoptics, He spoke to common Galileans; in John, to educated Judeans), and to the versatility of Jesus as a teacher, pp. 291-93.

¹¹Ibid., pp. 298-300.

¹²Ibid., p. 298. This is despite Brown's criticism that, as a supplement, John's gospel creates more problem than it solves, p. xliv. Even Brown admits that most of the problems are reconcilable; and

one wonders whether the early readers would have been struck with the discrepancies that come to the mind of the modern scholar.

[13]C. H. Dodd, Historical Tradition in the Fourth Gospel, pp. 423-24.

[14]Ibid., p. 60, n. 3.

[15]Cf. B. F. Westcott, The Gospel According to St. John, p. 36, for a slightly different outline.

[16]Brown, pp. 104-9.

[17]Ibid., p. 104. Cf. Isa. 54:4-9; 62:4-5 for possible Old Testament uses of the wedding feast figure.

[18]Dodd, p. 226.   [19]Morris, p. 176.

[20]Dodd, p. 226.

[21]Bernard, p. 77. Cf. a possible Old Testament antecedent in 2 Kings 3:11.

[22]Supra, p. 7; R. C. Trench, Synonyms of the New Testament, p. 32.

[23]R. C. H. Lenski, The Interpretation of St. John's Gospel, p. 191. See also Barrett, p. 159, who notes this is not the natural word for household servants and believes that John uses the word to recall "the activity of deacons in pagan and Christian cultus," an explanation that has neither support from the text or squares with John's theological motive.

[24]Lenski, p. 191, speculates Mary was perhaps manager of affairs of the feast.

[25]Ibid., p. 196.

[26]Bernard, p. 79; also Westcott, p. 79.

[27]The parallel story in Mark 14:3-9 and Matt. 26:6-13 places the incident after the entrace into Jerusalem. See Morris, p. 573, n. 4, for the suggestion that Matthew's and Mark's order does not reflect a precise dating of the stories but rather serves the author's purpose of contrasting the event with Jesus' plans for betrayal.

[28]Lenski, p. 837.

[29] Brown, p. 194. The story also completes a cycle of Jesus' ministry that began in Cana with the water-to-wine miracle. The similar pattern of this event--granting a request, reference to Jesus' glorification, belief by a group of people, and the following movement by Jesus to the temple--serves to remind the reader of Jesus' first miracle in Cana and the importance of faith in Jesus in light of His ultimate purpose.

[30] Dodd, p. 189.   [31] Ibid., p. 192.

[32] Brown, pp. 192-93; cf. also Barrett, p. 206.

[33] Supra, Chapter Four, pp. 132-34, for a discussion of the different details.

[34] Morris, p. 288.   [35] Dodd, p. 194.

[36] Brown, p. 90. Morris calls him a king's "officer," p. 289, and Barrett, a "person in the service of a king," p. 206.

[37] Brown, p. 90. Cf. Barrett, p. 206, who equates the nobleman with the centurion. R. V. G. Tasker, The Gospel According to St. John, Tyndale, p. 81, suggests that the nobleman may be Chusa (Luke 8:3) or Manean (Acts 13:1), a possible but unprovable equation.

[38] Κύριος can mean either "sir" or "lord," BAG, 4th rev. ed., s.v. "κύριος," pp. 459-61. The latter is Brown's preference, p. 191.

[39] Lenski, p. 354; Morris, p. 291, n. 114.

[40] Cornelius, being a centurion, provides the closer parallel with the nobleman.

[41] Morris, p. 416, n. 61.   [42] Supra, p. 8.

[43] John 18:36 is an exception, but Jesus uses it hypothetically.

[44] Lenski, p. 568. Morris, p. 431, says: "the authorities wanted an arrest but not a riot."

[45] Brown, p. 314; Bernard, p. 278. Morris calls them "temple police" but agrees they answered to the Sanhedrin, p. 416.

[46] So Morris, p. 431, n. 98, who appeals to οὕτως as support.

[47] Bernard, p. 287.   [48] Morris, p. 431.

[49] The scholarly discussion on the interrelationship of these units both with one another and with the synoptics, and the question of

the role of oral tradition in forming these accounts, is prodigious. The reader is encouraged to consult Brown, Dodd, and Morris for pertinent material on these issues.

⁵⁰Cf. Luke 22:52; Brown, p. 808; Lenski, p. 1175; Dodd, p. 73.

⁵¹Morris, pp. 775-76 shows the illegality of this trial. The high priest had no right to question the prisoner until all witnesses had first submitted evidence.

⁵²Lenski, p. 1202.   ⁵³Bernard, p. 601.

⁵⁴This behavior is also more in keeping, apparently, with the common view of these officers as violent men, as reported in the rabbinic ballad found in TB: Pes. 57a.

⁵⁵LXX translation of Prov. 18:35 and Isa. 32:5 shows ὑπηρέτης could be used of the king's officer.

⁵⁶Lenski, p. 1230.

⁵⁷Bernard, p. 611. Note that Matt. 26:53 does not use ὑπηρέτης.

⁵⁸Brown, p. 852.

⁵⁹Morris, p. 769; Westcott, p. 260; Tasker, p. 206. Lenski's objection to identifying the subjects as the apostles because they failed Christ at the crucial moment is hardly compelling, for Christ not only predicted their failure but also foretold their future authority (Luke 22:28-30). Brown's reluctance to interpret the subjects as disciples stems from Jesus' refusal to call them slaves any longer (John 15:15), a position which ignores Jesus' use of the slavery metaphor for the disciples again in John 15:20, and Jesus' use of δοῦλος not ὑπηρέτης in the context Brown appeals to, pp. 852-53.

⁶⁰Cf. John 17:12. Also note that in Annas' interrogation Jesus is questioned about His teaching and His disciples. He only responds about His teaching (18:19-21). Barrett, p. 431, sees Jesus' defense of the disciples as a prominent emphasis in this account.

⁶¹Brown, p. 852.   ⁶²Ibid., p. 876; Morris, p. 793.

⁶³Barrett, p. 431.   ⁶⁴Brown, p. 863; Morris; p. 767.

⁶⁵Dodd, p. 80, and Westcott, pp. 254-55, both suggest John felt free to add this detail because by the time the gospel was written it was no longer necessary to protect Peter from possible reprisals.

⁶⁶Dodd, p. 73. This is in contrast to the Matthean and Marcan accounts which place the attack after the arrest, suggesting Peter sought to help Jesus escape.

⁶⁷Barrett, p. 435.   ⁶⁸Brown, p. 812.   ⁶⁹Bernard, p. 589.

⁷⁰Lenski, p. 1187.   ⁷¹Westcott, p. 254.

⁷²D. Daube, "Three Notes Having to Do with Johanan ben Zaccai," JThS 11 (1960):61, postulates that Peter's attack was not intended to kill or maim the slave but rather to render him unsuitable for priestly service by slitting his ear (cf. Brown's understanding of the diminutive as "earlobe," p. 812). If true, this underscores the representative nature of the slave, for Peter would have intended to insult the high priest through an act of violence against his slave-representative. However, Morris may be right in asserting that Peter simply had bad aim!, p. 745.

⁷³See Dodd, pp. 82-88 and Brown, pp. 8369-39, for comparisons of this account with the synoptics.

⁷⁴Morris, p. 753. Note that Walter Grundmann, "Das Wort von Jesu Freunden (Joh. 15:13-16) und das Herrenmahl," NovT 3 (1959):65, argues that Peter's use of οὐκ εἰμί is to be contrasted with Jesus' authoritative ἐγώ εἰμί--possibly an additional irony in the chapter.

⁷⁵Trench, p. 34.   ⁷⁶Bernard, p. 603.

⁷⁷Lenski, p. 122; Bernard, p. 41; Brown, p. 44; Morris, p. 141; Edwin Yamauchi, "Slaves of God," BETS 9 (Winter 1966):46-47.

⁷⁸Supra, pp. 84, 143.

⁷⁹H. L. Strack and P. Billerbeck, Kommentar zum Neuen Testament aus Talmud und Midrasch, 5 vols., 1:121: "Alle Arbeiten, die ein Sklave seinem Herrn verrichtet, soll ein Schuler seinem Lehrer tun, aus genommen das Losen des Schuhwerks."

⁸⁰E.g., Mark places this dinner after the triumphal entry; John places it before. See Morris, pp. 574-75, for an explanation.

⁸¹Bernard, p. 413.

⁸²Brown, p. 451; Morris, p. 572. In the Lucan account the woman is an anonymous sinner who washes Jesus' feet first with tears and then with a liquid perfume. It occurs early in Jesus' ministry at the house of Simon the Pharisee and it illustrates forgiveness and love. In John (and the parallels) the woman who anoints Jesus' feet with an expensive

ointment is Mary of Bethany, not an immoral woman. It occurs late in
Jesus' ministry at the house of Simon the Leper (possibly the father of
Lazarus, Brown, p. 448), and the lesson Jesus draws is that such an
anointing anticipates His burial. Judas, not Simon, makes the protest.
See Morris, p. 573, for similarities of John and Mark; cf. also Dodd,
pp. 162-65.

[83] Barrett, p. 341.   [84] Morris, p. 577; Westcott, p. 177.

[85] Morris points out that a woman loosening her hair in public
would have been acting beyond conventional taste and deportment, p.
576. Cf. TB: Sot. 8a and Num. 5:18, where the loosing of hair was a
sign of shame associated with loose morals.

[86] Westcott, p. 177.   [87] Dodd, p. 60.   [88] Morris, p. 611.

[89] Brown, p. 562.

[90] A possible OT antecedent is Ezk. 16:9-10, "Then I bathed you
with water, washed off your blood from you, and anointed you with oil.
I also . . . put sandals of porpoise skin on your feet." Cf. Westcott
for this suggestion, p. 196. The figure, however, is more suitable of
a midwife than a slave since the activity suggests the birth of an
infant.

[91] Brown, p. 562.

[92] See Brown's discussion of the word μέρος. He cites LXX
references (Num. 18:20; Deut. 12:12; 14:27) to show heritage depicts
a God-given gift to the tribes and notes later NT references (Rev.
20:6; 21:8; 22:19) to show that heritage came to denote an eternal,
heavenly reward, pp. 565-66.

[93] Tasker, pp. 154-55. Brown also suggests, as possible evidence, that Peter's refusal to be washed may parallel his earlier
objections to the cross (Mark 8:32), p. 565.

[94] Brown, p. 568.   [95] Barrett, p. 364.   [96] Westcott, p. 190.

[97] Suetonius Caligula 26.   [98] Brown, p. 551; Barrett, p. 366.

[99] So Bernard, pp. 458-59. This best fits a reconstruction of
the events as recorded in all the gospels. Morris questions why John
does not record this dispute (p. 612); his likely answer is that the
footwashing better sets the tone for the entire discourse.

¹⁰⁰Lenski, p. 914.

¹⁰¹In addition to the references to John, the anonymous woman of Luke 7, and Mary of Bethany, see also Abigail (1 Sam. 25:41). Morris, p. 617, n. 23; Strack 2:557; Barrett, p. 366, who suggest that out of devotion wives might wash husband's feet, children wash parents', and even disciples tend rabbis', TB: Ber. 7b.

¹⁰²Bernard, p. 461.   ¹⁰³Barrett, p. 364.   ¹⁰⁴Lenski, p. 925.

¹⁰⁵Lenski's own rationale--that φωνεῖτέ designates more the way a person is spoken of than how he is addressed--is very difficult to support, ibid.

¹⁰⁶Brown, p. 553.

¹⁰⁷Ibid., Morris, p. 620. Brown also observes that this shift in emphasis reflects a general shift in the gospel itself: in the first half, the disciples use διδάσκαλος more frequently; in the latter half, they use κύριος, p. 553.

¹⁰⁸Brown, p. 568.

¹⁰⁹Although later saints did practice footwashing, 1 Tim. 5:10, to restrict the command to this one act would limit Jesus' point.

¹¹⁰Bernard, p. 370.   ¹¹¹Lenski, p. 928.   ¹¹²Barrett, p. 270.

¹¹³Lenski, p. 928; Barrett, pp. 465-66. The benediction in verse 17 confirms the importance of the disciple obeying this command. This "Johannine Beatitude" is similar to Matt. 24:46 which also repeats the theme of slavery: "blessed is the slave whom his master finds so doing (i.e., caring for the household) when he comes," Brown, p. 570.

¹¹⁴There is considerable debate over whether the Jews of v. 33 are the "believing" Jews of vv. 30-31. Morris, p. 454, holds the Jews of vv. 30-31, and 33 are identical but their belief was intellectual, and not one of trust; Brown affirms that the Jews of v. 33 are not believers and that vv. 30-31 are the work of later redactors to provide a consistent transition between paragraphs, pp. 354-55. It seems to this writer that the Jews of vv. 30-31 are true believers (the distinction between the use of εἰς and the dative should not be overstressed in this context) and the Jews in v. 33 are non-believers. This change of subject is not unreasonable in light of the composition of the multitude listening to Jesus: the Twelve, new disciples, onlookers, hostile Jews.

¹¹⁵It is Dodd who uses this phrase, but for a different reason: he believes it reflects the confrontation between Jewish and Gentile

elements in the early Church, p. 330.

[116]TDNT, s.v. "ἐλεύθερος, ἐλευθερόω, ἐλευθερία," by Heinrich Schlier, 2 (1964):496-98. The second proverb in John 8:35, "the son does not abide forever" may find theological expression in Paul's allegory of Sarah and Hagar (Gal. 4:21-31). In referring to their Abrahamic heritage (8:33) the Jews could have understood Jesus' figure as a reference to Abraham's two sons: Isaac the heir and Ishmael the outcast. If so, then Paul's allegory is a fine theological treatise on this portion of Christ's sixth Johannine discourse. Another suggested parallel is Heb. 3:5, where Moses, as the slave of the house, is contrasted with Christ, the son over the house, Bernard, p. 308. This is unlikely because: (a) the word for slave is not δοῦλος but θεράπων; (b) the slave is Moses, whereas in John 8 the focus is on Abraham; and (c) the contrast is highly pejorative in John 8 and only mildly negative in Heb. 3:5.

[117]Barrett, p. 285.

[118]TDNT, 2:487; Bernard, p. 305; Brown, p. 355.

[119]TDNT, 2:494-95.   [120]Morris, p. 456.

[121]Though Christ's declaration of Himself as the agent of freedom occurs only here in John, Luke 4:18 shows it was always an essential part of His ministry.

[122]Barrett, p. 285.

[123]Brown, p. 355; Cf., e.g., Josephus The War of the Jews 7. 3. 2-3. Note the irony of John 19:15, "We have no king but Caesar."

[124]Lenski, p. 633.

[125]Dodd, p. 380, and Brown, p. 355, prefer the textual reading which omits "of sin," a position that seems surprising in light of the overwhelming external evidence to the contrary. Cf. UBS Greek New Testament, 2nd ed.

[126]Bernard, p. 307; Barrett, p. 286.; Dodd, p. 386, says these are Stoic maxims.

[127]Dodd, pp. 380-82.   [128]Bernard, p. 307.

[129]Bernard, p. 305; Westcott, p. 134.   [130]Morris, p. 592.

[131]Brown, p. 467.

[132] Morris, pp. 590-91. Barrett's suggestion that this story functions to show that the mission of the church is to evangelize Greeks, while a valid application, seems too superimposed to be one of John's primary intentions, p. 352.

[133] See Dodd, p. 389; Morris, pp. 593-94; Westcott, p. 181; and Bernard, pp. 433-34.

[134] See Brown, pp. 473-74, for a complete analysis of the differences between these parallels.

[135] Brown, p. 475.   [136] Morris, p. 593.

[137] John Calvin, The Gospel According to St. John, Part 1, CC, p. 37; Morris, p. 593.

[138] "Soul" in this verse means "the immaterial part of man as it animates the body," Lenski, p. 863.

[139] Morris, p. 593.   [140] Brown, p. 467.

[141] This compels Dodd to say this use is non-Johannine, pp. 352-53, introduced because it was more easily transferable to the early church situation. If true, however, why are not the other references to slavery so changed?

[142] Barrett, p. 150.

[143] Lenski's translation captures the Greek: "If me anyone serves, me let him follow. And where I myself am, there also my own slaves shall be. If me anyone serves, honor him will the Father," p. 866. See also Morris, p. 594.

[144] Calvin, pp. 38-39.

[145] This dignity of service is suggested by Bernard, p. 454, and expanded by his "doctrine of διάκονια:" (1) a servant ministers to a master (Mark 1:31; John 12:2); (2) the servant is not thankworthy because he serves (Luke 17:9); (3) the path to pre-eminence and greatness is service (Mark 10:43; 9:35); (4) service to others will be the means of evaluating one's service to Christ (Matt. 25:44); and (5) Christ's own service of death may be the servant's lot.

[146] Brown, pp. 586-87.   [147] Barrett, p. 389.

[148] Cf. 1 Macc. 2:18, 3:28; 10:65.

[149] Morris, p. 675, n. 33; Strack, 2:564-65.

¹⁵⁰The disciples are also called friends in Luke 12:4, in a context which associates friendship with Christ with persecution from the world.

¹⁵¹Bernard, p. 488.

¹⁵²Brown, p. 683. Thus, Westcott's opinion that the believer's relationship to Christ is not essentially one of service but one of love is to be firmly rejected, p. 220. Service never ceases to be part of that relationship.

¹⁵³Barrett, p. 403.

¹⁵⁴The certainty of the hatred is seen in the simple first class conditional clause; the permanency is seen by the perfect, μεμίσηκεν; the basis is seen in their prior hatred of Christ. Morris, p. 678, n. 43.

¹⁵⁵Brown, pp. 693-95.

¹⁵⁶Lenski notes that its form is a litotes: a figure which expresses something by stating the negation of the contrary, p. 1056.

¹⁵⁷Morris, p. 679; Bernard, p. 492.

¹⁵⁸Brown, p. 687.

¹⁵⁹BAG, 4th rev. ed., s.v. "λατρεία," p. 468.

¹⁶⁰Brown translates it literally as, "to offer the service of offering worship to God," p. 691.

CHAPTER VI

CONCLUSION

What does it mean—practically, theologically, personally—to be a slave of Jesus Christ? To answer the question, this dissertation began an investigation of the slavery motif in the gospels that sought to identify the motif and to delineate the theological and ethical characteristics of one who is God's slave. Using the approach of biblical theology, an attempt has been made to overview lexical designations for service, bondage, and slavery; to analyze the Old Testament antecedents to spiritual slavery; to investigate the cultural contribution of Judaism, Greece, and Rome; and to examine in detail, and within their contexts, the gospel passages containing the motif.

It now remains to discuss briefly the role that the slavery motif in the gospels plays in biblical revelation and to organize the observations about being a slave of God into a logical and theological matrix.

The Role of the Slavery Motif
in the Gospels

It has been a persistent theme of this dissertation that a slavery motif runs through Scripture, from the עבד יהוה concept in the

Old Testament to the δοῦλος θεοῦ emphasis in the epistles. Since relatively little effort has been made to isolate and examine a similar motif in the gospels, some conclusions about the relationship of the gospels' slavery motif to the rest of Scripture is in order.

The gospels' slavery motif builds upon the Old Testament. As was observed earlier, the synoptics actually designate some persons (e.g., David, Israel, Simeon, Mary) as God's slave following Old Testament style. Additionally, both the synoptics and the Fourth Gospel continue the paradoxical emphasis that is present in the Old Testament: namely, that the slave designation describes not only humble service rendered to a superior but also denotes exalted privilege with him. This "double nuance" to the spiritual use of slavery is present in a variety of Old Testament contexts (from Moses, the prophets, and David, to the remnant, the nation, and the Suffering Servant).

All four gospels expand upon the slavery motif in the Old Testament. All, for example, extend the privilege of "slavery to God" to any disciple of Christ willing to pay the cost. Christ gives an open invitation for any to become great by traveling the road of humble service. All of the gospels also present Christ as the supreme example of the Servant: the synoptics by their more explicit application of the Old Testament Suffering Servant passages to Jesus; and John by Jesus' lowly act of washing the disciples' feet.

The synoptics present an eschatological perspective to the slavery motif. Consequently, they explain slavery to God in light of specific

promises of future rewards and punishments and the urgent necessity to
serve faithfully to attain future honor. Furthermore, the synoptics are
more specific on the kinds of service the slave of God performs (such as
hospitality, financial stewardship, feeding and clothing the needy,
showing mercy to others, etc.). By contrast, the Old Testament עבד theme
is less eschatological (except as it anticipates the Suffering Servant)
and less oriented to rewards and punishments, perhaps because being God's
slave was a sovereign pronouncement of one's relationship to God rather
than an opportunity to achieve.

The gospel of John expands upon the slavery motif in a slightly
different way. Although eschatological overtones are present (e.g., in
its allusion to eternal life), John's thrust is more soteriological.
Its emphasis, therefore, is more on the person and work of Christ and
upon the believer's obligation to follow His example. This is not only
seen in the footwashing incident, but also in John's particular emphasis
(both explicitly and implicitly) on the slave of God as God's representative. A related Johannine emphasis (that is present but not as accented
in the synoptics) is that slave representatives of Christ can expect to
receive the hostility which the world once directed to the Master. And
finally, this soteriological feature arises in John's use of the slavery
figure to depict bondage to sin, an unmistakable anticipation of Pauline
and Petrine theology.

In sum, the gospels provide a smooth yet ever expanding transition between the Old Testament and the epistles. They preserve the

somewhat paradoxical notion that slavery is both humble service and exalted privilege. Yet they expand upon it by extending the invitation of slavery to God to any who would follow Christ; by placing the present obligations into an eschatological, reward-oriented context; by specifically delineating the kinds of service the Master requires; and by constantly exalting the Suffering Servant. That Servant, who is also the Lord of Lords, is the perfect example to follow and the divine Master to obey.

A Profile of the Slave of God

A wide variety of implications about spiritual slavery have been drawn from many gospel passages. They must now be organized to give a satisfying portrait of the character and behavior of a slave belonging to Christ. To achieve completeness without redundancy, these implications will be presented in an outlined form below. The biblical support for each point (often in the form of an explanation or an example) will be included in the outline, although there is no attempt to be exhaustive in this documentation. Several key passages are used frequently since they usually contain a number of unique insights that are best displayed separately.

Summary: The slave of God faithfully and humbly serves in this present life in anticipation of reward and greater responsibility when the Master returns.

Emphasis #1: The slave of God's performance in this life

I. His present relationship with the Master

   A. Attributes of that relationship

      1. Exclusive loyalty to the Master
         Explanation: No man can serve two masters (Luke 16:13; Matt. 6:24)
         Example: Mary of Bethany's anointing of Jesus' feet with costly perfume (John 12:1-8)

      2. Accountability to the Master
         Explanation: The slave is to do what is expected of him (Luke 17:5-10)
         Positive examples: Faithful slaves in the parables (Luke 12:41-48; Matt. 25; Luke 19)
         Negative examples: The unjust steward (Luke 16:1-13); unmerciful slave (Matt. 18:23-35); and the unfaithful slaves of Luke 19 and Matt. 25.

      3. Inferiority to sonship in the Master's house
         Explanation: Slaves do not remain in the house forever while sons do (John 8:31-36)
         Example: The relationship of the nobleman's slaves to his son (John 4:46-54)

      4. Ownership by the Master
         Explanation: The slave does not choose the Master; the Master has chosen him (John 15:16)

      5. Being uninformed of the Master's intentions
         Note: This is one characteristic that is NOT true of the slave of God.
         Explanation: Since the slave does not know what the Master does, Jesus calls his newly informed disciples, "friends" (John 15:14-15)

   B. Attitudes of the slave toward the Master

      1. Submission
         Example: Mary, the mother of Jesus, willingly accept's God's purpose in a socially difficult situation (Luke 1:38)

      2. Humility
         Example #1: Mary of Bethany washes Jesus' feet with her hair (John 12:1-8)
         Example #2: The centurion considers his roof unworthy for the Lord (Luke 7:1-10; Matt. 8:5-13)

          Example #3: John the Baptist considers himself unworthy to untie the Lord's sandal thong (John 1:19-28)
          Example #4: Jesus washes the disciples' feet (John 13:1-20)

     3. Devotion
        Example: Mary of Bethany sits attentively at Jesus' feet (Luke 10:38-42)

  C. Activities of the slave for the Master

     1. *The principle:* Obedience
        Explanation: The slave's lot is nothing more or less than executing the Master's wishes (Luke 17:5-10)
     2. *The application:* Service to others
        Example and explanation: Serving others is equivalent to serving Jesus (Matt. 25:31-46)

II. His present relationship with other "slaves"

  A. His service toward others in need
    Explanation: serving the least of the brothers (Matt. 25)

  B. His deference toward others
    Explanation: The path to greatness is through being a slave (the "greatness" proverbs of Matt. 20:20-28; 23:1-12; Mark 9:33-37; 10:35-45; Luke 22:24-27).
    Negative examples: The disputes over greatness of the disciples (Mark 10; Matt. 20; Luke 22)
    Positive example: The footwashing by Jesus

  C. His mercy and forgiveness toward others
    Example: The parable of the unmerciful slave (Matt. 18:23-35)

  D. His reponsibility for others
    Example #1: The parable of the faithful slaves (Luke 12)
    Example #2: The parable of the doorkeeper (Mark 13:33-37)
    Example #3: The parable of the alert slaves (Luke 12:35-40)

III. His present relationship to the world

  A. He represents the Master to the world
    Example #1: The feast and supper parables (Matt. 22:1-14; Luke 14:15-24)
    Example #2: The wicked tenants parable (Luke 20:9-18; Matt. 21:33-46; Mark 12:1-12)

Example #3: The Johannine interplay of servants (ὑπηρέται) who represent the conflicting masters (John 18:1-- 19:6)

B. He communicates the Master's message to the world
Examples: The feast and supper parables; the wicked tenants parable

C. He can expect persecution from the world
Explanation #1: The slave is not greater than his Master (John 13:12-20; 15:17-27; Matt. 10:24-25)
Explanation #2: The one who hates his life will keep it to eternal life (John 12:25)
Examples: The feast and supper parables; the wicked tenant parable

IV. His present relationship to the task

A. Axioms about the task

1. Service requires listening as well as obeying
   Example: Mary of Bethany at Jesus' feet (Luke 10)

2. Service is to be performed faithfully but not ritualistically
   Example: Martha's service in contrast to Mary (Luke 10)

3. Service has future implications
   Explanation: The "greatness" proverbs (Matt. 20; 23; Mark 9:10; Luke 22): if you want to be great, be a servant; if you want to be first, be a slave
   Examples: Talents and minas parables

4. Service is exacting
   Explanation: The master is always served before the slave, and no thanks is to be expected (Luke 17)

5. Service has dignity
   Note: Dignity is a predicate because of who the Master is, not because the slave possesses special dignity.
   Example and explanation: The footwashing example of Jesus is to be followed by His slaves because He is the Lord and the Teacher.

B. Areas of service

1. Financial stewardship
   Example #1 and explanation: The unjust steward's shrewdness
                                  (Luke 16)
   Example #2: Women supporters of Jesus' ministry (Luke 8:3)

2. Hospitality
   Explanation: Receiving a brother like a child is a sign of
                  true slave service (Mark 9:36-37)
   Example: Mary and Martha; Peter's mother-in-law

3. Meeting of physical needs (hunger, thirst, nakedness)
   Exhortation: (Matt. 25)

4. Visitation of sick and imprisoned
   Exhortation: (Matt. 25)

C. Attitudes in discharging service

   1. Faithfulness
      Example #1: "Well done good and faithful slaves." (parables
                    of minas and talents, Luke 19; Matt. 25)
      Example #2: Parable of the faithful slaves (Luke 12)

   2. Patience
      Example: Parable of the wheat and the tares (Matt. 13:24-30)

   3. Expectancy
      Example #1: The alert slaves parable (Luke 12)
      Example #2: The faithful slaves parable (Luke 12)
      Example #3: The doorkeeper parable (Mark 13)

EMPHASIS #2: The slave of God's anticipation of the Master's return

I. His future position with the Master

   A. The Master and rewards
      1. The reward of commendation by the Master
         Explanation: If anyone serves me, the Father will honor
                        him (John 12:26)
         Example: "Well done good and faithful slave" (Luke 19)

      2. The reward of association with the Master
         Explanation: Where the Lord is, there will the servant be
                        (John 12:20-26)
         Example: "Enter into the joy of your Master" (Luke 19;
                    Matt. 25)

3. The reward of greater responsibility for the Master
   Explanation: Present faithfulness will be seen in future
               responsibility over what is of true value,
               what is great, and what is one's own (Luke 16)
   Examples: Authority over cities (Luke 19), over much (Matt.
               25) and over the 12 tribes of Israel (Luke 22:30)

4. The reward of exaltation by the Master
   Example: The Lord will gird Himself and serve the faithful
              slave (Luke 12:35-37)

B. The Master and punishment
   Explanation: There will be degrees of punishment depending, in
               part, on the slave's ignorance (Luke 12:46-48)
   Example #1: Deprived of responsibility (Luke 19)
   Example #2: Cast into outer darkness (Matt. 25)
   Example #3: Cut in pieces; placed with unbelievers (Luke 12)

II. His future relationship with the world
    Explanation #1: The hostile world which hated the slave will be
                judged at the Master's return. Parable of the
                rebellious citizens (Luke 19); parable of the
                wicked tenants.
    Explanation #2: He will have authority in the world (Luke 19:22)

III. His future relationship to the task
     Explanation #1: His task continues, but with greater responsibility
                 (Luke 19; Matt. 25)
     Explanation #2: He will have a greater interest in the task because
                 of its increased value, increased responsibility,
                 and increased personal right to possess it (Luke 16)

The Paradox of Slavery to God

Thus, the slavery motif in the gospels enjoys a rich and diverse application. It is suitable for coordinating many aspects of Christian behavior and capable of expressing even paradoxical facets of biblical truth into a harmonious cameo. Six of these paradoxes are briefly explained below as a summary picture of the slavery motif.

Paradoxes Regarding the Nature of Service

Humility versus dignity

By definition, the slave has no freedom to determine his destiny. He must serve the Master with unquestioning obedience even in socially demeaning or humiliating tasks. Yet this predicate of slavery is balanced in the gospels with the concurrent notion of dignity, a dignity which stems not from the intrinsic worth of the slave but rather from the worth of the Master. This dual emphasis on humility and dignity of service has some important implications for the contemporary theologies of liberation (including the Christian feminist movements).[1] While these movements rightly oppose exploitation of the weak, they often err by ignoring the biblical emphasis on humble service. They fail to see that such service has dignity only when it strives for theological and doxological ends, not social ones.

Obedience versus initiative

The need to be faithful and obedience to the Master under a variety of circumstances is juxtaposed by the encouragement to creatively further the Master's interests in the best way possible. Just as instructions given to the slaves with the talents and minas were clear but not exhaustive, the Master fully intends slaves to exercise their own judgment and select the appropriate means for accomplishing the Master's goals within the parameters of His Word and the working of His Spirit. Being a slave of God includes risk because commitment to the heavenly Master opens both the potential to greater reward for faithful service and the possibility for severe punishment for failure to obey.

Slaves versus friends

The believer is considered both a slave of God and a friend of God (even in the same biblical context). Friendship differs from slavery in that the friend is informed of the Master's purposes, while slaves remain uninformed. To be the slave of Christ, faithful obedience stemming from a heart of undivided loyalty should be a predicate of the believer's walk. But as Christ's friend, the Christian is the informed confidant who experiences intimate fellowship with his Lord.

Paradoxes Regarding the Eternal Perspective of Service

The present versus the future

The believer functioning in his capacity as a slave in this present life recognizes that such service, no matter how difficult or demeaning, is of a temporary duration; and that one's future relationship with the Master will be directly affected by one's present performance. The temporality of one's present service is important because of the hostility with which the world treats the slave (e.g., the wicked tenants, John 15:20). The promise of future blessing is a startling revelation which, while not the necessary or expected lot of the slave, makes the future a goal for which present service is rendered. The road to future greatness is tied to present service.

Hostility versus honor

There is a contrast between the way the world treats the slave of God now and the way in which the Master will vindicate His slave and reward him. The world which did not hesitate to mistreat the Master even to the point of death will not be less abusive to the Master's representatives. The motivation for enduring this abuse can be found in the promise of future honor and reward.

Serving versus being served

The ultimate paradox for the slave is that the one who faithfully serves the Master in this present world will, in the future, be served by the Master Himself, illustrating the extent to which the slave's faithful service to the Master is honored. The reversal of roles should not be totally unexpected. The same Jesus who urged the disciples to pursue greatness by following the path of lowliest service was also the Master who, in the midst of supper, laid aside His garments, took the towel and basin, and served the disciples through the menial washing of feet. His last supper promise to partake of the fruit of the vine only when He drinks it new with His slaves also anticipates the time when He will once again serve those who have so faithfully served their long-absent King in a hostile world.

Notes

[1] Paul K. Jewett, <u>Man as Male and Female</u>, pp. 144, 147-49. The analogy to the institution of slavery is seen as a most decisive—though by no means the exclusive—argument against hierarchical relationships between men and women. Jewett makes an assumption common to many: namely, that slavery as an institution is *ipso facto* sinful. A careful consideration of the spiritual imagery of slavery in the gospels and in Paul (with the dual components of humility and dignity) would seem, in this writer's opinion, to undermine that assumption.

BIBLIOGRAPHY

I. Books

Albright, William F., and Mann, C. S. *The Gospel According to Matthew.* The Anchor Bible. Garden City, N. Y.: Doubleday and Company, Inc., 1971.

Alford, Henry. *The Greek Testament: With a Critically Revised Text, a Digest of Various Readings, Marginal References to Verbal and Idiomatic Usage, Prolegomena, and a Critical and Exegetical Commentary.* Revised by Everett F. Harrison. 4 vols. Vol. 1: The Four Gospels. Chicago: Moody Press, 1958.

Allard, Paul. *Les Esclaves Chrétiens: depuis les premiers temps de l'Eglise jusqu'à la fin de la Domination Romaine en Occident.* N. Y.: Georg Olms Verlag, 1974.

Allen, Willoughby C. *A Critical and Exegetical Commentary on the Gospel According to Saint Matthew.* 3rd. ed. The International Critical Commentary. Edinburgh: T. & T. Clark, 1912.

Anderson, Hugh. *The Gospel of Mark.* Greenwood, S. C.: The Attic Press, Inc., 1976.

The Apocrypha and Pseudepigrapha of the Old Testament in English, with Introduction and Critical and Explanatory Notes to the Several Books. 2 vols. Edited by R. H. Charles. Oxford: At the Clarendon Press, 1913.

Archer, Gleason. *A Survey of Old Testament Introduction.* Chicago: Moody Press, 1964.

Argyle, Aubrey W. *The Gospel According to Matthew.* Cambridge: At the University Press, 1963.

Aristotle. *Nicomachean Ethics.* With an English translation by H. Rackham. The Loeb Classical Library. Cambridge, Mass.: Harvard University Press, 1968.

_____. *Politics.* With an English translation by H. Rackham. The Loeb Classical Library. Cambridge, Mass.: Harvard University Press, 1932.

Assman, Hugo. *Theology for a Nomad Church*. Translated by Paul Burns. Maryknoll, N. Y.: Orbis Books, 1976.

The Babylonian Talmud. Translated and edited by I. Epstein. 18 vols. London: The Soncino Press, 1961.

Bacon, Benjamin W. *Studies in Matthew*. New York: H. Holt and Co., 1930.

Barios, George A. "Chronology, Metrology, Etc." In *The Interpreter's Bible*, 1 (1952):142-64. Edited by George Arthur Buttrick. 12 vols. New York: Abingdon Press, 1952-57.

Barnes, Albert. *An Inquiry into the Scriptural View of Slavery*. New York: Negro Universities Press, reprinted, 1969. Reprint of the 1857 ed.

Barr, James. *The Semantics of Biblical Language*. London: Oxford University Press, 1961.

Barrett, C. K. *The Gospel According to St. John*. London: S. P. C. K., 1962.

Barrow, R. H. *Slavery in the Roman Empire*. New York: Barnes & Noble, 1928.

Bartchy, S. Scott. Μᾶλλον Χρῆσαι: *First Century Slavery and the Interpretation of 1 Corinthians 7:21*. Missoula, Montana: Scholars Press, 1973.

Bernard, J. H. *A Critical and Exegetical Commentary on the Gospel According to Saint John*. Edited by A. H. M'Neile. 2 vols. The International Critical Commentary. Edinburgh: T. & T. Clark, 1928.

Black, Matthew. *An Aramaic Approach to the Gospels and Acts*. 3rd ed. Oxford: At the Clarendon Press, 1967.

Blair, William. *An Inquiry into the State of Slavery amongst the Romans*. Edinburgh: Thomas Clark, 1833; reprint ed., Detroit: Negro History Press, 1969.

Blake, William O. *The History of Slavery and the Slave Trade, Ancient and Modern*. Colombus, Ohio: H. Miller, 1857.

Bömer, Franz. *Untersuchunger uber die Religion der Sklaven in Griechenland und Rom*. 4 Tiel. Wiesbaden: Verlag der Akademie der Wissenschaften und der literatur in Mainz in kommission bei Franz Steiner Verlag GMBH, 1957-63.

Brown, Raymond E. The Gospel According to John I-XII: A New Translation With Introduction and Commentary. The Anchor Bible. Garden City, N. Y.: Doubleday & Co., Inc., 1966.

_____. The Gospel According to John, XIII-XXI: A New Translation With Introduction and Commentary. The Anchor Bible. Garden City, N. Y.: Doubleday & Co., Inc., 1970.

Bruce, Alexander B. "The Synoptic Gospels." In The Expositor's Greek Testament, 1:1-651. Edited by W. Robertson Nicoll. 5 vols. London: Hodder & Stoughton, 1900-10; reprint ed., Grand Rapids: Wm. B. Eerdmans Publishing Co., 1970.

Bruce, F. F. New Testament History. New York: Doubleday & Co., 1972.

Buckland, W. W. The Roman Law of Slavery: The Condition of the Slave in Private Law from Augustine to Justinian. Cambridge: At the University Press, 1908, reprint ed., 1970.

Bultmann, Rudolf K. The Gospel of John: A Commentary. Translated by G. R. Beasley-Murray, P. W. N. Hoare, and J. K. Riches. Philadelphia: Westminster Press, 1971.

_____. The History of the Synoptic Tradition. Translated by John Marsh. New York: Harper & Row, 1963.

Bush, George. Notes on Genesis. New York: Ivison, Phinney, & Co., 1860; reprint ed., Minneapolis: James & Clock Publishing Co., 1976.

Buswell, J. O., III. Slavery, Segregation and Scripture. Grand Rapids: Wm. B. Eerdmans Pub. Co., 1964.

Butler, B. C. The Originality of Saint Matthew: A Critique of the Two-Document Hypothesis. Cambridge: University Press, 1953.

Caird, C. B. The Gospel of St. Luke. Westminster Pelican Commentaries. Philadelphia: Westminster Press, 1963.

Calvin, John. The Gospel According to Saint John, Part 1. Translated by T. H. L. Barker. Edited by David W. Torrence and Thomas F. Torrence. Calvin's Commentaries. Grand Rapids: Wm. B. Eerdmans Publishing Co., 1959.

_____. A Harmony of the Gospels: Matthew, Mark, and Luke, Part 1. Translated by A. W. Morrison. Edited by David W. Torrence and Thomas E. Torrence. Calvin's Commentaries. Grand Rapids: Wm. B. Eerdmans Publishing Co., 1959-74.

Carcopino, Jérôme. *Daily Life in Ancient Rome*. Translated by E. O.
    Lorimer. Edited by Henry T. Rowell. New Haven: Yale University
    Press, 1940.

Cassuto, Umberto. *The Documentary Hypothesis*. Translated by Isarel
    Abrahams. Jerusalem: The Magnes Press, 1961.

Chafer, Lewis Sperry. *Systematic Theology*. 8 vols. Dallas: Dallas
    Seminary Press, 1947-48.

Childs, Brevard S. *Biblical Theology in Crisis*. Philadelphia: Westminster Press, 1970.

Cicero. *Pro Archia*. With an English translation by N. H. Watts. The
    Leob Classical Library. N. Y.: G. T. Putnam's Sons, 1923.

Cole, Alan. *The Gospel According to Saint Mark*. The Tyndale New Testament Commentaries. Grand Rapids: Wm. B. Eerdmans Publishing
    Co., 1973.

Cone, James H. *A Black Theology of Liberation*. Philadelphia: J. B.
    Lippincott Co., 1970.

_____. *God of the Oppressed*. New York: Seabury Press, 1975.

Corpus Juris Civilis. 3 vols. Vol. 1: *Digesta*. Recogndvit, T. Mommsen.
    Retractavit, P. Krueger. Berolini: Apud Weidmannos, 1973.

Cranfield, C. E. B. *The Gospel According to Saint Mark*. The Cambridge
    Greek Testament Commentary. Cambridge: The University Press,
    1963.

Crook, John A. *Life and Law of Rome*. Ithaca, N. Y.: Cornell University
    Press, 1967.

Dabney, Robert L. *Discussions*. Edited by C. R. Vaughn. Vol. 3:
    Philosophical. Richmond: Presbyterian Committee of Publications,
    1892.

Danby, Herbert. *The Mishnah: Translated from the Hebrew with Introduction and Brief Explanatory Notes*. 2nd ed. London: Oxford University
    Press, 1938.

Davis, David Brian. *The Problem of Slavery in Western Culture*. Ithaca,
    N. Y.: Cornell University Press, 1966.

de Vaux, Roland. *Ancient Israel*. 2 vols. New York: McGraw-Hill Book
    Co., 1965.

Deissmann, Gustav Adolf. *Light from the Ancient East: The New Testament Illustrated by Recently Discovered Texts of the Graeco-Roman World*. Translated from the 4th German ed. by Lionel R. M. Strachan. New York: Harper and Row, 1927.

Derrett, J. Duncan M. *Law in the New Testament*. London: Darton, Longman and Todd, 1970.

Dodd, Charles H. *Historical Tradition in the Fourth Gospel*. Cambridge: At the University Press, 1963.

_____. *The Interpretation of the Fourth Gospel*. Reprinted paperback ed. Cambridge: At the University Press, 1970.

_____. *The Parables of the Kingdom*. Rev. ed. New York: Charles Scribner's Sons, 1958.

Driver, S. R. *A Critical and Exegetical Commentary on Deuteronomy*. The International Critical Commentary. Edinburgh: T. & T. Clark, 1895.

Edersheim, Alfred. *The Life and Times of Jesus the Messiah*. One vol. ed. Grand Rapids: Wm. B. Eerdmans Publishing Co., 1971.

Eichrodt, Walter. *Theology of the Old Testament*. 2 vols. Translated by J. A. Baker. Philadelphia: The Westminster Press, 1961, 1967.

Ellis, E. Earle. *The Gospel of Saint Luke*. The New Century Bible. Greenwood, S. C.: Attic Press, 1974.

Euripides. *Helen*. With an English translation by Arthur S. Way. The Leob Classical Library. Cambridge, Mass.: Harvard University Press, 1912.

_____. *Hippolytus*. With an English translation by Arthur S. Way. The Leob Classical Library. Cambridge, Mass.: Harvard University Press, 1964.

Fairweather, William. *The Background of the Gospels*. 3rd ed. Edinburgh: T. & T. Clark, 1920; reprint ed., Minneapolis: Klock & Klock Christian Pubs., 1977.

Farmer, William R. *The Synoptic Problem: A Critical Analysis*. New York: MacMillan, 1964.

Feine, Paul and Behm, Johannes. *Introduction to the New Testament*. Completely reedited by Werner Georg Kümmel. 14th rev. ed. Translated by A. J. Mattill, Jr. Nashville: Abingdon Press, 1966.

Finegan, Jack. *Light from the Ancient Past: The Archaeological Background of the Hebrew-Christian Religion*. 2nd ed. 2 vols. Princeton: Princeton University Press, 1959.

Finley, Moses I. *Ancient Slavery and Modern Ideology*. N. Y.: Viking Press, 1980.

_____. "The Extent of Slavery." In *Slavery: A Comparative Perspective*, pp. 3-15. Edited by Robin W. Winks. N. Y.: New York University Press, 1972.

_____, ed. *Slavery in Classical Antiquity: View & Controversies*. Cambridge: W. Heffer & Sons, Ltd., 1960.

France, R. T. *Jesus and the Old Testament: His Application of Old Testament Parables to Himself and His Mission*. Downers Grove, Ill.: Inter-Varsity Press, 1971.

Frank, Tenney, ed. *An Economic Survey of Ancient Rome*. 6 vols. Baltimore: John Hopkins, 1933-40.

Gager, John G. "Religions and Social Classes in the Early Roman Empire." In *The Catacombs and the Colosseum: The Roman Empire as the Setting of Primitive Christianity*, pp. 99-120. Edited by Stephen Renko and John J. O'Rourke. Valley Forge, Pa.: Judson Press, 1971.

Gayer, Roland. *Die Stellung des Sklaven in den Paulinischen Gemeinden und bei Paulus: zuglich ein social geschichtlich vergleichender Beitrag zur Wertung des Sklaven in der Antike*. Bern: Herbert Lang & Cie A. G., 1976.

Geldenhuys, J. Norval. *Commentary on the Gospel of Luke*. The New International Commentary on the New Testament. Wm. B. Eerdmans Publishing Co., 1966.

Glotz, Gustave. *Ancient Greece at War: An Economic History of Greece from the Homeric Period to the Roman Conquest*. Translated by M. R. Dobie. N. Y.: Barnes & Noble, 1965.

Gordis, Robert. *The Book of God and Man: A Study of Job*. Chicago: University of Chicago Press, 1965.

Grant, F. C. *Roman Hellenism and the New Testament*. N. Y.: Charles Scribner's Sons, 1962.

Green, H. Benedict. *The Gospel According to Matthew in the Revised Standard Version: Introduction and Commentary*. The New Clarendon Bible: New Testament. Oxford: At the University Press, 1975.

Greenridge, C. W. W. Slavery. London: George Allen and Unwin, Ltd., 1958.

Gulzow, Henneke. Christentum und Sklaverei in den ersten drei Jahrhunderten. Bonn: Rudolf Habelt Verlag GMBH, 1969.

Gundry, Robert Horton. The Use of the Old Testament in St. Matthew's Gospel. Leiden: E. J. Brill, 1967.

Guthrie, Donald. New Testament Introduction. 3rd rev. ed. Downers Grove, Ill.: Inter-Varsity Press, 1970.

Gutierrez, Gustavo. A Theology of Liberation: History, Politics and Salvation. Translated and edited by Sister Caridad Inda and John Eagleson. Maryknoll, N. Y.: Orbis Books, 1973.

Hasel, Gerhard F. Old Testament Theology: Basic Issues in the Current Debate. Grand Rapids: Wm. B. Eerdmans Publishing Co., 1972.

Hendricksen, William. Exposition of the Gospel According to Matthew. Grand Rapids: Baker Book House, 1973.

Hill, David. The Gospel of Matthew. The New Century Bible. Greenwood, S. C.: The Attic Press, 1972.

Hoehner, Harold W. Herod Antipas. Cambridge: At the University Press, 1972.

Homer. The Odyssey. 2 vols. With an English translation by A. T. Murray. The Leob Classical Library. Cambridge, Mass.: Harvard University Press, 1919.

Hooker, Morna D. Jesus and the Servant: The Influence of the Servant Concept of Deutereo-Isaiah in the New Testament. London: S. P. C. K., 1959.

Hopkins, Keith. Conquerors and Slaves. New York: Cambridge University Press, 1978.

Hughes, Philip Edgcumbe. "The Language Spoken by Jesus." In New Dimensions in New Testament Study, pp. 127-143. Edited by Richard N. Longenecker and Merrill C. Tenney. Grand Rapids: Zondervan Publishing House, 1974.

Hutchens, Robert M., gen. ed. The Great Books of the Western World. 54 vols. Chicago: Encyclopedia Britannica, Inc. Vol. 12: The Discourses, by Epictetus. The Dryden translation. Vol. 14: The Lives of the Noble Grecians and Romans, by Plutarch. Translated by George Long.

Jeremias, Joachim. *Jerusalem in the Time of Jesus: An Investigation into Economic and Social Conditions During the New Testament Period.* Translated by F. H. Cave and C. H. Cave. Philadelphia: Fortress Press, 1969.

_____. *New Testament Theology: The Proclamation of Jesus.* Translated by John Bowden. New York: Charles Scribner's Sons, 1971.

_____. *The Parables of Jesus.* Rev. ed. Translated by S. H. Hooke. New York: Charles Scribner's Sons, 1963.

Jewett, Paul K. *Man as Male and Female.* Grand Rapids: Wm. B. Eerdmans Publishing Co., 1975.

Johnson, Sherman E. *The Gospel According to Saint Matthew.* The Interpreter's Bible. New York: Abingdon Press, 1951.

Josephus, Flavius. *Complete Works.* Translated by William Whiston. Grand Rapids: Kregel Publications, 1960.

Kapelrud, A. S. "The Identity of the Suffering Servant." In *Near Eastern Studies: In Honor of William Foxwell Albright*, pp. 303-14. Edited by H. Goedike. Baltimore: John Hopkins Press, 1971.

Kautsky, Karl. *Foundations of Christianity.* Translated by Henry F. Mins. N. Y.: S. A. Russell, 1953.

Kehnscherper, Gerhard. *Die Stellung der Bibel und der alten Christlichen Kirche zur Sklaverei: ein biblische und kirchengeschichtliche Untersuchung von den altestamentliche Propheten bis zum Ende des Romischen Reiches.* Halle (Saale): Veb Max Niemeyer Verlag, 1957.

Keil, C. F. In vol. 1: *The Pentateuch.* Translated by James Martin. Commentary on the Old Testament. 10 vols. N. d.; reprint ed., Grand Rapids: Wm. B. Eerdmans Publishing Co., 1973.

Kitchen, Kenneth A. *Ancient Orient and Old Testament.* Downers Grove, Ill.: Inter-Varsity Press, 1966.

Koopmans, Jochem J. *De Servitute Antiqua et Religione Christiana.* Capita Selecta. Groningae-Hague: J. B. Wolters, 1920.

Knight, Douglas A. *Rediscovering the Traditions of Israel: The Development of the Traditio-Historical Research of the Old Testament, With Special Consideration of Scandinavian Contributions.* Society of Biblical Literature Dissertation Series. Missoula, Mont.: Scholars Press, 1975.

Ladd, George E. *A Theology of the New Testament*. Grand Rapids: Wm. B. Eerdmans Publishing Co., 1974.

Lane, William L. *The Gospel According to Mark: The English Text With Introduction, Exposition and Notes*. The New International Commentary on the New Testament. Grand Rapids: Wm. B. Eerdmans Publishing Co., 1974.

Leaney, Alfred R. C. *A Commentary on the Gospel According to Saint Luke*. New York: Harper and Brothers Publishers, 1958.

Lee, Clarence L. "Social Unrest and Primitive Christianity." In *The Catacombs and the Colosseum: The Roman Empire as the Setting of Primitive Christianity*, pp. 121-38. Edited by Stephen Benko and John I. O'Rourke. Valley Forge, Pa.: Judson Press, 1971.

Lee, Robert Warden. *The Elements of Roman Law, with a translation of the Institutes of Justinian*. 2nd ed. London: Sweet & Maxwell, 1949.

Lehman, Chester K. *Biblical Theology*. 2 vols. Scottsdale, Pa.: Herald Press, 1971-74.

Lenski, Richard C. H. *The Interpretation of Saint John's Gospel*. Minneapolis: Augsburg Publishing House, 1961.

_____. *The Interpretation of Saint Luke's Gospel*. Minneapolis: Augsburg Publishing House, 1961.

_____. *The Interpretation of Saint Matthew's Gospel*. Minneapolis: Augsburg Publishing House, 1961.

Leupold, Herbert C. *Exposition of Genesis*. 2 vols. Grand Rapids: Baker Book House, 1942.

Lévy-Bruhl, Henri. "Theorie de l'Esclavage." In *Slavery in Classical Antiquity: Views and Controversies*, pp. 151-170. Edited by M. I. Finley. Cambridge: W. Heffer and Sons, Ltd., 1960.

Lewis, Naphtali, and Reinhold, Meyer, eds. *Roman Civilization: Sourcebook II: The Empire*. New York: Harper and Row, 1966.

Lindhagen, Curt. *The Servant Motif in the Old Testament*. Upsalla: Almquist and Wiksells Boktrychkeri Ab, 1958.

Linnemann, Eta. *Parables of Jesus: Introduction and Exposition*. Translated from 3rd ed. by John Sturdy. London: S. P. C. K., 1966.

Longenecker, Richard N. *Biblical Exegesis in the Apostolic Period*. Grand Rapids: Wm. B. Eerdmans Publishing Co., 1975.

Louis, Paul. *Ancient Rome at Work: An Economic History of Rome from the Origins to the Empire*. Translated by E. B. F. Wareing. N. Y.: Barnes & Noble, 1965.

Maine, Henry J. S. *Ancient Law: Its Connection with the Early History of Society and its Relation to Modern Ideas*. London: Oxford University Press, 1931.

MacMullen, Ramsey. *Roman Social Relations, 50 B.C.-A.D. 284*. New Haven, Conn.: Yale University Press, 1974.

M'Neile, Alan Hugen. *The Gospel According to Saint Matthew*. London: MacMillan & Co., Ltd., 1955.

Marshall, I. Howard. *The Gospel of Luke: A Commentary on the Greek Text*. Grand Rapids: Wm. B. Eerdmans Pub. Co., 1978.

Meadows, Jack. "A History of Jewish Interpretation of the Suffering Servant of Isaiah 52:13-53:12." Th.M. Thesis, Dallas Theological Seminary, 1967.

Meyer, Eduard. *Die Sklaverei im Altertum*. Dresden: V. Zahn and Jaensch, 1898.

Moltmann, Jurgen. *Theology of Hope: On the Ground and Implications of a Christian Eschatology*. Translated by James W. Leitch. New York: Harper and Row Publishers, 1967.

Montgomery, James A. *A Critical and Exegetical Commentary on the Book of Kings*. The International Critical Commentary. Edinburgh: T. & T. Clark, 1951.

Moore, George F. *Judaism in the First Centuries of the Christian Era*. 2 vols. New York: Schocken Books, 1958.

Morris, Leon. *The Gospel According to John: The English Text With Introduction, Exposition and Notes*. The New International Commentary on the New Testament. Grand Rapids: Wm. B. Eerdmans Publishing Co., 1971.

_____. *The Gospel According to Luke: An Introduction and Commentary*. The Tyndale New Testament Commentaries. Grand Rapids: Wm. B. Eerdmans Publishing Co., 1974.

_____. *The Revelation of Saint John: An Introduction and Commentary*. The Tyndale New Testament Commentaries. Grand Rapids: Wm. B. Eerdmans Publishing Co., 1969.

_____. *Studies in the Fourth Gospel*. Grand Rapids: Wm. B. Eerdmans Publishing Co., 1969.

Mounce, Robert. *The Book of Revelation*. The New International Commentary on the New Testament. Grand Rapids: Wm. B. Eerdmans Publishing Co., 1977.

New Testament Apocryphal Books. 2 vols. Edited by Wilhelm Schneckmelcher and Edgar Hennecke. Translated by A. J. B. Higgins, et. al. Edited by R. McLachlan Wilson. Philadelphia: Westminster Press, 1963.

Nineham, Dennis E. *Saint Mark*. Westminster Pelican Commentaries. Philadelphia: Westminster Press, 1963.

North, Christopher R. *The Suffering Servant in Deutero-Isaiah: An Historical and Critical Study*. 2nd ed. London: Oxford University Press, 1956.

Nygren, Anders. *Agape and Eros*. Translated by Philip S. Winston. London: S. P. C. K., 1957.

Orlinsky, Harry M. "The So-Called 'Servant of the Lord' and 'Suffering Servant' in Second Isaiah." In *Studies on the Second Part of the Book of Isaiah*, pp. 1-133. Supplements to Vetus Testamentum, vol. 14. Leiden: E. J. Brill, 1967.

_____. "The So-Called 'Suffering Servant' In Isaiah 53." In *Interpreting the Prophetic Tradition*, pp. 229-32. Edited by H. M. Orlinsky. New York: Hebrew Union College, 1969.

Perrin, Norman. *What is Redaction Criticism?* Philadelphia: Fortress Press, 1969.

Petronius. *Satyricon*. Bound with Seneca's *Apocolocyntosis*. With an English translation by Michael Heseltine. The Loeb Classical Library. Cambridge, Mass.: Harvard University Press, 1951.

Philo. *On the Virtues (De Virtutibus)*. With an English translation by F. H. Colson. The Loeb Classical Library. Cambridge, Mass.: Harvard University Press, 1939.

Plato. The Laws. 2 vols. With an English transation by R. G. Bury.
The Leob Classical Library. Cambridge, Mass.: Harvard University
Press, 1926.

_____. Phaedrus. With an English translation by Harold North Fowler.
The Leob Classical Library. Cambridge, Mass.: Harvard University
Press, 1971.

Plummer, Alfred. A Critical and Exegetical Commentary on the Gospel of
Luke. 5th ed. The International Critical Commentary. Edinburgh:
T. & T. Clark, 1922.

Pritchard, James B., ed. Ancient Near Eastern Texts Relating to the Old
Testament. 3rd ed. with supplement. Princeton, N. J.: Princeton
University Press, 1969.

Reicke, Bo. The New Testament Era: The World of the Bible from 500 B. C.
to A. D. 100. Translated by David E. Green. Philadelphia:
Fortress Press, 1968.

Ridderbos, Herman. Paul: An Outline of His Theology. Translated by John
R. DeWitt. Grand Rapids: Wm. B. Eerdmans Publishing Co., 1975.

Robertson, Archibald T. Word Pictures of the New Testament. Vol. 1:
Matthew and Mark. New York: Harper & Row, 1936.

Robinson, Theodore H. The Gospel of Matthew. The Moffatt New Testament
Commentary. Garden City, N. Y.: Doubleday, Doran & Company,
Inc., 1928.

Rostovtzeff, Mikhail. The Social and Economic History of the Roman
Empire. 2 vols. 2nd ed. Revised by P. M. Fraser. Oxford:
At the Clarendon Press, 1957.

Rupprecht, Arthur A. "The Cultural and Political Setting of the New
Testament." In The Expositor's Bible Commentary, 1 (1978):483-
98. Edited by Frank E. Gaebelein. 12 vols. Grand Rapids:
Zondervan Publishing House, 1978.

Russell, Kenneth C. Slavery as Reality and Metaphor in the Pauline
Letters. Rome: Catholic Book Agency, 1968.

Rowley, H. H., ed. The Servant of the Lord and Other Essays on the Old
Testament. London: Lutterworth, 1952.

Ryrie, Charles C. A Biblical Theology of the New Testament. Chicago:
Moody Press, 1959.

Schlaiter, Robert. "Greek Theories of Slavery from Homer to Aristotle." In <u>Slavery in Classical Antiquity: Views and Controversies</u>, pp. 93-132. Edited by M. I. Finley. Cambridge: W. Heffer and Sons, Ltd., 1960.

Schlatter, Adolf. <u>Der Evangelist Matthaus</u>. Stuttgart: Calver Verlag, 1963.

Schmid, Joseph. <u>The Gospel According to Mark</u>. The Regensburg New Testament. Translated by Kevin Condon. Staten Island, N. Y.: Alba House, 1968.

Schweizer, Eduard. <u>The Good News According to Matthew</u>. Translated by David E. Green. Atlanta: John Knox Press, 1975.

_____. "Zum Sklavenproblem im Neuen Testament." <u>Evangelische Theologie</u> 32 (Oktober 1972):502-6.

Segundo, Juan L. <u>Liberation of Theology</u>. Translated by John Drury. Maryknoll, N. Y.: Orbis Books, 1976.

Seneca. <u>Moral Essays</u>. 3 vols. With an English translation by John W. Basone. The Leob Classical Library. Cambridge, Mass.: Harvard University Press, 1970.

_____. <u>Epistulae Morales</u>. 3 vols. With an English translation by Richard M. Gummere. The Leob Classical Library. Cambridge, Mass.: Harvard University Press, 1962-70.

Sherwin-White, A. N. <u>Racial Prejudice in Imperial Rome</u>. Cambridge: At the University Press, 1967.

_____. <u>Roman Society and Roman Law in the New Testament</u>. Oxford: At the Clarendon Press, 1963.

Solle, Dorothee. <u>Political Theology</u>. Translated by John Shelley. Philadelphia: Fortress Press, 1974.

Stott, John R. W. <u>The Preacher's Portrait: Some New Testament Word Studies</u>. Grand Rapids: Wm. B. Eerdmans Publishing Co., 1961.

Strack, Hermann L., and Billerbeck, Paul. <u>Kommentar zum Neuen Testament aus Talmud und Midrasch</u>. Vol. 1: <u>Das Evangelium nach Matthaus</u>. Vol. 2: <u>Das Evangelium nach Markus, Lukas und Johannes und die Apostelgeschichte</u>. München: C. H. Beck, 1924-26.

Stendahl, Krister. <u>The School of St. Matthew and its Use of the Old Testament</u>. Uppsala: C. W. K. Gleerup, Lund, 1954.

Streeter, Burnett W. The Four Gospels: A Study of Origins, Treating of the Manuscript Tradition, Sources, Authorship, and Dates. London: MacMillan & Company, Ltd., 1964.

Suetonius. Caligula. With an English translation by J. C. Rolfe. The Leob Classical Library. Cambridge, Mass.: Harvard University Press, 1964.

Talmon, Shemaryahu. "The 'Desert Motif' in the Bible and in Qumran Literature." In Biblical Motifs: Origins and Transformations, pp. 31-63. Edited by Alexander Alrtmann. Cambridge, Mass.: Harvard University Press, 1966.

Tasker, R. V. G. The Gospel According to Saint John. The Tyndale New Testament Commentaries. Grand Rapids: Wm. B. Eerdmans Publishing Co., 1960.

_____. The Gospel According to Saint Matthew. The Tyndale New Testament Commentaries. Grand Rapids: Wm. B. Eerdmans Publishing Co., 1961.

Taylor, Vincent. The Gospel According to Saint Mark. 2nd ed. New York: St. Martin's Press, 1966.

Tenney, Merrill C. New Testament Times. Grand Rapids: Wm. B. Eerdmans Publishing Co., 1965.

Thompson, George H. P. The Gospel According to Luke in the Revised Standard Version, With Introduction and Commentary. The New Clarendon Bible: New Testament. Oxford: At the Clarendon Press, 1972.

Thompson, J. A. The Bible and Archaeology. Grand Rapids: Wm. B. Eerdmans Publishing Co., 1972.

Thornwell, James H. The Collected Works of James Henley Thornwell. Vol. 4: Ecclesiastical. Edinburgh: Banner of Truth Press, 1974.

Treggiari, Susan. Roman Freedmen During the Late Republic. Oxford: At the Clarendon Press, 1969.

Trench, Richard C. Synonyms of the New Testament. 9th ed. Grand Rapids: Wm. B. Eerdmans Publishing Co., 1953.

Vogt, Joseph. Ancient Slavery and the Ideal of Man. Translated by Thomas Wiedemann. Cambridge, Mass.: Harvard University Press, 1975.

Vos, Geerhardus. *Biblical Theology: Old and New Testaments.* Grand Rapids: Wm. B. Eerdmans Publishing Co., 1948.

Warfield, Benjamin B. *The Inspiration and Authority of the Bible.* Edited by Samuel C. Craig. Philadelphia: The Presbyterian and Reformed Publishing Co., 1970.

Watson, Alan. *The Law of Persons in the Later Roman Republic.* Cambridge, Mass.: Oxford Press, 1967.

Weaver, Paul Richard Carey. *Familia Caesaris: A Social Study of the Emperor's Freedmen and Slaves.* Cambridge, Eng.: At the University Press, 1972.

_____. "Social Mobility in the Early Roman Empire: The Evidence of the Imperial Freedmen and Slaves." In *Studies in Ancient Society*, pp. 121-40. Edited by M. I. Finley. London and Boston: Routledge and Kegan Paul, 1974

Weiser, Alfons. *Die Knechtsgleichnisse Der Synoptischen evangelien.* Munchen: Kösel-Verlag, 1971.

Weld, Theodore Dwight. *The Bible Against Slavery. Or, an Inquiry into the Genius of the Mosaic System and the Teachings of the Old Testament on the Subject of Human Rights.* Pittsburgh: United Presbyterian Board of Publication, 1864; reprint ed., Detroit: Negro History Press, 1970.

Westcott, B. F. *The Gospel According to Saint John.* Reprint ed. Grand Rapids: Wm. B. Eerdmans Publishing Co., 1973.

Westermann, Claus. *Isaiah 40-66: A Commentary.* Translated by David M. G. Stalker. The Old Testament Library. Philadelphia: Westminster Press, 1969.

Westermann, William L. "Slavery and the Elements of Freedom in Ancient Greece." In *Slavery in Classical Antiquity: Views and Controversies*, pp. 17-32. Edited by M. I. Finley. Cambridge: W. Heffer and Sons, Ltd., 1960.

_____. *The Slave Systems of Greek and Roman Antiquity.* Philadelphia: The American Philosophical Society, 1955.

Wiedemann, Thomas, ed. *Greek and Roman Slavery.* Baltimore: The Johns Hopkins University Press, 1981.

Wolff, Hans Walter. *The Anthropology of the Old Testament.* Translated by Margaret Kohl. Philadelphia: Fortress Press, 1974.

Zimmerli, Walther, and Jeremias, Joachim. The Servant of God. Naperville, Ill.: Allenson, Inc., 1965.

II. Dictionaries, Encyclopedias, and Biblical Texts

Baker's Dictionary of Theology. Edited by Everett F. Harrison. 1972 edition. S.v. "Biblical Theology," by Geoffrey W. Bromiley, pp. 95-97.

Biblia Hebraica. Edited by Rudolf Kittel. 6th ed. 1937.

The Compact Edition of the Oxford English Dictionary: Complete Text Reproduced Micrographically. 2 vols. 1971 edition.

A Dictionary of the Bible. Edited by James Hastings. 1903 ed. S.v. "Servant, Slave, Slavery," by Owen C. Whithouse, 4:461-69.

Dictionary of World Literature, J. T. Shipley, ed. S.v. "Motif," p. 274.

Encyclopedia Judaica. 1971 ed. S.v. "Slavery," by Haim H. Cohn, 14:1655-59.

A Greek-English Lexicon of the New Testament and Other Early Christian Literature. By Walter Bauer. Translated by William F. Arndt and Wilbur Gingrich, 4th rev. ed.

The Greek New Testament. Edited by Kurt Aland, Matthew Black, Carlo M. Martin, Bruce M. Metzger, and Allen Wikgren. 2d ed.

A Hebrew and English Lexicon of the Old Testament. By Francis Brown, S. R. Driver, and Charles A. Briggs.

The Interpreter's Dictionary of the Bible: An Illustrated Encyclopedia. Edited by George A. Buttrick. 1962 ed. S.v. "Biblical Theology, Contemporary," by Krister Stendahl, 1:418-32; s.v. "Slavery in the Old Testament," by Isaac Mendelsohn, 4:383-91.

The Interpreter's Dictionary of the Bible: An Illustrated Encyclopedia. A Supplementary Volume. Edited by Keith Grim. 1976 ed. S.v. "Slavery in the Old Testament," by Walther Zimmerli, pp. 829-30; s.v. "Slavery in the New Testament," by Wayne G. Rollins, pp. 830-32.

Lexicon in Veteria Testamenti Libres: A Dictionary of the Hebrew Old
    Testament and of the Aramaic Parts of the Old Testament in
    English and German. Edited by Ludwig Koehler and Walther
    Baumgartner.

The New American Standard Bible, 1973 ed.

The New Bible Dictionary. Edited by J. D. Douglas. 1962 ed. S.v.
    "Slave, slavery," by E. A. Judge and K. A. Kitchen, pp. 1195-99.

The New International Dictionary of New Testament Theology. Edited by
    Lotar Coenen, Erich Beyreuther and Hans Bietenhand. Translated,
    with additions and revisions, by Colin Brown, gen. ed. 1975-
    1978. S.v. "Serve," Klaus Hess, 3 (1978):544-53; s.v. "Slave,
    servant, captive, prisoner, freedman," by Gervais T. D. Angel,
    Hans-Georg Link, and Rudolf Tuente, 3 (1978):589-99.

Septuaginta. Edited by Alfred Rahlfs, 3d ed.

Synopsis of the Four Gospels: Greek-English Edition of the Synopsis
    Quattuor Evangeliorum, with the Text of the Revised Standard
    Version. Edited by Kurt Aland. Stuttgart: United Bible
    Societies, 1972.

Theological Dictionary of the New Testament. Edited by Gerhard Kittel
    and Gerhard Friedrich. Translated and edited by Geoffrey W.
    Bromiley. 1964-74. S.v. "δικαοέω, διακονία, διάκονος," by
    Hermann W. Beyer, 2 (1964):81-93; s.v. "δοῦλος," by Karl H.
    Rengstorf, 2 (1964):261-80; s.v. "ἐλεύθερος, ἐλευθερόω,
    ἐλευθερία," by Heinrich Schlier, 2 (1964):487-502; s.v. "παῖς,"
    by Albert Oepke, 5 (1967):636-54; s.v. "Παῖς θεοῦ," by Walther
    Zimmerli and Joachim Jeremias, 5 (1967):654-717.

A Theological Wordbook of the Bible. Edited by Alan Richardson. S.v.
    "Servant," by J. Y. Campbell, pp. 223-25.

The Vocabulary of the Greek Testament Illustrated from the Papri and
    Other Non-Literary Sources. Edited by James Hope Moulton and
    George Milligan, 1972 ed.

Zondervan Pictorial Encyclopedia of the Bible. Edited by Merrill C.
    Tenney. 1975 ed. S.v. "Bethsaida," by Robert L. Alden, 1:542-
    43; s.v. "Jericho," by Howard M. Jamieson, 3:451-55; s.v. "Jesus
    Christ," by Donald Guthrie, 3:497-583; s.v. "Job," by Elmer B.
    Smick, 3:600-16; s.v. "Nethinium," by Wilber B. Wallis, 4:414;
    s.v. "Slave, slavery," by Arthur A. Rupprecht, 5:453-60; s.v.
    "Tiberias," by Edward M. Blaiklock, 5:745-46; s.v. "Tyre," by
    Edward M. Blaiklock, 5:832-35; s.v. "Zealot," by John H. Bratt,
    5:1036-37.

III. Periodical Literature

Argyle, A. W. "Did Jesus Speak Greek?" *Expository Times* 67 (December 1955):92-93 and 67 (September 1956):383.

Ballard, Paul H. "Reasons for Refusing the Great Supper." *Journal of Theological Studies* 23 (1972):341-50.

Barr, James. "Which Language Did Jesus Speak?" *Bulletin of the John Rylands Library* 53 (1970):9-29.

Barbour, R. S. "Uncomfortable Words (VIII): Status and Titles." *Expository Times* 82 (February 1971):132-42.

Berger, P. L. "The Sociological Study of Sectarianism." *Social Research* 21 (1954):467-83.

Bishop, Eric F. F. "Jesus and Capernaum." *Catholic Biblical Quarterly* 15 (October, 1953):427-37.

Brown, Robert McAfee. "Who is the Jesus Christ Who Frees and Unites?" *Ecumenical Review* 28 (January 1976):6-21.

Bucher, Glenn R. "Theology for the 'Oppressor.'" *Journal of the American Academy of Religion* 44 (1976):517-34.

Campbell, Ernest T. "They Also Serve Who Lead." *Princeton Seminary Bulletin* 2 (1978):3-8.

Chavasse, C. "The Suffering Servant and Moses." *Church Quarterly Review* 165 (1965):152-63.

Coates, George W. "Conquest Traditions in the Wilderness Theme." *Journal of Biblical Literature* 95 (June 1976):177-90.

Cone, James H. "Revelation and Social Existence." *Theology Digest* 23 (Autumn 1975):251-53.

Crossan, John Dominic. "The Parable of the Wicked Husbandmen." *Journal of Biblical Literature* 90 (1971):451-65.

_____. "The Servant Parables of Jesus." *Semeia* 1 (1974):17-62.

Daube, D. "Three Notes Having to Do with Johanan ben Zaccai." *Journal of Theological Studies* 11 (1960):53-62.

Davidson, J. A. "Sacrament and Servanthood." *New Pulpit Digest* 56 (January 1976):57-59.

de Goedt, Michel. "L'Explication de la Parable de l'Ivraie." Revue Biblique 66 (1959):32-54.

Deist, Ferdinand. "The Exodus Motif in the Old Testament and The Theology of Liberation." Missionalia 5 (August 1977):58-69.

Derrett, J. Duncan M. "Law in the New Testament: The Parable of the Talents and the Two Logia." Zeitschrift für die neutestamentliche Wissenschaft 56 (1965):184-95.

_____. "'Take thy bond . . . and write fifty' (Luke xvi.6): The Nature of the Bond." Journal of Theological Studies 23 (1972):438-40.

Dodd, C. H. "Some Problems of New Testament Translation." Biblical Translator 13 (July 1962):145-57.

Durand, J. J. F. "Liberation for Reconciliation." Missionalia 5 (August 1977):108-10.

"Editorial." Interpretation 23 (1969):78-80.

Egnell, Ivan. "The 'Ebed-Yahweh Song and the Suffering Messiah in 'Deutero-Isaiah.'" The Bulletin of the John Rylands Library 31 (1948):54-93.

Eissfeldt, Otto. "The Ebed-Jahwe in Isaiah XL-LV in the Light of the Israelite Conception of the Community and the Individual, the Ideal and the Real." Translated by A. R. Johnson. Expository Times 44 (January 1933):261-68.

Ellison, E. L. "The Hebrew Slave: A Study in Early Israelite Society," Evangelical Quarterly 45 (1973):30-35.

Emerton, J. A. "Did Jesus Speak Hebrew?" Journal of Theological Studies 12 (1961):189-202.

Falk, Z. W. "Manumission by Sale." Journal of Semetic Studies. 3 (April 1958):127-8.

Farmer, William R. "A 'Skeleton in the Closet' of Gospel Research." Biblical Research 6 (1961):18-42.

Finley, M. I., "Between Slavery and Freedom." Comparative Studies in Society and History 6 (1963-64):245.

Fitzmeyer, Joseph A. "The Story of the Dishonest Manager (Lk. 16:1-13)." Theological Studies 25 (1964):23-42.

Fretheim, Terrence E. "On Being a Servant." *Princeton Seminary Bulletin* 66 (October 1973):59-64.

Ginsberg, H. L. "The Oldest Interpretation of the Suffering Servant." *Vetus Testamentum* 4 (1954):400-4.

Goldingay, John. "The Man of War and The Suffering Servant: The Old Testament and the Theology of Liberation." *Tyndale Bulletin* 27 (1976):79-113.

Goodspeed, Edgar J. "Paul and Slavery." *Journal of Bible and Religion* 11 (1943):169-70.

Grintz, Jehoshua M. "Hebrew as the Spoken and Written Language in the Last Days of the Second Temple." *Journal of Biblical Literature* 79 (1960):32-47.

Grundmann, Walter. "Daw Wort von Jesu Freunden (Joh. 15:13-16) und das Herrenmahl." *Novum Testamentum* 3 (1959):62-69.

Gundry, Robert H. "The Language Milieu of First Century Palestine." *Journal of Biblical Literature* 83 (1964):404-8.

Buillet, Jacques. "La Polemique contre les Idols et le Serviteur de Yahve." *Biblica* 40 (1959):428-52.

Haran, Menahem. "The Gibeonites, the Nethinim, and the Sons of Solomon's Servants." *Vetus Testamentum* 4 (1961):159-69.

Hellwig, Monika. "Liberation Theology: An Emerging School." *Scottish Journal of Theology* 30 (1977):137-51.

Herzog, Frederick. "Liberation and Imagination." *Interpretation* 32 (July 1978):227-41.

Horn, Gilbert J. "Servanthood Vis-a-vis Sophistication." *Princeton Seminary Bulletin* 66 (Summer 1974):68-71.

Hustado, Larry W. "The Ministry as Servanthood." *Trinity Studies* 4 (Spring 1975):67-75.

Hyatt, J. Philip. "The Sources of the Suffering Servant Idea." *Journal of Near Eastern Studies* 3 (1944):79-84.

Jeremias, Joachim. Review of *Jesus and the Servant*, by Morna D. Hooker. *Journal of Theological Studies* (1960):140-44.

Jones, A. H. M. "Slavery in the Ancient World." *The Economic History Review* 9 (1956):185-99.

Jones, David C. "Diakonia." *Covenant Seminary Review* 4 (1978):90-94.

Kessler, M. "The Law of Manumission in Jer. 34." *Biblische Zeitschrift* 15 (1971):105-8.

Kruse, Colin G. "The Servant Songs: Interpretative Trends since C. R. North," *Studia Biblica et Theologica* 8 (April 1978):3-27.

Lauffer, Siegfriend. "Die Sklaverei in der griechich-römischen Welt." *Gymnasium* 68 (1961):370-95.

Lemche, N. P. "The 'Hebrew Slave.'" *Vetus Testamentum* 25 (1975):129-44.

_____. "The Manumission of Slaves--The Fallow Year, The Sabbatical Year, the Jobel Year." *Vetus Testamentum* 26 (1976):38-59.

Lipinski, Edouard. "L'Esclave Hebreu." *Vetus Testamentum* 26 (January 1976):120-24.

Lyall, F. "Roman Law in the Writings of Paul--The Slave and the Freedman." *New Testament Studies* 17 (October 1969):73-79.

McGaughy, Lane C. "The Fear of Yahweh and the Mission of Judaism: A Post-Exilic Maxim and Its Early Christian Expansion in the Parable of the Talents." *Journal of Biblical Literature* 94 (June 1975):235-45.

MacKay, John A. "The Form of a Servant." *Theology Today* 15 (October 1958):304-14.

Manley, Michael. "From the Shackles of Domination and Oppression." *Ecumenical Review* 28 (January 1976):49-65.

Marshall, I. Howard. "Luke xvi.8--Who Commended the Unjust Steward?" *Journal of Theological Studies* 19 (1968):617-19.

Mendelsohn, Isaac. "The Conditional Sale into Slavery of Free-Born Daughters in Nuzi and the Law of Exodus 21:7-11." *Journal of the American Oriental Society* 55 (1935):190-95.

_____. "State Slavery in Ancient Palestine." *Bulletin of the American Schools of Oriental Research* 85 (February 1942):14-17.

Meyners, J. Robert. "Liberation 200 Years On." *Chicago Theological Seminary Register* 66 (Fall 1976):79-113.

Millikan, Bill. "Where Have All the Servants Gone?" Faith at Work 88 (February 1975):32-33.

Minear, P. S. "A Note on Luke 17:7-10." Journal of Biblical Literature 93 (1974):82-87.

Morgenstern, Julian. "The Suffering Servant: A New Solution." Vetus Testamentum 11 (1961):292-320, 406-31.

Mudge, Lewis S. "The Servant Lord and His Servant People." Scottish Journal of Theology 12 (1959):113-28.

Newell, Jane E., and Newell, Raymond R. "The Parable of the Wicked Tenants." Novum Testamentum 14 (July 1972):226-37.

Ngally, Jacques. "Jesus Christ and Liberation in Africa." Ecumenical Review 27 (July 1975):212-19.

Osborne, Robert T. "Jesus and Liberation Theology." Christian Century 93 (March 1976):225-27.

Palmer, Humphrey. "Just Married, Cannot Come." Novum Testamentum 18 (October 1976):241-57.

Pascal, C. Bennett. "Rex Nemorensis." Numen 23 (April 1976):23-39.

Patrick, Dale. "The Moral Logic of Election." Encounter 37 (Spring 1976):198-210.

Payne, D. F. "The Servant of the Lord: Language and Interpretation." Evangelical Quarterly 43 (July 1971):131-43.

Pidoux, G. "Le Serviteur Souffrant d'Isaïe 53." Reformed Theological Review 7 (1956):36-46.

Pinnock, Clark. "Liberation Theology: The Gains, The Gaps." Christianity Today 20 (January 16, 1976):13-15.

Plasterer, George. "A Bibliographic Essay." Asbury Seminarian 32 (July 1977):40-48.

Price, James L. "The Servant Motif in the Synoptic Gospels." Interpretation 12 (1958):28-32.

Rabinowitz, Jacob. J. "Manumission of Slaves in Roman Law and Oriental Law." Journal of Near Eastern Studies 19 (1960):42-45.

Reeve, Jack V. "Preparing Professional Servants." *Lexington Theological Quarterly* 13 (July 1978):87-96.

Reumann, J. "'Stewards of God'--Pre-Christian Religion Application of Οικονόμος in Greek." *Journal of Biblical Literature* 88 (1958): 339-49.

Richardson, Peter. "Paul Today: Jews, Slaves, and Women." *Crux* 8 (November 1970):30-37.

Rosenburg, R. A. "Jesus, Isaac, and the Suffering Servant." *Journal of Biblical Literature* 84 (1965):381-88.

Roth, W. M. W. "The Anonymity of The Suffering Servant." *Journal of Biblical Literature* 93 (1964):171-79.

Rowley, H. H. "The Servant Mission: The Servant Songs and Evangelism." *Interpretation* 8 (1954):259-72.

Ryan, William F. "The Church as the Servant of God in Acts." *Scripture* 15 (1963):110-15.

Sass, Gerhard. "Zur Bedeutung von δοῦλος bei Paulus." *Zeitschrift für die neutestamentliche Wissenschaft* 40 (1941 Juni):29-31.

Sanks, T. Howland and Smith, Brian H. "Liberation Ecclesiology: Praxis, Theory, Praxis." *Theological Studies* 38 (March 1977):3-38.

Scharbert, J. "Stellvertretendes Sühnleiden in dem Ebed-Yahweh Liedern und in altorientalischen Ritual Texten." *Biblische Zeitschrift* 2 (1956):190-213.

Sellin, Ernst. "Die Lösung des deuterojesajanischen Gottesknechtstratsels." *Zeitschrift für die altestamentliche Wissenschaft* 14 (1937):177-217.

Shenk, Joseph C. "Missionary Identity and Servanthood." *Missiology* 1 (October 1973):505-15.

Spicq, C. "Une Allusion au Docteur de Justice dans Mattheu 23:10." *Revue Biblique* 66 (1959):201-26.

_____. "Le Vocabulaire de l'Esclavage dans le Nouveau Testament." *Revue Biblique* 85 (April 1978):201-26.

Stek, John A. "Salvation, Justice and Liberation in the Old Testament." *Calvin Theological Journal* 13 (November 1978):133-65.

Sugden, Christopher M. M. "A Different Dream: Jesus and Revolution."
    Theological Student Fellowship Bulletin 71 (Spring 1975):15-22.

Szakats, Alexander. "Slavery as a Social and Economic Institution in
    Antiquity With Special References to Roman Law." Prudentia
    7 (May 1975):33-45.

Thomas, Carol G. "On the Origin of the Institution of Slavery." The
    Ancient World 1 (September 1978):109-10.

Tourney, R. J. "Les Chants du Serviteur dans la Second Partie d'Isaie."
    Revue Biblique 59 (1952):355-85, 484-512.

Treves, Marco. "Isaiah LIII." Vetus Testamentum 24 (January 1974):98-
    108.

Urbach, E. E. "Halakhot Regarding Slavery as a Source for the Social
    History of the Second Temple and the Talmud Periods." Zion
    25 (1960):141-89.

van Wyk, J. A. "Latin American Protestant Theology of Liberation."
    Missionalia 5 (August 1977):86-91.

Ward, James M. "The Servant Songs in Isaiah." Review and Expositor 65
    (1968):133-46.

Westermann, William L. "Two Studies in Athenian Manumission." Journal
    of Near Eastern Studies 5 (1946):92-104.

Wilder, Amos N. "Eleutheria in the New Testament and Religious Liberty."
    The Ecumenical Review 13 (July 1961):409-20.

Willesen, Folker. "The Yalid in Hebrew Society." Studia Theologia 12
    (1958):192-210.

Wilshire, Leland E. "The Servant-City: A New Interpretation of the
    'Servant of the Lord' in the Servant Songs of Deutero-Isaiah."
    Journal of Biblical Literature 94 (September 1975):356-67.

Wolff, Hans Walter. "Masters and Slaves: On Overcoming Class-Struggle
    in the Old Testament." Interpretation 27 (July 1973):259-72.

Woudstra, Marten H. "A Critique of Liberation Theology by a Cross-
    Culturalized Calvinist." Journal of the Evangelical Theological
    Society 23 (March 1980):3-12.

Yamauchi, Edwin. "Slaves of God." Bulletin of the Evangelical
    Theological Society 9 (1966):31-49.

Young, Edward J. "Of Whom Speaketh the Prophet Thus?" Westminster Theological Journal 11 (1949):133-35.

_____. "Origin of the Suffering Servant Idea." Westminster Theological Journal 13 (1950):19-33.

Zeitlin, S. "Slavery During the Second Commonwealth and the Tannaitic Period." Jewish Quarterly Review 53 (1962):185-218.

Zimmerli, Walther. "The Theme of the Servant of Yahweh in Primitive Christian Soteriology and its Transposition by St. Paul." Catholic Biblical Quarterly 16 (1954):385-425.